I0130088

POWER CIRCUITS

POLYAMORY
IN A POWER DYNAMIC

RAVEN KALDERA

POWER CIRCUITS

POLYAMORY IN A
POWER DYNAMIC

RAVEN KALDERA

Alfred Press
Hubbardston, Massachusetts

Alfred Press
12 Simond Hill Road
Hubbardston, MA 01452

Power Circuits: Polyamory In A Power Dynamic
© 2010 Raven Kaldera
ISBN 978-0-9828794-1-2

All rights reserved.
No part of this book may be reproduced in any
form or by any means without the permission of
the author.

Printed in cooperation with
Lulu Enterprises, Inc.
860 Aviation Parkway, Suite 300
Morrisville, NC 27560

*Dedicated to my boy, my bitch, my wife,
and all my friends-with-benefits,
my leather family,
and all the brave people who walk this road.*

Contents

Part I
Background and Basics

Dreams and Disasters

Max and Jennifer have had a dominant/submissive relationship for a year now, and have been living together for six months. When Jennifer moved in, Max collared her and told her that she was his slave. She found it wonderfully romantic ... until some months later Max decided that he wanted a second slave girl, and went hunting for one. Jennifer protested, then wept, and begged him not to do it. Both went online and asked advice; on one Internet forum Max was told that he was the master and thus Jennifer should do whatever he told her, and on another forum Jennifer was told that she should leave him if he didn't agree to be monogamous. Both shouted their competing advice at each other, and by the time the night was over, they had broken up and Jennifer had given back her collar. He was sure that she wasn't really submissive. She was sure that he didn't care about her. Both went back online to complain about the other one, and to start over again with other people.

When Master Keith comes to the club, or to leather events, or local BDSM conferences, he's always accompanied by one of his three faithful boys—jack, rumi, and garry. He's had them for 14, 9, and 7 years, respectively, and is clearly loving toward all of them. At the same time, they always seem to know their place and never seem to have relationship drama in public. His alpha slave, jack, is also his domestic partner and they are clearly in love ... and jack often points out hot guys that Master Keith might like to play with. His other two slaves adore him and adore jack, their "big brother", and have something of a relationship with each other. One of them, garry, has a vanilla partner named Jude who lives alone, and sometimes accompanies them to events. The vanilla partner never seems to mind that Master Keith has first dibs on garry's time.

What people at the clubs and events don't see is all the work that each of these men have done in order to make their leather family run smoothly. Master Keith puts in a great deal of time and thought and effort to make sure that each of his boys gets enough special attention, and understands why they don't get more. There are clear rules and protocols set out so that they can bring up resentments and insecurities without feeling blamed, and they are encouraged to communicate regularly. At least once a week, Master Keith has a household meeting where they go over problems and work things out. Their master rules this meeting with an iron hand, requiring honesty and openness but not allowing anyone to attack anyone else. If there are problems, they are solved and new rules are set up to prevent future occurrences. When garry brought Jude in, Master Keith invited him to the household meetings and made sure that his needs were heard and met. New boys, or outside partners, who are unwilling to respect the commitment of the household dynamic or whose emotional problems create drama are broken off. The seamless appearance of the household is not maintained without a great deal of work.

David and Gail had been married for six years, and during the last two years they had remade the marriage into a master/slave relationship. Somewhere along the line, David began to dream of having a second slave girl, or maybe even more—a whole household of slaves. Gail was not thrilled with the idea, but she didn't want to lose her marriage or the master/slave dynamic, so when David brought another submissive—Diane—home and let her move in, Gail bit her tongue at first and didn't talk about the great pain and insecurity that it caused her. David, enthusiastically caught up in his dream of having two women serve him, assumed that everything was all right.

But it wasn't. Gail's resentment leaked out, and she could not help but be rude to Diane. At night, she cried herself to sleep, and when David wanted sexual service, she got sick to her stomach. For her part, Diane was new to both polyamory and being a full-time submissive, and while she accepted David's word that she should just be a good girl and get along with Gail, she secretly fantasized about having him all to herself. These fantasies escalated when she saw Gail acting out and disobeying from her resentment toward

David. She and Gail argued over household management, as they had been raised in different styles of home-care.

David quickly found himself tired of constantly mediating battles, so he made himself scarce when arguments started, or told them both to shut up. His fantasy began to crumble as his girls fought more and more, and he did not know what to do in order to make them get along. Both felt betrayed by him and acted out more and more. David alternated between being dictatorial and punishing them both severely for acting out (which only made them feel as if he didn't care about their feelings) and withdrawing in frustration in front of the television. It was only a matter of time before he found a new girl on the Internet and walked out on both women, leaving a broken marriage and broken hearts.

Mistress Silver has two male slaves and an egalitarian husband, all of whom live with her. She and her husband opened up their marriage to polyamory when it became clear that Silver strongly desired a power-dynamic relationship, and her husband Rory wasn't interested. Over the years she has collected George and Carl, carefully evaluating them to find out if they were going to be able to adapt to her unusual household. While Rory has no authority over the other men, he had to like them and not feel competitive with them. George and Carl are guys that he can treat as buddies, even though they are his wife's slaves; he respects and likes them as people, and the feelings are mutual. The household is currently looking for a female slave to add to their polyamorous family.

For her part, Mistress Silver has had to work hard to create a context of female domination that did not follow the classic "porn story" of the cruel and unfeeling mistress whose power lies in not giving a damn about the discomfort of her male submissives (a story often built on the assumption that if she showed caring feelings they would revert to sexist patterns and attempt to bully or take advantage of her). She has learned that multiple relationships work best when everyone is encouraged to communicate their emotions, even the ones that seem unacceptable. ("I'm sorry, Mistress, but today I'm just furious with you.") At the same time, she has had to work hard not to become so addicted to the power dynamic that she loses interest in her egalitarian relationship with her husband, or lets her dominance leak over into that arena. Polyamory has taught her how to sort out romantic "in-love" feelings from sexual lust, and from warm "family love". It has also forced her to discipline herself enough to overcome the passive-aggressive patterns that she learned from her mother as a girl. If she hadn't grown a lot in a short time, she would never have been able to juggle her current household.

Denise and Sarah were in a mistress/slave relationship with each other. They met Dawn, another dominant, and CJ, her female "boy", at a leather conference. They all got along as friends and hung together for some months, and then Denise and Dawn got sexually involved. Their partners didn't mind at first, but eventually Dawn confessed that Denise triggered feelings of wanting to submit in her, and Denise collared Dawn one night without any word to Sarah or CJ. Problems arose immediately—Sarah had assumed that her partner would be having an egalitarian relationship, and having to share her mistress with another sub made her feel insecure. This was exacerbated by Denise giving over many of the services that Sarah performed to Dawn, who was eager to experience service.

CJ, on the other hand, felt betrayed by her mistress because she was no longer sure of the chain of command—as her mistress's mistress, did Denise have the right to give her orders? She hadn't consented to that, and felt threatened by everything Denise asked of her that was even remotely dominant. She ended up arguing with Denise in public, resentfully subsiding when her collared mistress ordered her to stop. Denise and Dawn spent much of their time comforting each other over what to do with their suddenly disobedient slaves; they both compared Sarah and CJ unfavorably with Dawn (newly in the sub position and enthusiastically trying to be perfect at everything). Eventually CJ gave back her collar and left. Dawn moved in with Denise and Sarah, and wanted to be Denise's girl but Sarah's mistress as well. Denise agreed, but Sarah resented it, and acted out until Denise kicked her out.

Denise and Dawn lived happily and monogamously for a year, and then Dawn met Terra, a sub who made her remember how good it was to be dominant. Terra wanted to be Dawn's slave but not Denise's, and the resulting argument tore Denise and Dawn apart.

Master Vince is the unquestioned Daddy of his leather family of five. His wife Alicia is submissive to him, but is a dominant Mama to the rest of the family. Fran is a slave, and Corie is a "little girl" of both Vince and Alicia. Their newest sub is Dani, a butch "little boy" who is a new brother for Corie. All five of them work and contribute their money to the running of the household; Dani, who does not yet live with them, contributes only a little money and a lot of chores. There is a thirty-page rulebook that everyone can refer to, but the number-one rule is Daddy Knows Best. Vince has not merely declared this rule to be so; he's insisted that each member of the household watch him carefully from the beginning in order to earn their trust. When he and Alicia were first starting out with polyamory, he took her to support groups, read books on the subject with her, and questioned many successful leather families about their journeys. He made sure that Alicia had supportive polyamorous friends to talk to about her fears, and he worked hard to make peace with her insecurities before they went looking for anyone new. The two interviewed new slaves as a couple, and Alicia had a strong say in picking each of them. If any didn't get along well with Alicia, they were kindly sent on their way in the early stages.

Vince juggles different sets of rules for different levels of power dynamic. Alicia is submissive to him in some areas, but not others—the running of the daily household is unquestionably hers and Vince does not interfere. Fran is property, and has given up her ability to defend any limits; her rules are different from those of Corie, who is a submissive "little girl" but has negotiated limits in various areas such as sexual preference—Corie is straight and does not have to have sex with Alicia or Dani, while Fran has agreed to have no limits in that area, all preferences aside. Dani's rules and limits are still being worked out while she is in her probationary period; she is bisexual and a switch, and would like to be allowed to have some authority over Fran, but Master Vince has told her that she has to earn that privilege. Dani also plays part-time with a dominant that Master Vince knows and respects; the two of them have good communication with each other and work out Dani's schedule so that there are no stepping on toes.

The Master keeps a keen eye on everyone's interactions, and when there are resentments, he uses his authority to make everyone involved sit down and work it out, with him as mediator. No one is allowed to get away with passive-aggressive or manipulative behavior; honesty and communication is rewarded. All his women have been trained to let him know when they're having a bad day, when they're feeling in need of attention, and when they need a beating. This means a lot of work with each of them, getting them to be self-aware rather than simply acting out from unconscious issues. In the process, Vince has had to become more self-aware himself, and has learned a great deal of conflict resolution and how to read people. This has given him a better ability to manage his women, and increased their trust in him.

These six vignettes of polyamory and power dynamic are composites of actual situations. If you've lived this challenging relationship combination yourself—successfully or unsuccessfully— you might recognize one or more of these vignettes. Perhaps you've been in one, or one like it. Perhaps you wanted to be in one that was like the working relationships, but ended up in a scenario like one of the disasters. There are, certainly, disasters. Their sad stories litter the table whenever people start to talk about combining these two difficult lifestyles. (Of course, no one talks about the successful ones, the ones that are still going on after a decade or more. There's no need to talk about contentment. It's pain that people need support for, so it's pain that people hear.)

There are a variety of reasons for the failures, but the biggest one is that people jump into polyamory with no idea how to make it work. Polyamory can be an immensely rewarding lifestyle for the right people, but it takes a lot of work and a lot of relationship skills. We barely have models for doing monogamy in a healthy and respectful way; we have almost no models for the complexity of polyamorous relationships. Similarly, many if not most of the models we have for power-dynamic relationships are derived from pornography, and what makes for hot porn doesn't necessarily make for useful reality. The deeper and more absolute the power dynamic is, the fewer healthy role models we have for it. While there are no statistics, master/slave relationships anecdotally seem to have a very high attrition rate during the first year or so.

If these two lifestyles are difficult enough to handle by themselves, trying to do both at once is a feat not unlike juggling flaming torches while riding a unicycle. Add to this the fact that some models of M/s (and especially the porn models) can seem to make irrelevant the basic format of "classical" polyamory. It's no wonder that there are so many disasters. Actually, what's amazing is that anyone manages to make it work at all. There's a huge grey area around power dynamics and polyamorous protocol (which is why, when I wrote my book on polyamory, I left out the entirety of the power dynamic question as it would have muddied the waters). This book is an attempt to fill that void, and perhaps prevent at least some future disasters.

And yet people do manage to make this work. When I went to clubs or leather events, I saw them. I saw them together for year after year, coming back to the same conference annually without a breakup, so it must be working somehow. When I built my own road through this minefield, I remembered the polyamorous families I'd seen that worked. If they could do it, I could do it. I just had to learn how.

Currently, I live in a house with my two partners—Bella, my egalitarian wife of 16 years, and Joshua, my slaveboy of 9 years. I love them both, and they fill different roles in my life. They are not involved with each other, so this is what we refer to as a V-relationship. I'm the center, the fulcrum, so it's on me to put in the extra effort to make it work. I also have Ruth, a part-time sub in service to me who is married to her wife Lizzie and is actually owned by yet someone else (I have permission from both Lizzie and Ruth's owner to have her in part-time service to me). I asked her what title she wanted and we decided that she was my Bitch. In addition, I have occasional liaisons with two male friends, when any of us gets around to it in our busy schedules, which is something like twice a year. It's a running joke that the mating call of the polyamorous is "Get out your calendars!" Certainly the issue of scheduling, and giving each relationship enough time and attention, is a common demon in our lifestyle.

We live together on the same farm with a couple of housemates, and the three of us all sleep in the same bed. However, we are not all three involved in a D/s relationship. My wife is not interested in being submissive to me (and thus she shouldn't have to), and she has no authority over Joshua just because she is married to me. She knows that we're in this relationship, although she rather sees it as an elaborate game that he and I are playing. She had no problem with Joshua moving in; we've been poly for all 15 years of our marriage and she generally likes him as a person. The polyamory is not a problem.

Her initial big discomfort with the situation was a worry that having someone to wait on me would make me lazy and entitled, and that I wouldn't do my share of the housework. Living in a group house of equals means that we have to act as if we are independent adults in terms of handing out chores; just because I have a slave doesn't mean that I can just order him to do my stuff for me all the time, because the other housemates see that as an unfair advantage. So I may be the only master who does shifts washing dishes and doing laundry, for the sake of domestic harmony. (This is something that often makes other owners who live alone with their slave cross their eyes in disbelief.) It also reassures my wife that I am not letting slaveownership make me into a tyrant or a couch potato.

Since my disabling disease has progressed, however, and Joshua now does the PCA/nursing for me (which would drive her nuts), she's happy with the fact that I have someone to take care of me physically. It's easier to have a slave to drive you around, take you to health care appointments, cook you special food, and get up with you in the middle of the night when you're ill again than to pay professionals to live in and deal with it. Since we don't have a lot of money and I couldn't afford that anyway, we all see Joshua as a health necessity for me. Also, since Joshua works and supports me, she can spend her own income as she pleases and not have to support me, which always made her uncomfortable. That means that we don't argue over money like we used to, so it's less stress on the marriage. So is not having to depend on her for kinky sex she isn't particularly interested in.

The boy himself, when asked by another s-type how he felt about being second priority in my life (well, fourth really, if you count my jobs first and my daughter second), wrote this:

> As far as insecurity goes, I have never been left any doubt as to which of my master's needs I am and am not fulfilling. If he were to get a slave that met his needs in places where I fall short of the mark, I would be very thankful. It might be painful to be reminded of areas where I am struggling, but those are issues I would need to get over whether there was another slave or not. It is not my job to fulfill all of my master's needs. It is my job to serve him to the best of my ability. I have learned what happens when I lament my "failings" and doubt my worthiness of my master ... he ignores me or tells me to knock it off. "You won't be able to wash any dishes with your hands nailed to that cross, boy."

I have been successfully polyamorous for a very long time—since I was 15 and first lost my virginity, in fact. I don't base "success" on whether I stayed with anyone in the beginning—that was 30 years ago—but even most of my early lovers are considered part of my family, and I'm friends with them. (The surviving ones. The lover I lost my virginity to, and with whom I created our daughter, passed away from cancer mere days before these words were written. We parted amicably after 8 years and were family to the end.) I base "success" on the fact that when I broke up with anyone, it wasn't over polyamory problems—and my last two serious relationships are still with me and going strong.

This was helped by the fact that all my partners are experienced at polyamory, and indeed I won't be sexual with anyone who's not. Breaking in a heretofore monogamous person is a delicate art on the level of defusing a nuclear bomb, and it requires a great deal of skill and patience that I'm just not willing to deal with these days. (In spite of this, I am including a section on dealing with a heretofore monogamous slave, for those who like to defuse warheads in their copious spare time.) Both my wife and my boy had been poly long before they met me, and were old hands at it. They are also two of the least sexually jealous people I know, for which I thank the Gods regularly. So with 30 years of experience in polyamory—and in power dynamics; I've had 8 submissives and a slave, at various points—I'm jumping into the fray to share what I learned, and to showcase what other people have learned.

Definitions

Before we go any further, we need to define our terms. Since most of the key terms in this book are controversial and debated in the very demographics that use them as labels, it's especially important that we be clear about which definitions I am using for the purpose of this book, in reference to any given piece of regular jargon. We should disclaimer, however, that this book was written by many hands, and many worldviews. As an anthology, it has to keep the authentic voice of each author. That means that the definitions given in this introduction may not be those of everyone else; they are simply the definition of my "anchor" pieces. We apologize for any confusion this may create.

(Some of the following definitions were drawn from Raven and Joshua's book *Dear Raven and Joshua: Questions and Answers About Master/Slave Relationships*.)

Polyamory: A term coined by Morning Glory Zell-Ravenheart, and first published in her essay *A Bouquet Of Lovers*. The word is a combination of Greek and Latin meaning "many loves", which often annoys linguists who think that it should be written as *multiamory* or *polyphilia* in order to stick to one language. Zell-Ravenheart defined it as open, honest, ethical nonmonogamy, and that is how we are defining it here. We do not choose to judge the intensity or worthiness or level of affection of any consenting adult sexual interaction, because we don't think that we or anyone else has the right to decide whether anyone else's relationship should be considered "love". Only the people involved can really make that decision.

Poly: An abbreviation for polyamory or polyamorous.

Polyfidelity: A closed group of more than two lovers who do not seek sexual or romantic liaisons outside of the group.

Partner: Someone who has a regular committed romantic and sexual relationship with someone else, as opposed to someone who is a friend whom they occasionally have sex with, or someone who is still in the uncommitted dating phase, or someone with whom they had a one-night stand.

Primary Partner: A partner who is the top priority in someone's life, for whatever reason. Usual reasons are seniority and/or legal marriage. Similarly, a "secondary partner" is one step down in priority. Some poly folks even refer to "tertiary partners" although most find other words for that level of priority. Not all poly folks structure their relationships in this hierarchical way; some prefer to make all their partners an equal priority. The primary/secondary structure is somewhat more prevalent among power-dynamic poly folks, as they tend to be much more comfortable with hierarchies.

Fluid Bonding: Also called "body fluid monogamy", the practice of limiting any activity which involves the exchange of bodily fluids to only one partner. Some poly families practice body fluid polyfidelity—keeping the exchange of fluids within the poly relationship and using barriers with outsiders.

V-Relationship: Two people who are involved with a third person, but not with each other. The most common polyamorous structure. Another style is the "triangle", where three people are all involved with each other; the "square", like a triangle but with four people; and the "chain" or "line marriage" where there is a long string of people with two partners each, none also involved with each other. When it gets more complicated than that, my bitch Ruth likes to call it a "molecule".

Compersion: In modern poly jargon, compersion is the ability to feel nothing but pleasure in the fact that your partner is being made happy by other lovers. It is rather the opposite of jealousy.

NRE: New Relationship Energy, that burst of brain drugs that you get when you're first involved with someone. If NRE goes far enough to make you forget your existing partner's needs, we call it Shiny New Lover Syndrome.

Poly Family: Three or more people involved in polyamory with each other who consider themselves a family. Some poly families include former lovers. Many poly folk consider their poly family to be a modern version of the old-fashioned genetic extended family, or the clan or tribe.

Leather Family: A chosen family, who may or may not consider themselves poly, that considers itself to hold to the traditional culture of "Leather". This is, according to them, not just about BDSM practice but about upholding certain standards of behavior and forms of earlier "Leather Culture". Not all members of a Leather Family may be sexual with each other; Leather Families can contain nonsexual service relationships as well. Some folk, however, refer to themselves as a Leather Family without any cultural markers other than polyamory, BDSM practice, and some sort of power dynamic. The definition of "Leather culture" is also in flux and debate.

BDSM: Bondage/Discipline, Dominance/Submission, Sadism/ Masochism. The umbrella term.

Power Dynamic: A relationship structure with deliberately chosen and negotiated inegalitarian power distribution. Some people use the term "power exchange", but others dislike the word "exchange", as they feel that the power goes one way rather than being exchanged. I prefer "power dynamic" and will be using that term in this book.

Top vs. Bottom: This is referring to S/M play, and anywhere you see it used in this book, that will be the case. The top is the active partner in S/M play, and the bottom is the one who things are done to. These terms can also be used as verb forms—e.g. "to top someone" or "to bottom to someone". S/M play roles are irrelevant to power dynamic roles; submissives can enjoy sadistic or sexually aggressive play and dominants can enjoy sexual passivity or masochistic sensation. These terms refer only to fun activities and not to how a relationship is structured.

Dominant/Submissive, or Dom/sub, or D/s: This refers both to personality traits and to chosen roles (as in "it's not very dominant to be passive-aggressive at your submissive"). The dominant is the one who is in charge of the situation, be that an hour-long scene or a lifetime. Since these words also refer to personality traits (usually differentiated by such language as "being *a* submissive" as opposed to "being *the* sub in that scene" or something similar) we believe that one can be a dominant or a submissive while still alone and unpaired. In a D/s relationship, there can be as many limits set by the submissive as the dominant is willing to go along with. The level of D/s can range from cursory to limited and specific to deep and broad, but there is generally an understanding that the sub is bound only by their word and could walk out at any time, should they wish to do so.

"Domme" is a term for a female dominant, but not all female dominants use it, especially since it has a "femme" quality. More butch (or at least less femme) dominant women sometimes prefer "Master" or "Sir". In complement, "Dom" refers specifically to a male dominant. When it comes to genders in general over the course of this book, we've tried to alternate them for both submissives and dominants. I'll also refer to dominants in general as "D-types" in this book.

Master/Mistress/Slave, or M/s: These are the most controversial terms, the ones that people argue over fairly intensely. "Slave", especially, is a term that is bitterly fought over in various areas of the BDSM demographic. In our book *Dear Raven and Joshua*, we spent a lot of wordage going over all the possible definitions for both words that we'd heard, no matter how contradictory they were. If you're interested in reading further on this definitional conundrum, we invite to you check it out. However, we'll spare you the list here and simply say that the term "slave" is generally self-applied by a person who lives in (or desires to live in) a level of transfer of authority and control over their lives to another person that is greater than that of a submissive. How much greater? As there's no central authority to enforce standards of who's a sub and who's a slave ... it's whatever people decide themselves, in their own relationships, confusing as that is when people try to compare experiences. (Also, some people living on the bottom side of a power dynamic prefer "slave" to "submissive" because they feel that the latter term implies a personality trait that they do not have, generally being aggressive people who happen to surrender to only one human being.)

Similarly, "Master" (or the feminine "Mistress", although some women also use the term "Master"), refers to someone who has (or desires to have) a level of authority and control over someone transferred to them that is greater than that of a "dominant". Some people (including my slaveboy and myself) see these terms as relational, like "husband" and "wife"; you can't be one without having the other. Other people (including many whom I like and respect greatly) see them as personality traits, much like "dominant" or "submissive", and feel that one can be a master or slave even if one has no partner and has never been in a power dynamic.

To be completely honest with all the confused people who are reading this right now, there is no great consensus about these terms in the various branches of the widespread and scattered BDSM demographic. There isn't even a consensus among people who take on those labels, and often there isn't a consensus among people in a single M/s-oriented group. We've seen some bitter and furious fighting over who has the right, or should bestow the right, to carry these labels. Sometimes this fight has driven people out of groups, or split groups up. At this time in the ongoing self-discovery of the M/s and D/s demographic, there's no neutral ground with respect to defining yourself ... and especially others.

So, for the purposes of this book, we aren't going to try very hard to do so. When you see me writing, you'll know what my definition is—a relational title with a very high level of authority transfer. (Very high. But then Joshua and I practice O/p and IE—see below.) When you read other people's essays, they will have their own definitions. In some cases, they were gracious enough to give them.

(I'll also refer to Masters and Mistresses as M-types in this book, as an abbreviation. I will sometimes use the term s-type, which can encompass both slaves and submissives.)

Owner/Property: These terms are used similarly to the terms above, but with the strong connotation that one party owns—fully possesses—the other party, with all the responsibilities that go along with owning something. In some circles, the O/p tag has been adopted by those who feel that the M/s tags are quickly becoming meaningless due to the vast numbers of part-time fetishists calling themselves "Masters" and "slaves". The O/p label seems—in my observation—to have started in the European BDSM scene, and this dynamic has a much stronger emphasis on absolute control, and absolute permanence, as opposed to a voluntary service arrangement. The slave is chattel, albeit probably the most valuable piece of property that the owner has, and considers themselves a "possession" of the owner. My boy Joshua like to sign his Internet posts to BDSM lists this way: *Joshua, a wholly owned subsidiary of Raven Kaldera*. That's his way of describing it.

Internal Enslavement, or IE: The term "Internal Enslavement" was coined by Tanos, a master in the UK who founded the website *The Slave Register*. According to him, Internal Enslavement is "both a process and a set of practical techniques which use detailed examination of a slave's thoughts, emotions and past experiences to establish and maintain a solid and inescapable state of ownership. This is achieved through control of the slave's psychological states, in contrast to external enslavement, which is made inescapable by physical forces rather than the slave's internal psychological state."

Total Power Exchange, or TPE: The current accepted definition of Total Power Exchange, coined by Steven S. Davis in the mid-1990's, is "a relationship in which no impediment to the exercise of the owner's power is accepted ... Such things as safewords, contracts, negotiated limits, and anything else which recognizes, acknowledges, or formalizes limits on the owner's power are inimical to TPE."

The difference between these two terms is one of specificity. Total Power Exchange is just what it says it is: a (usually 24/7 live-in) M/s relationship in which one person has given all authority over to the other one. But it is still an umbrella term, and under that strict definition, there can be a lot of leeway. While the early proponents of TPE felt that the definition didn't count unless it was a live-in 24/7 relationship, later D/s folk adapted it to cover part-time relationships, as long as the TPE model stood whenever the people in question were together.

It also leaves open the question as to whether the submissive in question is a voluntary submissive ("Every day I have the choice as to whether I leave this relationship, and I choose to stay..."), an honor-bound submissive ("I could theoretically leave, but I've promised to stay..."), or a psychologically bound slave ("I can't leave, because I can't bring myself to disobey any more..."). In contrast, Internal Enslavement is more specific. It is a system whereby the slave is slowly conditioned into a state where they are psychologically unable to disobey. This is done with their consent, and is usually an open collusion between both parties.

Scene: There are two meanings to this word, and no real way to get around either of them. The first meaning refers to a single discrete episode of BDSM play ("...I got beaten pretty hard in that scene we had last week..."). The second, usually differentiated by calling it *the* scene, refers to the greater BDSM community in one's given area ("...switches seem to abound in the scene around here..."). Unfortunately, members of a wide variety of other subcultures also refer to what they are involved in as "the scene".

Munch: Informal term in the BDSM community for practitioners getting together nonsexually for a group outing, usually to a restaurant.

Protocol: A set of rules about the behavior of a Master/slave couple (or more than a couple). Protocol can cover everything from how people are to speak to each other to how people are to move their bodies. "High protocol" generally refers to a relationship with extremely formal behavioral interactions, whereas "low protocol" has more casual interactions. Protocol does not necessarily refer to ethics, morality, or how the household is to be run on a daily basis— for instance, "You will greet me by kneeling and placing your head between my boots" would definitely be considered protocol, whereas "This is the kind of laundry softener that we use" might not.

M/s Household: I believe that this term started out by meaning a group of people who all lived together under one roof, and who were all involved in a power dynamic with each other. However, more recently, it seems to have taken on a meaning similar to "Leather Family", as the members no longer have to live together or necessarily be directly involved with the dynamic, just with each other. I've seen it used as almost analogous to "clan", with some D/s or M/s practices.

Most D/s people who don't have much experience with polyamory tend to imagine it as being one dominant with a "stable" of submissives, but in actuality the range of variety in kinky polyamorous families is huge. As well as the aforementioned situation, there are paired (and occasionally unpaired) dominants who share one or more submissives, slaveowners with vanilla partners, hierarchies with people at the top and bottom and switches in the middle, and even submissives with an egalitarian partner and a dominant. There is also great variety in the levels of power dynamic between relationships with any given partner; a dominant might have one egalitarian lover, one full-time slave, one full-time submissive with significantly more rights and limits, and a part-time sub that they see occasionally. Many ongoing polyamorous families end up looking more like constellations than simple geometric forms.

Border Wars:
Polyamory, Swinging, and BDSM

People who are polyamorous, in general, tend to be socially progressive and are often involved in numerous (especially sexually) progressive groups. While this is certainly not true across the board, it does seem to be the majority situation. It's as if coming out of one closet makes it easier to throw open the doors of another, or dive into that unknown swimming pool you've always eyed with fascination. However, to assume that all sexually progressive groups have the same worldview, politics, or values is often to make a mistake that creates scuffles and dust-ups along the frontier's edge.

Swinging Into Kink

One of those dividing lines has traditionally been between polyamory and the "swinging" demographic. While both feature ethical, honest nonmonogamy as their "front line", the swinger demographic has traditionally been older (45-65-year-old) upper-middle-class to upper-class professionals who place no value on being out of any closets, and who tend to be sexually conservative. BDSM was largely "too way out" for most of them; kinky swingers tended to get together privately rather than showing off their perversions in public swinger's clubs. Heterosexuality was the unquestioned norm. Female-female eroticism was accepted so long as it was secondary to heterosexuality, but male-male eroticism was taboo.

To be fair, nearly all of these values seem to come less from any homogenous "swinging culture" and more from the inherent values of the age and class of people who are most into it. As that demographic is replaced on the bottom by people who came of age further past the sexual revolution, things are slowly changing. Today, swinging isn't always the rigid dynamic expressed in most of the stereotypes. Former swinger (now poly slave) AJ recounted his experiences to me:

When I was in the swinger's community, there was a strong emphasis on the importance of your primary relationship. Swinging was seen as something that enriched your marriage and enhanced your sexual relationship with your spouse, not as a substitute for a healthy and enthusiastic sexual relationship. One of the fundamental cornerstones of that community is that swinging is not a threat to your marriage, and your marriage *always* comes first. We never used the words "primary" and "secondary", because your spouse was always assumed to be your only primary. And if you hit it off with someone but your spouses didn't get along, you didn't go any further with it.

Playing with other people is something we did as a *couple*, not as two individuals. You never set up a date without your spouse. In fact, on the rare occasion one member of a couple couldn't make it to a party, the other one wouldn't even suggest going alone. The person staying home would have to offer, and repeatedly assure them it was okay. You couldn't seem too eager to be at a party without your spouse, or people would talk. No one wanted to be seen as a home-wrecker.

Swinging isn't just about sex. It starts out being just about sex, but then you get to know each other. You start spending time together outside the bedroom. You go on vacation together. Some couples even move in together as a foursome, or move next door. (I think the best setup is sharing a duplex.) I only met one real "threesome" of swingers. They'd been a foursome, two couples who'd been swapping for years. Then one of the husbands passed away, and the widow moved in with the other couple. You could tell the husband really loved and cared about the widow, and the two women were like sisters. It was really a beautiful relationship.

Old-time swingers who've totally opened their relationship seem bemused when poly folks go on about negotiation, and scheduling, and all this complicated stuff. They seem to have a really natural and easy way of going about it. Maybe because they've been doing this for decades! It seems like the poly community is mostly younger folks.

BDSM, too, is starting to horn its way into swinging. While it is still too outré for most swinging clubs, private clubs and organizations for swingers who practice BDSM are springing up all over the Internet. "Adventurous sex" headlines are lumping them all together, and they are definitely getting jumbled together in the process, more than simply in print. BDSM-swinger Eddie reported to me:

> I'd wanted to play with submissive sex for decades, but I was worried that my wife wouldn't approve. When I did tentatively bring it up to her, she didn't like the idea—it's not her thing, and she just wasn't into being a dominatrix. Since I love her more than I love submissive sexplay, I left it alone for years. Eventually we ran into a couple we liked as people—a dominant woman and her submissive husband—who I brought over to talk to my wife. I hoped that maybe the dominant woman of the couple would be able to tell her about some of the delights of female domination, of having a man under your heel.
>
> Instead, by the end of the evening, all three of them were talking about swinging, and how some swing couples were into whipping, dominance and submission, etc., but not all of them. They both assured her that swinging was a safe place to be married and stay married, that "running off together" was not acceptable. They suggested that we look for a couple where the wife wanted to explore domination but the husband just wanted good old-fashioned sex, and they sent us to the right places to advertise. So within a week, instead of my

wife of 28 years wanting to dominate me, I was facing down a lovely woman with a whip while my wife got it on with her husband in the next room. When I came out later, she just said, "Did you spank him good?" and when she received an affirmative, she laughed and said that she was glad I'd gotten what I wanted. I asked her if she had had fun and she told me that it was great.

Now we have a regular relationship with three other couples we met through swinger's organizations. One is the couple we first met, and the others are dominant women with submissive husbands who are allowed to have vanilla sex with women of their wife's choosing—which usually means my wife because she is not dominant and is thus no competition. I get to submit to them, and our sessions usually end with them ordering me to "make sure to service my wife beautifully between now and the next time." She has reported that I am much more considerate of her in bed now, because I have to be! And the other guys are very attentive to her as well, and she knows that our marriage is safe. So it is the best of both worlds.

Polyfolk, for the most part, regard swinging as a different world, and not one that they generally want to be associated with. While there is more crossover than most polyfolk might like to admit—from swing couples who leave the club scene and move in with each other to poly couples who play with swinging because they can—there is still a perceived gap between the two. They are usually demographically different, for one. Polyfolk tend to be younger, or if they are the same age as the swingers they came out of a counterculture lifestyle rather than a professional one. Polyfolk also tend to be more interested in education than preserving a closeted status quo, more open to GLBT members (and more likely to have openly bisexual practices), and more likely to have progressive politics.

While women have a lot of power in swinging—the emphasis on protecting one's marriage is very much a female-safety social mechanism—it's subtle power, and the overriding initial aesthetic seems to be one of satisfying male desires. Of course, many former swingers admit that while it's usually the husband who initiates the move into swinging, many a couple finds themselves with the wife having a wonderful time and the husband pulling back due to jealousy or performance anxiety. In contrast, the polyamory demographic is setting a new standard for men and women in relationship.

Gender Battles On The Sexual Frontiers

A recent article on polyamory in America in Newsweek's online magazine[1] came to the interesting conclusion that, far from being the male-horndog-screwing-around-uncaringly-on-the-hapless-women stereotype that many outsiders fear, polyamory is shaping up to be a surprisingly woman-centered (and, the article dares to say, feminist) practice. The article comments, "It's easy to dismiss polyamory as a kind of frat-house fantasy gone wild. But in truth, the community has a decidedly feminist bent: women have been central to its creation, and 'gender equality' is a publicly recognized tenet of the practice." The article's author, Jessica Bennett, commented in a blogpost that "...the key to poly relationships is gender equality, and women have been central to the creation of the practice ... The way these families make their relationships work is perhaps the most feminine of all of this: by good old-fashioned talking."[2]

Academics who are watching the polyamory demographic are commenting similarly, often in something like wonder. Elisabeth Sheff, in her article *Polyamorous Women, Sexual Subjectivity and Power* in the *Journal of Contemporary Ethnography* points out that "...multiple-partner relationships have always gone on, but they have rarely had the gender equity characteristic of poly

---

[1] http://www.newsweek.com/id/209164/page/2
[2] http://www.doublex.com/blog/xxfactor/feminist-roots-polyamory

relationships." [3] It seems that in order to make the potentially woman-exploiting practice of nonmonogamy woman-safe, women have stepped in to create the boundaried, honest, processing-laden, love-focused practice of polyamory. Most of the "primary texts" of the polyamory demographic have been written by women, usually women with progressive politics (but also a large percentage of sexually kinky women). This is not to disparage the written contributions of non-female poly authors (being as I'm one of them), but women have contributed the lion's share of the most-read works.

In the provocative online essay "Polyamory and Feminism", poly writer Pepper Mint points out that polyamory media incidences get the most positive public attention when they are clearly woman-focused—i.e. where the subjects are not only egalitarian but focused around a female figure with multiple partners. It seems that this allays the fears of egalitarian female watchers while not turning off too many male watchers, whereas a man with several girlfriends (or at the extreme, a far-right-religious man with multiple wives) loses the approval of more women than the watching male fantasists make up for. Pepper Mint theorizes that, given this media statistic, the political arm of the polyamory movement should "...ensure that media exposure of polyamory foregrounds women who have multiple partners." Pepper Mint also condemns allying with religious polygamous groups for this reason, stressing that:

> Perhaps most importantly, the current surprisingly high credibility of polyamory depends on the status of women within polyamory. I have seen this repeatedly in discussions among people who are new to polyamory: their acceptance of polyamory often hinges on how women are treated. If they think that polyamory is yet another excuse for men to exert a double standard, they are turned off. (And many of them do think this despite the actual situation within polyamory, because nonmonogamy historically has been dictated by the

---

[3] http://jce.sagepub.com/cgi/content/short/34/3/251

desires of men.) If it can be made clear to them that women are significantly involved, they are impressed.[4]

While the polyamory demographic is considerably less political than, say, the GLBT demographic, it is just now starting to be more political, and to think about the possibility of gaining social and perhaps legal acceptance someday. These new considerations, along with the strong ethic of strict egalitarianism (in order to contrast with historical sexist models) and the pervasiveness of women's-choice-as-ethical-touchstone as a moral starting point, has created what may be the best possible principles for polyamory to succeed politically against huge cultural odds.

On the other hand, this ethic seems at least at first glance to fly in the face of power-dynamic relationships, especially ones with female submissives. Feminists have had a hard time—for a very long time—with the conundrum of women freely choosing to put themselves into submissive positions in relationship. Some younger (or kinkier) feminists will cautiously agree that feminism is about having unlimited choices for women, even if some of those choices aren't ones that they approve of or would choose for themselves. (Some female submissives, especially lesbian or bisexual ones, identify as staunch feminists themselves on the same grounds.) Others are unable to see far enough past the position of submission to see that choice as anything but social programming-based delusion.

The first great public clash between feminism and BDSM was the infamous leatherdyke controversy of the 1980s, best described in the anthology *Coming To Power* by the lesbian SM group Samois. Before that point, the feminist movement (which was never a monolithic movement, really, but a number of loosely related ideologies that differed widely on many matters) and the fledgling BDSM demographic had moved in very separate worlds. It was not surprising that lesbian-feminism was the place where they would clash; SM dykes were "the enemy within the ranks" rather than "the

---

[4] http://freaksexual.wordpress.com/2007/03/27/polyamory-and-feminism/

enemy without", and generally considered themselves staunch feminists who had made free choices as adult women, and wasn't that was feminism was about?

The initial clash, however, ended not with any sort of conclusion, but with SM dykes drifting away from the lesbian-feminist ranks. The latter subcategory of the women's movement more or less disintegrated over the next decade, with members mostly moving into other areas of activism, and SM dykes avoided feminist groups in favor of GLBT-oriented ones. The dialogue stalled in mid-argument and was not picked up again, at least not there.

BDSM (by now it had gotten its whole acronym) was debated thoroughly in gay-lesbian political circles, but its existence seemed to fall into an oubliette of "something a few unimportant weirdoes do" for most other groups. The polyamory movement developed from a demographic that was middle-class, intellectual, well-educated, politically progressive, sex-positive, and largely heterosexual, with or without bisexual tendencies. Queers—especially ones who move mostly within the GLBT community rather than bisexuals who hang mostly with a straight-to-bi crowd—are a more recent addition in the past decade. Feminism and egalitarianism is, to this day, a closely-held tenet—and one which has become a barrier to any kind of political alliance with polygamous religious sects, many of whom are the ones actually ensconced in active legal situations.

After so many years apart, when BDSM practitioners began to make their way into poly political and social communities, there wasn't much of a ripple at first. Kinky sex didn't faze the polyfolk ... but then the people with the full-time power dynamics started poking in, and the ideologies (emphasis on the plural) of master/slave families seemed to be an awkward fit. On an online forum discussing the clash of demographic cultures, "Sin" explained:

> I allowed a non-kink poly group to dominate my life
> for 10+ years. As one of the co-facilitators of ongoing
> community events, I tried to introduce the aspects of
> BDSM to those who seemed interested through

discussions and hands-on-demonstrations. But no-go. Those few of us within that community who were *living* the leather lifestyle were pushed off to a separate room, much like a circus sideshow. I finally withdrew from that community, and am seeing it all much more clearly now from the distance.

The biggest difference I have experienced is this: it appears that many (most?) vanilla polyfolk see the entire world as their playground or candy store. I fear that our community may be just another cruising scene for them. I've witnessed similar behavior in the Neo-Pagan community as well: non-Pagan poly folk showing up at the events to cruise—not at all serious about the religion at hand! We are just another flavor of playtoy. I hope I was not guilty by association all of those years. I've burned my "poly" card. As for where the poly community "developed its values and social mores", I believe it all started as a natural expression of more love. Today it seems to be a game of more numbers—who's got the fullest calendar, or most "complicated" lifestyle.

On the other hand, some inexperienced D/s practitioners shoot themselves in the foot when they get it into their heads to look for new partners in polyamory groups. My partner and I have been able to educate some hardcore-egalitarian polyfolk, perhaps not into appreciating but certainly into being more comfortable with our dynamic. However, this doesn't happen by dragging D/s customs (and especially online D/s customs, which are their own arcane behavior) into a community that doesn't have the background knowledge to see it as anything more than pretentious, rude, and possibly sexist (if submissive women are involved, in fact or fantasy). D/s practitioners who brave those shores need to step carefully and leave the jargon, and the attitudes, out of it. Anita Wagner, a poly activist, writes:

A controversy arose over the last couple of days on a polyfidelity list about a new member who is a submissive in the BDSM lifestyle's introduction. In it she referred to herself in the third person and made other references that caused some of the non-kinky poly list members distress ... I recall a time when a BDSM master joined a poly list I was on, and his manner of writing about himself felt to me very off-putting. Though I didn't condemn him or even address the issue to my recollection, I do recall feeling offended that this man seemed to expect people not of his lifestyle to address him in terms that acknowledged his self-identified superiority.[5]

Regardless of how frequently outsiders to both demographics pretend that we're all one mass of sex-kink, that's not the case in real life. Most polyfolk are not kinky, any more than most people are. Of the ones that play with SM, most are not interested in power dynamics outside of "play". Most will neither understand nor appreciate being recruited nonconsensually into a "scene" with power-dynamic-seekers using their stage to play "roles" that, without education, may make them uncomfortable. I've always felt that part of both mastery and service was courtesy, and part of courtesy is not making people unnecessarily uncomfortable. While there are certainly prejudices we as power-dynamic people face when building bridges with this community (for all the political reasons I've listed), there's no point in making it worse by waving inappropriate roleplay in their faces. It's a "when in Rome" custom.

I do believe that with enough time, effort, gentle education, and people willing to be good examples, useful bridges can be built between all these communities. But if you're in a power dynamic relationship and you're walking into a polyamory group (since the

---

[5] http://practicalpolyamory.blogspot.com/2007/04/why-bdsm-poly-community-customs.html

sparse traffic is largely one-way at the moment), try to be that good example. I would suggest holding to these rules:

+ Be a courteous guest, bother to take the feelings of the tribe you're visiting into account, leave the jargon at home, and act like you would in any public space. (Assuming you're not the sort who drags your significant other around on a leash in the grocery store. Remember that people in public did not agree to be nonconsenting audiences to your scenes. All the serious, long-term, stable power-dynamic relationships I know are well aware how to behave in public, and don't find it necessary to pull such childish pranks.)

+ Act and speak like an ordinary human being, including on the Internet. No slashed caps, no lower-case pronouns, no "yes master". This is really aimed at the unowned subs, and the masters/mistresses who require these things of their s-types. Don't make them do things in public that will make people uncomfortable, at least not until you've been there a good long while and folks know you as people.

+ Bring up the fact that you're in a power-dynamic relationship, sure, but remember that you might have to do education if asked, and be prepared to educate in a way that makes you a good example. The best way to start is for the s-type to interact in ways that proves they are a thinking person with their own opinions. They don't have to openly disagree with their dominant, but they should be able to interact normally with other people. The dominant should interact in ways that prove they are secure, friendly, easy to approach, and don't expect anyone else to act submissive toward them or give them special respect. In other words, let them get to know you as people first, without clouding the issue with the trappings of your power dynamic. If it's really a grounded, reality-centered dynamic, you should be able to make it invisible when necessary, while still very much in place. "Honey, would you please hand me a cup of soda? Thanks, hon," can be code for "Get me a drink, slave," and no one needs to see more than that. Also, it helps if both parties look happy about each other and their lives, and are openly affectionate and loving to each other. (It's especially effective if the dominants are openly affectionate and loving toward the submissives. Dominants who sit in the corner looking sullen and occasionally giving a sharp order to their s-types are going to be looked at askance. That's just the way of things.)

✦ Understand the background values of the group, and don't disparage them—they have the right to hold the values that they hold, and you won't be able to walk into a group and change those anyway. As someone who is personally a feminist myself—and, yes, I am also a slaveowner with an M on my driver's license, and I don't see those things as necessarily conflicting—and who comes from a long history of progressive sexual values, I am very much in favor of people having the choices that they want in their lifestyle. That includes the choice to turn some or all of their lives over to some worthy person that they have chosen.

I believe that the best way to bridge this ideological gap is not to decide that "this philosophy is in opposition to what I believe, and so I think it's stupid," but to reiterate, again and again, that both sets of base values come from a place that is much closer than either group might think. The polyamory demographic's holy grail is about having a wide range of relationship choices for all people. BDSM's holy grail is consent, and even people in extreme power dynamics lay their ethical keystone on the fact that the slave signed up for this life enthusiastically and honestly wants to be there. Both groups want to be able to choose the life they love, and that makes them content, without outside interference. Go over this ground again, whenever it's necessary. Remind people that just because a choice isn't one you'd take doesn't mean it's a bad choice. Remind them how their choices look to people who don't approve of them. Go over it every time, *before* you start explaining or justifying why you prefer this lifestyle yet again. It sets the stage for the explanation to come, and it puts out another stone for the bridge.

D/s and M/s Within BDSM

The BDSM demographic is an enormous umbrella over a huge diversity of people. There's no way to generalize about any of us except to say that the way we conduct either the context or the activities themselves of our love lives is considered to be outside the norm. Most BDSM people are in it for the kinky sex, and there's nothing wrong with that. (Let it be said that I am totally in favor of all forms of kinky sex between consenting adults. Go for it.) Some of those folks play with power dynamics as part of a scene, but everyone involved knows that it's not serious. A smaller number are serious about it while it's happening, but keep it well boundaried inside the bedroom.

A smaller number yet bring it outside the bedroom, and negotiate its effect on their regular lives. Here's where it starts to get suspicious for everyone else, even the "kinky everyone else". Most people will be all right with a little bit of play extending into daily life, so long as it's still considered "play", so long as it doesn't intrude on the notice of others (which is actually not an unfair preference), and so long as it can be abandoned on a moment's notice by anyone involved who doesn't feel like doing it at the moment. However, at this point the intensity levels of power dynamics increase, and that starts to make a lot of people uncomfortable.

Before we go any further with this explanation, I'd like to make an Enormous Disclaimer. First: There is no one right level of intensity to a power dynamic. Every relationship must be custom-designed by the people involved in it, and created to their satisfaction and no one else's. Having a more intense dynamic does not mean that you are better, cooler, more impressive, or "doing it the real way". Saying that one must have a certain level of power dynamic involved is like saying that the only way to be a good Catholic is to be a monk or nun. (Even the Pope wouldn't say that.) If you are feeling bad about your dynamic because you think that it isn't intense enough to look impressive next to someone else's, I've got a rolled-up newspaper for you to beat yourself with.

Second: Very few people who have very intense dynamics would say that they're better than everyone else because of it, or that you, the reader, ought to do things the way they do it. The miniscule number of people who *might* say that are the assholes that one finds in about equal proportion in any demographic, and secure adults simply learn to tune them out. (Sometimes those assholes cruise for potential partners, and give people a hard time if they won't agree to their chosen dynamic. Again, ignore them and walk away, and understand that this is not the entirety of M/s people by a long shot.) If you think that everyone with a power dynamic more intense than your own is constantly judging you as some kind of weakling ... well, you get the rolled-up newspaper too. And if you decide that I'm saying that, then you get a whole series of newspapers, because I'm not. In fact, I'm stating it here: The relationship is good when it's good for everyone involved, not when it matches anyone else's standards. Period. Got it?

(In fact, I'll tell you what's *really* impressive. What's impressive is having a solid, stable, mindful, negotiated power dynamic *of any level of intensity* that has been going on for more than a decade, with the same people involved, and is still going strong. That's what's impressive, OK? Work towards *that*.)

Now we can get back to the implications of dynamic levels. Once you pass the 24/7 line, people begin to get suspicious, as I said. There are still plenty of people who openly claim that 24/7 D/s or M/s relationships don't exist, or can't really work, and that those of us who claim to actually be doing it are lying or deluded. Still others claim that while they may exist, they are inherently unhealthy for all participants—and, in some cases, the "abuse" term is thrown about to describe them. Proponents of this view—including, and perhaps most sadly, others in the BDSM demographic—quote lists of characteristics assigned to codependent relationships and point out their similarity to some of what we do. (As of right now, I have gone onto the Internet, that fertile source of most of these lists, and found 16 of them in 15 minutes of Googling. None are alike. Many of them contradict each other. The only things that they all have in common are the ideas that at least one person in the codependent relationship is *not happy there*, and *is made to feel bad about themselves*. This common denominator, by definition, rules out every one of the successful long-term master/slave relationships that I know personally, regardless of intensity, and that's all I have to say about that.) Within the BDSM demographic itself, people with 24/7 power dynamics have to tread carefully, and if they are of the sort where slaves willingly give up their paychecks, their votes, their ability to breed ... or their right to decide who does or does not have sex with whom ... even some 24/7 people start getting uncomfortable.

In his keynote speech to the Master/slave Conference in D.C. in 2008, Master Skip Chasey said:

> Don't think for a moment that the larger kink community has got our backs. We're the outsiders among the outsiders, and the reality is that those of us whose D/s proclivities extend beyond the dungeon are more often than not considered suspect by our leather brothers and sisters, who view us as a threat to their social acceptance.
>
> I can tell you from first-hand experience that while our legal system is sometimes willing to turn a blind eye with respect to one's SM activities in connection with family law and guardianship matters—after all, everyone knows that SM is just "kinky sex," right?—that's unfortunately not the case when it comes to evaluating the qualifications of persons who participate in Master/slave relationships. M/s is still virtually always a disqualifying taboo. Because of the heightened scrutiny we receive from the powers that be, many in the leather community would like nothing better than to sever the link between them and us.

If you think I'm simply paranoid, then perhaps you're unaware that at the 1998 Leather Leadership Conference, a policy statement on the issue of "SM vs. Abuse" was drafted containing some imprecise verbiage that could be interpreted as a condemnation of the dynamic that underlies virtually every Master/slave relationship. And when a few years later that problem was brought to the attention of the kink community's leading national advocacy organization, who at the time was widely promoting that policy statement, their leadership responded by saying, and I quote, "Those people"—meaning us—"are on the fringe. We don't care about them."

When I wrote the book *Pagan Polyamory* on the subject of polyamory in the Neo-Pagan religious community, I put out a lot of flyers at Pagan religious events, looking for people to interview about their relationships. I also began to get the first angry mail (I won't call it hate mail, exactly, but it was on the way there) from people in a group that I actually belonged to (my religious community) as opposed to the right-wing fundamentalists from whom I was quite accustomed to getting hate mail. People in my own religious community rejected the idea of polyamory, and especially the idea that it might be made legitimate. This reaction made me realize that I needed to add a chapter on polyamory's political reception in Paganism, and that meant that I had to poll people who didn't approve, to find out why they felt so strongly about it.

After some discreet polling, I discovered that people's opinions fell into three major categories. First, there were the converts who had brought Judeo-Christian mores from their upbringings, and just hadn't questioned them. (For the record, I suppose I should say that there is no theological reason in Paganism to bar polyamory, which is probably why it's spreading so fast there.) They honestly believed that monogamy was "correct", in a cosmic sense as well as a personal one. Since they no longer followed faiths that mandated it, theirs was simply a deeply-held personal conviction of what looked "right" to them, because that was what they had observed growing up. The second group was more political; these individuals were openly worried that if we allowed polyamory as a practice to be acceptable in our faith, we'd look bad to outsiders who wouldn't understand. "They'll think we're all sluts," was the frequent comment.

The third group was a little more problematic. The entirety of this group seemed to be women (although I wouldn't rule out the existence of men who would feel the same way; the problem just seemed to be more widespread among women) who were scared that if polyamory was accepted as a practice, their husbands and boyfriends would want to pressure them into doing it. They clearly felt that they would not be able to hold their own personal boundaries on the matter without great trauma, and really wanted a social standard that they could point to and say, "See? Our community agrees that this is wrong. If I talk to everyone else in it, they will tell me so." In essence, they were asking the community to legislate their relationship boundaries for them.

These same attitudes can be seen in the divisions between people in full-time power dynamics and the rest of the BDSM demographic. Many people in kink communities have feelings about the essential necessity of egalitarian relationships that are just as solid as those in polyamory communities. In some cases it's even more important to them, because they may justify the practice of playing with power and vulnerability during sex by reminding themselves and everyone else that they are only giving up power or receiving someone else's power for a short and heavily rule-bound period, and across the breakfast table everyone is equal. People who don't have that justification might have the potential to go very wrong, and even if most of them aren't, there's a certain amount of "if this is dangerous in the hands of some, then we shouldn't encourage it for anyone". After all, there's no certifying body that scrutinizes people's power-dynamic relationships and determines their health and worthiness, so what's stopping the Bad People from reading about this and using it as a justification to do Bad Things?

My argument for these folks depends largely on their backgrounds. If the values in question are the strongest emotional hook they've got to hang their justification of their kink on, there may be no way to cross that bridge except for a "well, let's just try to agree to disagree courteously, all right?" If it isn't that pivotal to assuaging their inner guilt, I'll use concepts that I got both from doing HIV activism in the GLBT demographic and kink activism/education itself: We all know that telling people not to do that sex thing they really want to do is less effective in the long run than teaching them how to do it safely. Forbidden fruit just looks tastier, but with the right education, people can learn how to get what they want without hurting each other. While some skeptics might not believe that there is a way to do a 24/7 power dynamic safely, one could argue that at the least, showing would-be masters and slaves a model with high standards of trust, honor, honesty, communication, good judgment, and extensive pre-negotiations, and encouraging them not to settle for less will give them the skills they need to weed out not only the Bad People but the Simply Unsuitable People whose desires and expectations do not match theirs.

The second negative opinion has relevance as well. The general BDSM leadership is well aware how bad the demographic looks to most ordinary vanilla citizens. While some elders grumble about the mystique that is lost via the new culture of rainbow floggers, fundraisers, and Fun Flogging 101, there is the point that this is what needs to happen in order to have any chance of becoming normalized in society. We have, as a demographic, now breached the ring-pass-not where we can no longer hide, and bureaucracies that were once only vaguely aware of us as a faint bogeyman are now watching with disapproval. We have court case precedents, many of them detrimental to us. We can't go back, and the only way forward may well depend on making us look as far from sinister as possible. Those of us who live in full-time power dynamics make awfully sinister villains, if you're trying to hang the mask on someone. It's understandable that BDSM leaders with their eyes on the prize at all costs would prefer that we vanish into the woodwork until the prize is won. Understandable, but not fair.

My answer to this group is exactly the same answer I gave to the anti-poly Pagans who were worried that we'd give them a bad name. I wrote this in an open letter to an angry Pagan and put it up on my website:

This is a question that the queer community has been dealing with for some time: who do we dump in order to "look better" to right-wing fundamentalists? After years of angry (and justified) infighting, the queer community is finally coming to the realization that we can never dump enough "fringe groups" to look good to them. The fact that we are queer at all damns us. The Pagan demographic will, similarly, have to come to this decision. The fact that we are a sex-positive, queer-positive religion means that we will never have their blessing, polyamorists or no.

That doesn't mean that all hope is lost, though. In Massachusetts, the state where I live, gay marriage was just legalized. I have faith that it will be a long, slow tumble across the country over the next few years. It's just a matter of time. The first stone has fallen, and the rest will follow. My point is that Massachusetts has one of the most inclusive queer movements in the country - we don't turn away the leatherfolk, the transsexuals, the drag kings and queens, the polyfolk in order to look respectable – and we won. We won. That says that it's possible to win without sacrificing any of your children at the gate.

Why did we win? By being inclusive, we got the sheer numbers to do so. We cannot convert most of the enemy, but we can outnumber them by gaining like-minded allies. By like-minded, I mean groups who are also pro-diversity, and who do not make rules about who their allied groups can have as members. Because that's one of the deepest tenets ... that diversity is sacred, a truth that we can see reflected in Nature. By gaining allies who believe similarly, we gain the numbers to win. By not sacrificing our more controversial members, we show those allies ... that we are not merely paying lip service to that ideal.

The third group's objection was, and is, the hardest to face down: people who fear that they will be pressured to accept a power dynamic that is more intense than they are comfortable with. As in my polyamory survey, it seems to be made up primarily of women, with only a few men also complaining. In the BDSM demographic, it seems to be entirely submissives, slaves, or would-be slaves. This is not surprising, being as s-types are the ones who have the most to lose by being roped into a relationship that is not congruent with their desires and values. Submissives also tend to be people who want to please, and may have a harder time with being assertive, especially in the face of a charismatic dominant or one that they are emotionally invested in. It may be that they have an even harder time holding their boundaries intact than did the egalitarian Pagan women who complained to me, and even more of a dependence on "but this is the way that the People Worthy Of Respect say it's to be done, Master!"

I had the hardest time of all finding something effective to say to this group this first time around, and I'm still working on it when faced with BDSM people. Saying, "It's your responsibility to find out what your options are, choose the one that's right for you, and not settle for anything else even in the face of loneliness, horniness, romantic softcore porn, or pressure from a potential or existing partner," is cold comfort and not useful for a submissive who is facing that pressure (even if only in paranoid fantasy) and panicking. The only useful thing I have come up with goes back to my first answer: Teaching about M/s models with high standards helps would-be slaves to see that they are allowed to have standards from the beginning, before they make any agreements, and that indeed they *should* have them. It's how they can keep themselves safe.

I do believe that part of any discussion on M/s education needs to start with the kind of Enormous Disclaimer that I stated earlier in this section. If there has to be a Community Standard for people to lean on, rather than "24/7 Master/Slave Lifestyles Are Dangerous And We Shouldn't Be Doing Them," how about "Everyone Has The Right To Agree Only To The Relationship Style That They Want To Have, And No One Can Tell Them That They Should Be Having Something Different." Even if they do have a screen name of Master Lord High Domly-Dom or Mistress Goddess Dominique Eternally Ruthless. It's not just that people will be less threatened by something they don't want to do when there's an ethic in place stating that free choice of relationship styles is an inalienable right that you are expected, and commended, for holding your personal line about. It will give our submissives a little more spine and a lot more surety, and that's a good thing. After all, it's a greater honor to give up something strong than something flaccid.

At this point, the polyamorous people with no interest in power dynamics who are reading this book out of curiosity will be noticing something: You've seen this kind of reflexive "if-this-is-OK-someone-will-make-me-do-it" fear before. I chronicled its existence in the Neo-Pagan community, but it can easily be found in many other places directed at polyamory by frightened monogamous people with poor boundaries. You understand the concept of an ethic of free choice of relationship, that people should be allowed to choose the structure that works best for them, and not bow to the ideas of outside standards, right? See, we're not that different after all. In the end, we all want something that looks remarkably alike when seen from an objective distance. It's just the details that differ, and we can all agree that those are, and should be, custom-fitted for each batch of warm bodies and minds, however we choose to organize ourselves in relation to each other.

M/s and Sexism

The first thing that most polyfolk think of when they imagine a negative master/slave relationship is usually a male-dominant, female-submissive dynamic where both parties believe that those roles are "natural for their gender" and that everyone else would be better off if they emulated that pattern. I'm not saying that such couples don't exist, but they are few and far between, just as there are fringe extremists in every group that the vast majority rolls their eyes at. There is a slightly larger cadre of M/f couples who, as one of them put it, "know that's not true for the rest of the world, but it's true for our household." In other words, they are creating a small world of their own with its own rules, separate from the outside world. That's basically what every M/s couple does in one way or another. After all, there is no "certifying body" to decide that I am the person best suited to be in charge of Joshua; that's just something that we two decided together.

Unfortunately, there are a few loud and obnoxious people who like to tell people that their way is right, and they often happen to fall into that first category. I remember going to a presentation at a sex-positive conference which turned out to be run by just such an individual, complete with a slideshow of cringing slave girls and silhouettes of mammoths and sabertooth tigers (apparently to indicate that M/f relationships were some sort of "primal" pattern), and talk about how women really want to be in a cage when a sabertooth tiger comes for them. After the presentation, however, all the people who had come because they were already in some kind of power dynamic were sighing and shaking our heads, and trying to calm the distressed vanilla organizer and reassure her that this wasn't the usual way things worked. I believe that most of this sort of thing comes out of people wanting desperately to get some kind of legitimate justification for their kink, which I also believe is the wrong tack. Kink ought to be justified by the explanation of We Enjoy This And It Harms No One, and it needs nothing else.

Obviously, the gamut of GLBT power dynamics and female-dominant/male submissive relationships don't fall into this category at all. However, some male masters with female slaves —while not trying to universalize their experience to others—describe themselves as having an "old-fashioned" or "traditional" or "1950s" relationship. This helps them to "pass" in public with the wife doing deferential things for the husband that might raise eyebrows in this more egalitarian era. (Then they complain when militantly egalitarian people don't find that acceptable either.) Except that when we're talking about actual master/slave relationships of the sort that I and my friends practice, I don't think that description actually applies.

When looking at the M/s practices of the people I respect, regardless of gender combinations, I find that we put a great deal of thought into the headspace and well-being of our slaves. We dig into their minds and ponder their thoughts. We communicate constantly. We go to a huge amount of trouble to figure out what's best for them, and how to get them to come to a place of comfort with our wishes and expectations. We make sure that they are suitable for this life before we take charge of them. We worry about our honor, and acting rightly toward our slaves, and earning—and keeping—their trust.

"Traditional marriage", of the type where husband had full chattel rights over wife, was not anything like that. The religious and civil rulings that hemmed in the wife made it irrelevant. The husband did not need to earn her trust—she was often handed to him willy-nilly as a girl and could not leave because the community would bring her back. He did not take her feelings into account, nor was he encouraged to by society and male "gender norms" of the time—in fact, he was discouraged from this. Her submission to whatever situation she found herself nonconsensually (and possibly unhappily) in was maintained not merely (or even mostly) by him, but by her upbringing and the other female members of her family. Even if she was miserable and unsuited for that life, he was not required to do anything about it. (Romantic love was not necessarily always an expected thing, either.)

Even in a kindly and well-suited marriage, the sort of transparency and communication and shaping that experienced M/s practitioners do was unheard of. Intimacy was not a high value in relationships—following the social rules was instead. Couples might go their entire lives not speaking to each other about their inner lives, and that was normal, and it worked because the expectations were low and the social rules held everything in place—like a supporting web, or like a prison, depending on the person.

It is the last 40 years, from the sexual revolution on, that influences our approach to M/s relationships today more than many would like to admit. The emphasis on equality and the shaking off of social norms placed a greater emphasis on communication and emotional intimacy (as being normal) to replace those bonds, and we utilize that today, those "forced" relationship skills. The kind of master/slave relationship techniques that are discussed in detail at support groups and conferences by M/s teachers and mentors, these would have been unnecessary and unthinkable in former times. Some people may idealize and euphemize the past in ways that are unrealistic, but the truth is that we have more to thank from the sexual revolution than from its preceding eras for most of what makes modern M/s work. And this, too, is true for polyamory as well.

Starting Gate:
Before The Relationship

When I first got into a power-dynamic relationship, I had been polyamorous for fifteen years already. I had a pretty good handle on that, and I knew how to communicate and process and resolve conflict (and how to screen out people who were not going to be able to handle polyamory, one of the most important skills of all). My first power-exchange relationships were fairly lightweight in terms of how much power and authority anyone was giving up. (They seemed pretty heavy at the time, but compared to where I am now, they were only two steps away from egalitarian. Still, it was an excellent place to start.) I treated the polyamory as I would with any egalitarian partner, because that was what I knew how to do. Everyone's needs were taken equally into account, and I did not press my will on my subs when it came to poly issues. When it came time to talk about the relationships, we communicated like equals.

Later—and that meant a few subs later—I became curious about how a strong power dynamic would change the nature of "classic" polyamory. After all, if someone is willingly giving up authority over how their life will be lived, does that include who their partner has sex with, or brings into the home? Would the "veto power" polyamory clause that my wife and I had with each other be meaningless in such a relationship? I decided to find out. I went online—this was earlier in the saga of the Internet, and while there were email lists there weren't a lot of specialized forums in the early '90s—and looked for something that combined these two axes. I found a single list, labeled "Poly and BDSM" or something like that, and got on it.

I was taken aback to find out that all the people on the list (or at least all the ones who were posting) were submissive heterosexual women, most of whom identified as slaves, and whose dominants/masters had pushed polyamory onto them whether they wanted it or not—and none of them seemed to want it. The list seemed to be bogged down in one long argument over whether when

Master tells you that you have to put up with him finding other slavegirls, you can't complain or you're not a good slave. No one seemed to have worked the problem out successfully. Some were in the process of dumping their dominant male partners; some had recently done the dumping and were warning the other women that future "masters" had to be forced to remain monogamous. Most were hanging on but generally miserable. I found none of the happiness that I'd run across in vanilla polyamorous demographics, to my dismay. I left the list, shaking my head.

It was my first introduction to the single most popular form of poly-and-power disaster. I still see it happening, over and over. Part of the problem is that people in M/s relationships (and specifically the ones in charge) often have very little idea how much work even egalitarian polyamory is. The polyamory community and the subset of the BDSM demographic that practices serious power dynamics don't cross very often, for reasons I covered in the last chapter. This means that many masters and mistresses don't actually get to talk with experienced polyamorous families about what works and what doesn't, and they end up blindly attempting to reinvent the wheel, losing a lot of wheels in the process.

According to the pornography models, the M-type is supposed to be able to wave his or her dominant hand and all the s-types will just magically get over their ingrained issues and adapt gracefully to being part of a harem. In reality, this is rarely the case. (If ever. I'm not saying that it's impossible, because nothing is impossible, but it's highly improbable at the least.) Porn doesn't tell stories about jealous fits and processing and ulterior motives and passive-aggressive behavior, because that's not sexy. In porn, masters are always right even when they're acting stupidly or pathologically, and slaves can always be beaten into liking something.

In reality, interestingly enough, forced polyamory does seem to be the single most frequent subject for so many (especially female) slaves to be laying down very unsubmissive lines about, even if they claim to be slaviest slave on the block. I hear "If my Master decided not to be monogamous with me, I'd leave him (or throw a fit or whatever)" far, far more often than I hear stuff about physically damaging behavior or moral issues or whatever. It really seems to haunt the thoughts of many submissives.

I think it's because polyamory is an ambivalent ethical issue. Activities that involve endangering the physical health of the sub, or clearly immoral issues (making the sub steal or kill for you), well, those are going to be weighed in on as "bad" by nearly everyone. There will be a huge amount of social pressure on the M-type to refrain from doing such things, and plenty of support for an s-type who is inflicted with them. But many people think that polyamory is perfectly fine, that there's nothing inherently wrong with it, as long as everyone involved has given consent. Certainly many people in the BDSM demographic practice it, including many BDSM "celebrities". There's a lot of precedence for (bad) poly in BDSM porn. This situation can frighten the submissive who doesn't want this relationship structure. They may feel that their preferences will not be taken seriously, either by the dominant or by the community that sets the social standards. This can explain the panicky note in the voice of many a submissive when they declare that any breach of monogamy by the dominant would be an immediate deal-breaker.

After all, if you as a sub give up even some of your choices and authority to someone else, ideally you're doing that because you've already inspected their values and lifestyle, and are confident that any large and life-impacting decision they make would be one that you would very likely agree with. Once you give up even some of your authority, it's that much harder for you to fight your D-type or M-type if they make a decision that you hate—and having to do so may well ruin your trust in them and in the dynamic.

There's another layer to this which is probably even more frightening to many subs. People change, including dominants. People's wants and needs change, and they come to learn more about themselves. Sometimes that means that the most consistent and dependable dominant will suddenly discover that they like something that they didn't think they ever would ... and I've seen that thing be polyamory so many times that it's not funny.

No, I'm not saying that every master who promised monogamy to their slave at the beginning, before the collar went on and the enslavement started, is going to suddenly change their mind and start realizing that they would really prefer to be polyamorous 15 years down the road. Certainly not; some people are monogamous because that's what suits them best. But some are monogamous for other reasons, reasons that don't suit them and that they may eventually discard, and that's frightening to the sub who wants everything set in stone at the beginning of the relationship, never to change, especially after they no longer have much (or any) recourse. Of course that's frightening. Giving yourself to someone else is a huge act of trust.

And yet ... it happens. People change. Dominants change, and as I said polyamory is one of the more frequent ways that I've seen them change ... and what's the submissive with the desperate need for monogamy to do? The hard truth is that it's the dominant's job to do whatever it takes to slowly lead them into a place of being OK with that (after first having made a realistic decision about whether it's even workable and healthy with this person), and it's also true that many dominants do not have the experience or the wherewithal to do that, and that's hard on the sub. But I think that every submissive needs to understand that they are taking a leap of faith, and that their dominant may change in the future.

In fact, I think that there ought to be part of the pre-claiming negotiations that sounds like, "So I know that you're swearing that everything you like now you'll always like and everything you don't want now you'll never want. But what if that changes after I'm collared? What will you do to help me be all right with that? Because just ordering me to like it and telling me that I'm a lousy slave if I can't manage is not going to be terribly effective."

I know that's an area where most people don't want to tread—it's like being a vanilla couple and saying, "So on the off chance that we get divorced, can you convince me that you'd be a kind and reasonable ex?" Everyone wants to pretend that this never happens ... but it does, and it takes a brave couple to look at that before the commitment of whatever kind happens.

Let's begin with the obvious. Before a power dynamic is determined, both parties need to talk honestly about polyamory, and how they feel about that. I hear a lot of "Yeah, Master has always said that he'd like to be poly someday, but I don't think I could deal with that, so I'm just hoping that he won't." This is a slave who clearly went into the relationship without due diligence. They're sitting around hoping that the person who controls most (or all) of their life won't do something that they believe will bring them great grief and trauma … even though that person in control of them has intimated that they might do just that. This is a recipe for one of those aforementioned disasters.

Even the most dedicated slave is still human, and if they would not be comfortable with polyamory in a vanilla relationship, that doesn't change just because they get owned. On the other hand, really-truly-owned slaves sometimes end up poly whether they like it or not, because yes, they give up the right to decide who will be sexually exclusive with whom, or to have any control over their partner's bits. I think that this is especially difficult for monogamously-inclined submissives in romantic relationships with their partners, who have a starry-eyed idea that this will be in many ways like a vanilla bodice-ripper except kinkier.

If the single would-be master or mistress is not one hundred per cent set on absolute monogamy, the would-be slave has the right to ask the would-be master or mistress these questions, and get an honest and thoughtful reply:

+ If the right person came along, would you be polyamorous?

+ If the right person came along, would you be polyamorous even if it meant that I would feel terrible and hate it?

+ If the right person came along, would you be polyamorous even if it meant that I would leave (assuming that I still could)? Would you give me up because I could not adapt to polyamory?

+ If I was not in a psychological state to be able to leave, or I really wanted to try and make this work, what would you do to help me past my emotional pain?

✦ Are you looking to merely have casual sex, or are you ideally looking for another serious relationship?

✦ Have you ever been polyamorous in the past? How did that work out? If there were problems, what contributed to them? (Beware the dominant who simply blows this off by saying that they were all crazy, or something like that.)

✦ What relationship skills did you learn during those relationships that you found valuable?

✦ If you've never been polyamorous in the past, and you want to try it, how are you going to prepare yourself for it?

✦ If I'm willing to try it, but I have reservations, how are you going to prepare me for it? What resources can you find me? Books, support groups, friends, mentors?

✦ If additional people were brought into the relationship, would I be allowed to help choose them? Interview them? How much influence would you give my preferences? Veto power? Put up and shut up? Something in between?

✦ Would there be contracts with them as well? What would they look like?

✦ What would my position be in relation to them? What would that entail?

✦ What would be expected sexually of me in a poly situation?

✦ What would I be sexually allowed in a poly situation? Could I have an outside lover? What would that require with regard to my priorities?

✦ What kind of safe sex rules would be used? What kind of pre-sex testing would be required? How do you intend to keep us all safe in this way?

✦ If there are limits around "sex", on you or on me or on anyone else involved, what does "sex" mean to you?

Where's the line? Does nongenital BDSM play count? Sex toys in orifices? Oral sex? Be specific.

✦ Are my ideas about what constitutes "sex" going to be taken into account at all?

✦ If I am to be the primary relationship, what will I get that's special for me?

✦ How will you convincingly demonstrate to potential partners that I am your primary relationship?

✦ If I believe that a new partner does not really respect our primary bond—e.g. is hoping that we'll break up so that they will have you all to themselves—will you take my fears seriously? What indications of this lack of respect would you take seriously? What would you do about it?

✦ If we have children, how will the poly situation be handled?

✦ If I have massive insecurities once we get into this, what will you do to help me get past them?

✦ If we have fights, how will the conflict resolution be handled? How much experience do you have in conflict resolution? Are you willing to get more training before becoming a polyamorous dominant?

✦ If we have a partner move in, how will the household management decisions be handled? How much say will they have? Will they be just a "roommate" in terms of how much clout they have in things like cleaning, decorating, having friends over, etc., or will they have more?

✦ What kind of time and attention do you intend to give another partner, and how much would I continue to receive? Do you have that much time and attention to give?

If you as the would-be master are reading this and thinking, "Damn, this sounds like a hell of a lot of work," you're right. And you know what? This communication session, with all these questions, *is just the beginning.* If you're having trouble giving clear answers to these questions, maybe you need to learn more about how this process works before you jump in. While it does get easier, it doesn't stop being work.

Many submissives get into relationships with dominants who already have primary relationships. In 90% of those cases, it's called "cheating", especially with online or long-distance relationships. The dominant's primary (and usually married) partner generally has no idea what is going on, and the dominant in question wants to keep it that way. Many folks involved in such situations have long lists of reasons why this is a good and necessary thing. Personally, I cannot see that level of dishonesty as either loving or respectful. However, whatever the reasons, this is not polyamory. One of the basic tenets of polyamory is that honesty about other partners is necessary for healthy relationships, period. Some spouses do a "don't ask, don't tell" sort of thing, but the information needs to be available to them if they ask. And besides, it's not a good thing to be someone's dirty little secret. That gets old fast, and it never seems to stay a secret anyway. There's also that many people who claim to have a "don't ask, don't tell" relationship are actually cheating, but the new partner has no way of verifying this if they can't talk to the existing partner. D/s and M/s relationships require more trust than an egalitarian relationship, and there can't be that level of trust without a high level of communication between all partners.

On the other hand, if a heretofore monogamous submissive has fallen head over heels for a dominant who is openly polyamorous and already has at least one relationship, then even more talking needs to happen before any contracts are finalized. While this couple can skip the first eight questions, the rest all still apply. On top of that, they need to discuss other questions as well. The very first one should probably be "When will I be able to discuss our potential relationship with your partner(s)?" If the answer isn't, "Let's set a date for everyone to talk about it—here, let's check the calendar ..." then the potential submissive should probably turn the other way and start walking.

Some other questions that they might also discuss:

✦ How much of your time and attention will I have, compared to your existing partner(s)?

✦ Is there a chance of me evolving into a partner equal to your existing partner(s) or is that just not going to happen? (This doesn't have to be a deal-breaker; it depends on the needs of the person asking. Some people are fine being eternal secondaries; some would prefer something more.)

✦ If I'm not the primary partner, who will I be in public when family or neighbors come over? The nanny? The maid? The roommate? The friend? Do you intend to acknowledge me as a partner?

✦ Will I be allowed to be affectionate in public with you?

✦ When we go to events where people are aware of our situation (e.g. kink events or poly events) how will you handle things? Will I be required to act (or not act) in ways that show my secondary status, especially if your existing partner is present?

✦ Is there a hierarchy? Where am I in it? Will your existing partner(s) have authority over me? If the two of you disagree, who wins? If I don't like what they want me to do, what recourse will I have?

✦ If there are children between you, what relationship will I have to them?

✦ *(To the existing partner)* What are your fears regarding adding me to the relationship? What can I do to alleviate them? Is there anything I can do to make this easier?

✦ *(To the existing partner)* How do you see the power dynamic between the two of you? Do you approve of the power dynamic that we are negotiating?

The submissive also needs to do some realistic soul-searching about their own personality and needs, and how well they would be able to cope with polyamory. It helps if they can come up with some reason besides "this dominant won't take me if I won't go along with it." Bea Amor, in her article *Polyamory in BDSM: What To Expect As A Submissive*, writes:

> Polyamory is not something you involve yourself in because it will please your dominant. You have to want to be in a relationship with more than one person and perhaps more than one gender. It has to come from inside you and you have to ensure that when you involve yourself with a dominant that has candidly stated that he wants more than one submissive or slave, or get involved with a couple, that you are very sure of yourself and not at all prone to jealousy ... The critical thing is to ensure that all the parties know exactly what is expected of them.[6]

What if the dominant wants monogamy and the submissive is hoping that in time they'll be able to talk them into polyamory? I wouldn't stake the next few years of your life on it. Monogamous dominants are generally pretty intractable; their unwillingness to let anyone else touch their toys can be legendary. If you're hoping for polyamory and looking at a monogamous dominant, my advice to you is to leave them to all the desperate-for-monogamy subs, and go find yourself one of the desperate-for-polyamory dominants.

This is a fairly rare situation, for obvious reasons. Still, it happens. It can also happen that a newer master or mistress starts out fully intending to be polyamorous, but the possessive joy of owning someone completely takes them by surprise and they find themselves wanting to be monogamous, or at least to not let the slave have sex with anyone else. This possibility needs to be discussed as well, even if the dominant believes "that will never happen!" However, this possibility shouldn't be counted on by the sub who secretly desires monogamy.

---

[6] http://www.associatedcontent.com/article/950809/bdsm_101_polyamory_in_bdsm_what_to_pg2.html?cat=7

Rights And Limits:
Intensity Levels Explained

Whether the s-type has the "right" to demand that their owner be monogamous, or whether they have veto power over new relationships, or whether they can have other relationships of their own, depends on how many rights they are allowed and how absolute the dynamic is. Different relationships on this continuum will have widely varying agreements.

We don't believe in saying that subs or slaves or masters or mistresses "ought" to have certain rights or limits. These are all negotiated in intensely personal ways between the people involved, and the only way to judge is if everyone involved says that they're completely happy with the situation. Beyond that, it's up to them. There is no one "right" way to do this. There's only the ways that work to make everyone content with their choices, and the ways that make someone in the relationship miserable. That will be different for everyone.

One definitional note: Throughout my section of this book, you will see me refer to the defining factor in comparing levels of power dynamic as *intensity*. I chose this term after a great deal of thought. I needed something to describe how much control the dominant in the relationship has over their opposite number, how much authority has been given up and in how many areas. *Intense* seemed to be a word that could usefully describe the quality of an escalating power dynamic. (*Extreme* seemed pretentious, and made me roll my eyes.) However, this term has no bearing on the sexual or emotional intensity of the relationship, and should not be misunderstood as such. People with a low-intensity power dynamic (or none at all) can be intensely in love with each other, and have an intense sex life. It's possible for people in a high-intensity power dynamic to not be in love or be having sex with one another at all. These areas are irrelevant to each other.

This is a sampling of points on that continuum:

✦ **Only In Scene.** The couple is generally egalitarian, and only occasionally play at a power dynamic during kinky sex. They negotiate as equals outside a scene about sexual contact with others.

✦ **Part Of My Time Is Owned.** The s-type is part-time, and the dominant only has authority over limited and specific parts of their life, and monogamy/polyamory is not one of them. They must negotiate as equals in this area.

✦ **All The Time, But Not Everything.** The s-type is full-time, but the dominant still only has authority over limited and specific parts of their life, and monogamy/polyamory is not one of them. They must negotiate as equals in this area.

✦ **My Sex Life Is Owned.** The s-type has given over authority in almost all areas of their life, including polyamory, but the dominant has promised them specific sexual expectations
(such as monogamy, or that they will have certain rights should polyamory occur; for instance remaining the primary partner or helping to select new partners) and it is agreed that the s-type has the right to walk out should the dominant break their word.

✦ **Everything Is Owned: No Recourse.** The slave is owned property, and willingly gave up their right to decide on such issues or enforce such limits. They must depend on the dominant's honor and the promises that they have made, and if those promises are changed they have no recourse.

Obviously, what level of intensity the dynamic will have should be negotiated beforehand. In fact, for a single submissive approaching or being approached by a single dominant, it should be negotiated thoroughly and agreed on to both parties' satisfaction before they even get to the poly questions in the Starting Gate chapter. Each of those questions will then be discussed from the standpoint of that level of intensity. The new s-type needs to be realistic with themselves about what they can handle when it comes to polyamory. My advice to the s-type is to imagine, in living color, the worst-case scenario allowed by the level of power dynamic that the two of you are negotiating. Mull it over for a good long while. If you're not quite ready to give up that level of trust, that's all right. Trust can't be demanded too soon. It might get to that level after several years, but there's nothing wrong with you if you need time to get there. If you can't imagine yourself ever handling it well, get that out on the table before you commit. It's better to wait for the right person than to invest yourself in someone whose desires are not congruent with your own.

Only In Scene

The five points on the continuum above are probably not the entirety of that continuum, but they will do for a start to discuss the polyamory situation in more depth. Point 1 is essentially an egalitarian relationship with temporary negotiated power dynamic in the bedroom. It is usually assumed that, while Joe is tied up, Sue the temporary dominant is not going to decide to bring someone into the bedroom to have sex with either her or Joe without having previously negotiated this act (and who is acceptable, and what level of sex they can have with whom, etc.) to the satisfaction of both parties ... unless, of course, that couple has negotiated otherwise.

It should also be negotiated as to what kind of protection and responsibility the temporary dominant will give to the temporary submissive for the duration of the scene. For example, if a third party is brought in to play and that person does something to make the sub uncomfortable, what are the rules? Should the sub drop out of role and yell at them, or should they communicate their distress in a suitably submissive way to the dominant and trust them to handle it? This decision should be made well ahead of time by both parties, based on variables such as:

✦ Is the submissive uncomfortable about giving up any power
in a situation that is not absolutely guaranteed to be safe?
(While this may feel to the eager dominant like a way of
saying, "I don't trust you to protect me," it's not a good idea
to pressure your play partner to be more vulnerable than
they are comfortable with. Trust can't be demanded, only
earned, and sometimes there may be a whole raft of past
experiences in the way that can't just be shoved aside at
will.)

✦ Is the dominant one hundred per cent sure about their
ability to firmly, confidently, and graciously handle the
situation? This includes knowing their partner extremely
well, enough to tell exactly how distressed they are without
forcing them to be further vulnerable in an uncertain
situation, and being able to guess the motivation and
potential ignorance of the third party. It requires calm
confidence that does not waver, but also does not get
triggered into anger—that's weakness, not good dominance.
Getting triggered and blowing up at someone is a good way
to make the person you're in charge of to be less likely, not
more, to speak up and potentially ruin the evening. If the
dominant isn't ready for that level of responsibility, and
would rather their partner just speak up and state their
problem like an equal, then that is what should happen.
(There's no shame in the dominant not wanting to go
further than they're comfortable with, either, something
that often escapes enthusiastic submissives. A sub should
never castigate their dominant for not wanting to be more
of a controller than they feel able to comfortably manage.
It's better to get a smaller level of competent, contented
control than a greater level of incompetent, uncomfortable
and possibly resentful control.)

✦ Can third parties be brought into the scene without prior
equal negotiation? In other words, will they be brought in
only beforehand with neither person "in role", or will the

submissive trust the dominant to handle it and take their wishes into consideration while they're in a vulnerable position?

✦ How are other poly partners in a poly family to treat both temporary dominant and temporary submissive while they are in role, should they be present during a scene? How will those boundaries be respected? What authority would they have over the submissive during scenes, if any? If they are not into power dynamics and are made uncomfortable by having to interact with them during a long or space-invasive scene, how will this be handled?

We've seen scenes that went pretty badly because other people were brought in, familiar or unfamiliar, and there was not enough negotiation between the initial people doing the scene. One thing that can go wrong is that some (certainly not all) submissives lose the ability to properly negotiate in "subspace", and can expect—and need—a great deal of protection from the dominant. We've heard of at least one scene where a gay dom took a sub boy into a party and offered him to a half-dozen other men. While the boy thought this was a hot idea and didn't object, later while he was "out of it" from hours of being in a very submissive headspace, a couple of the men decided to have unsafe sex with him. Later, when he had his head on straight again, he confronted the dominant about it. The dominant said something to the effect of "But you didn't seem to complain about it at the time!"

It's a reminder that if the temporary dominant is holding the submissive's limits, he/she needs to know what those limits are, and know to what extent he/she is authorized to negotiate those limits with others. In general, however, I strongly suggest that the two people in question negotiate with any other human beings before a scene, when both are acting as an egalitarian team and can put their opinions and perceptions on the table. This goes for threesomes and other poly groups negotiating with outsiders as well. ("I'd like you to co-top James with me; are you all right with our other partner Alicia watching?") Since technically people at this level are equals outside of a very tiny percentage of their lives—however exciting a percentage that may be—they may get carried away in the heat of a scene and forget that their dynamic hasn't been negotiated to be nearly as intense as they are pretending it is in the moment. At the very least, trusting the dominant alone with poly negotiations should not be a feature of the relationship in its early stages. Trust needs time—years, even—to be built up, and so does experience.

Part Of My Time Is Owned

At the second level of intensity, the dynamic is part-time—often this consists of people who do not live together, or who have children or high-powered jobs or other obstacles—and the dominant has full authority during specific times or over specific areas of the submissive's life ... but polyamory is not one of them. Perhaps the submissive has agreed to contact the dominant three nights a week, to keep a "slave journal" that the dominant has access to, to wear certain clothing, etc. ... but no one has any say over limiting or expanding the other's sex life. The people in the dynamic may also have other partners who require things of them as well.

When my boy Joshua counsels s-types who have partial dynamics, he advises them that it's better and more satisfying for both parties if the dominant is given full and complete authority over certain specific areas—even if those are only small and seemingly inconsequential ones—and the submissive does their absolute best to completely surrender those activities to the dominant's will, rather than giving up half-assed submission in a greater number of areas that must constantly be readjusted and interrupted. This also helps both parties feel better about the activities that cannot (and perhaps should not, for those individuals in that situation) be given over to another's authority. Assuming that polyamory is not one of these areas—for example, the dominant of a married submissive is unlikely to be able to order that sub to have sex with another party without the negotiated approval of their spouse—then everything needs to be conducted as equals, with equal respect.

Some points to consider when setting boundaries for this sort of relationship:

✦ Make sure that the dynamic doesn't leak into other areas. The current boundaries were probably set for common-sense reasons, but a power dynamic is a very seductive thing, and people in the midst of new relationship energy combined with a new power dynamic can desire a situation to change beyond common sense. Be warned that the submissive is often the biggest culprit in pushing to stretch the boundaries too hard and too fast and too inappropriately. It's almost a running joke among power-exchange people that in the early phases of a relationship, the submissive is yelling "More—harder—faster—more!" while the dominant is trying to curb their overenthusiasm and keep things at a reasonable pace without making the sub feel bored or betrayed. It usually falls on the One In Charge to keep the reality boundaries in place: "Oh, if only we could…" "Yeah, but we can't. Let's concentrate on what we *can* do." It's one of the official duties of the One In Charge, in fact.

✦ If the dominant is the one who is pushing past previous agreements, the submissive should worry, because they are vulnerable to being pushed beyond their own boundaries if they don't hold to them strongly. It might be time, in that case, to meet as equals and have a discussion on the matter, perhaps with mediators experienced in power dynamics who can help the submissive keep from just giving in on the matter. The reason that I stress this is because poly issues are so often one of the main areas where a dominant who is unfairly trying to push, will push. If either party in a relationship with this level of power dynamic wants to add people or change relationship structures, it needs to be discussed as equals, with no pressure of "… but real slaves just do what their masters tell them." It's not about "real". It's about what's negotiated for this particular relationship, which is just as "real" as any other relationship if the people in it decide that it is.

+ If the power dynamic has specific times when the submissive must obey the dominant (e.g. "I want all your Saturdays" or "When you go to BDSM clubs, you are mine first" or "Every night from 7 to 9 you are to text with me"), what is the role of other partners not involved in the power dynamic? It's not fair to put someone into a submissive position and then expect them to mediate on the spot between two conflicting commitments. ("I don't give a damn what she says about texting her from 7 to 9, I need the computer now to answer a business email, and then I wanted us to go out and get some dinner!")

+ Similarly, if the power dynamic has specific activities where the submissive must obey the dominant, those must also be negotiated with existing partners. Activities that impinge on another partner in some way that makes them uncomfortable need to be reevaluated. For example, the submissive may dream about being put in chastity and not allowed sex for weeks at a time, but if there's another partner who would be upset by this, then it's not realistic. Sometimes other partners can be convinced to go along with things to a certain extent, but no more—the dominant's egalitarian partner might be all right with the submissive doing the dishes and washing the floor every time they come over, but not if the submissive uses titles on them that they didn't consent to, or is naked and wearing only a large buttplug. Remember that no other partner should be a nonconsensual party to a scene if they don't want to be. I bring up the chastity rule because I know two examples using that particular desire, both in situations where the submissive had a dominant who didn't live with them, and an egalitarian partner who did. In the first case, the partner was fine with them being put in chastity every other week because they were satisfied with the submissive having sex with them in ways that didn't involve the sub's genitals during that time, and they rather liked the extra enthusiasm when the dominant unlocked the chastity harness and sent the sub to their partner's bed with orders to perform superbly well or else. In another situation, the partner was so unhappy at the idea of not having access to their partner's genitals, and so turned off by the idea of someone else having control over their partner's genitals, that the chastity idea was scrapped.

✦ If this is a couple who live together in a house with other adults, some of whom may be poly partners of one sort or another, how are the other partners to know when the submissive is "on duty"? There should be a clear signal—perhaps the presence of a collar or some other obvious, clearly visible sign—and they should all know what is appropriate in that situation, and be comfortable with it. The same goes for other partners who live separately but come over frequently, and are likely to visit during times when the dynamic is going on.(One note to remember: Teasingly encouraging the submissive to disobey the dominant's orders can be a sign of discomfort, although it may be difficult to get them to admit it.)

All The Time, But Not Everything

At this level, the two are dominant and submissive 24/7, and it is usually (although not always) live-in. However, it has been negotiated in the beginning that certain things are not under the dominant's authority. Examples might be the rearing of children from a prior relationship, or the submissive's job or career or schooling, or the submissive's home and domestic situation, or what area they will live in ... or who will have sex with whom. When things scale up to full-time, many of the problems found in levels 1 and 2 vanish, in that there isn't a start-and-stop pattern ... but it means that even more care has to be taken with other existing partners, should there be any. At this level, almost all dominants will be the submissive's primary partner, although in rare cases this is not true (and those cases require complete approval from the actual primary partner). Most of the submissives will be the dominant's primary partner, although some aren't.

Considerations for people on this level may be:

+ If the submissive is constantly under the authority of someone else, then it is entirely up to the dominant to make life decisions that respect the needs and desires of any pre-existing partners of that submissive.

+ While the dominant may not have a final say over submissive's poly activities, in a relationship at this level, he or she usually has a good deal of influence. Of partners I've known who were at this level, the dominants did have authority over the practice of safe sex, and many had authority over such things as how often a sub would see another partner, or how much time would be spent on them. When negotiating with a potential new lover, the submissive needs to be open about their D/s status, and exactly what that entails in terms of their time and activities. With a part-time relationship, the sub could theoretically see an outside lover only during times when they aren't "on duty"; when "on duty" is 24/7, there is no such time and any new partners will have to deal with this. We suggest that the potential partner first hear it from the sub, and if that doesn't weed them out, it's time to negotiate with the couple together and work out their priority in the sub's life.

+ At this level, the issue of transparency varies. (See the section on communication and transparency for a more thorough explanation of this phenomenon.) However, this is the first level at which total transparency is a frequent option, although some subs will still opt for privacy limits. Transparency can be very off-putting to another partner who may not want their sex life, their personal foibles, and everything that falls from their lips to be discussed with the dominant. Limits may have to be negotiated around this issue. If the dominant is not willing to compromise on transparency, then the sub is going to have to get used to a new form of behavior—every time that someone says, "Don't tell anyone, but-" they will have to put up a hand and say, "No, don't tell me—I can't promise to keep a confidence from (dominant)."

✦ Taking charge of someone's life 24/7 is a serious responsibility that requires a lot more time and effort than that of a more autonomous lover. New partners of the dominant, assuming that they are not also submissives, will have to understand the priorities involved. Frankly speaking, if someone turns over authority of much of their life to you, it is your duty to actually put in the time it takes to manage that life, as well as your own life. This means a lot of energy put into knowing their mental state and everything that is going on in their life, at least in all the areas where you have authority. An egalitarian partner may not understand the level of communication and effort necessary. (Even experienced poly processers have raised their eyebrows when I describe M/s processing, training, etc.) They may feel as if being more autonomous means less attention, and this will have to be worked out either by deeper understanding of the situation or more time put into their relationship.

My Sex Life Is Owned

At this level, the slave—and here I'm going to arbitrarily switch to the word slave, not because that's where all or even most other people draw the line but because this feels to me like a good place to switch over—has given their master/mistress authority over every part of their sex life. However, certain conditions still apply.

In her 2009 keynote speech at the master/slave conference, Laura Antoniou pointed out that:

> *Of course there are limits*. Don't be obtuse. The first "for instance" that comes out of anyone's mouth (or keyboard) usually involves amputation, am I right? "Oh, yeah? What if your mistress wanted to chop your ding-dong off, huh?" See, the answer to that is *not* "I would do it and hate it." The answer is *not* "That's a stupid example." Hey, you said no limits, not "no limits except for stupid examples." So the first "what if" is usually amputation or mutilation. They generally don't get to death for another five minutes or so. And almost no one mentions my favorite limit tester, moose vomit enemas.
>
> The real answer is that when we form deeply intimate bonds based on mutual respect, attraction, esteem and trust, *we pre-select for matching values*. A bottom who says they have no limits – assuming they are not a complete idiot on collarme.com, but say a bottom in a relationship right now, looking adoringly at their top – is saying, in effect, "I trust this person so much that I know they would never tell me to sell my children into sexual slavery/donate my brain to science tomorrow/ tell me to watch Glenn Beck for 24 hours straight."
>
> The top who says "no limits" really means that they trust their bottom to take a leap of faith with them. No limits doesn't mean a top is stocking fava beans and a nice chianti to serve roast slaveboy with. But it does mean they have found someone whose trust, faith and backbone are so admirable they can go places they would not even think of with someone less experienced or less well matched. This isn't no limits. It's pretty close

to matching limits. (Hey, if they were perfectly matched, it would get boring.)[7]

This is really the point where we have to talk about rights and limits. Up until now, it has been assumed that the slave has given up certain limits but kept others, including perhaps the most crucial things in their life. It has been assumed that their rights in the relationship were decided between the two of them as a compromise, if weighted a bit on the M-type's side at the last level. At this point, there's practically nothing left that the master/mistress does not have authority over. (There may still be a couple of big areas like kids or job, but at this level it's common for decisions on those to be handed over as well, or at least their word carries huge weight.) When we go past Level Three on this chart, it becomes absolutely imperative that the slave has thoroughly inspected the master's values and ethics in the beginning, before things get this serious. It is important, as Laura Antoniou says above, that they have limits that the slave is in congruence with. That goes for polyamory too, because at this level the M-type is setting the rules for everything about it—who will fuck whom and when, how people will be chosen and vetoed, whether there will be new partners and how they will be integrated. It's a matter of honor for the master/mistress—they are promising that the relationship rules will be XYZ, and the slave is trusting that they won't suddenly decide to break their word and change the rules ... because if that happens, the slave might decide to walk out.

I believe that this is the level where most of those angry female slaves on that early Internet list were coming from—they had given over authority for their sex life to their master, assuming that there would be monogamy because their master had made that promise to them ... and then he had changed his mind. Since negotiating about polyamory is no longer done as equals at this level, a sudden policy change for no reason other than "I feel like it" can cause a lot of resentment.

Considerations for people on this level may be:

---

[7] http://www.masterslaveconference.org/MsC2010/pages/history-speeches.html

✦ Listening to the slave's opinions about partners. At this level, the slave's opinions can theoretically be bypassed if the M-type desires, but they should keep in mind that a slave is a resource to use, and that includes their perspective. Even if the slave does not have any part in making the final decision about a potential new partner, their perspective may be valuable ... assuming that they are not caught in the throes of insecurity. One M/s couple who were just starting out interviewing new partners asked me whether my slaveboy had any part in the interviewing of new partners. I explained that we did it as a team. First, that reinforces the feeling of "teamwork" rather than "replacement" for the slave (who is in a more vulnerable position), and second, I found his opinion useful. He is especially good at seeing behavior problems in submissives that I might miss, because he comes at it from the bottom side and has a deeper understanding of what it is to be that sort of person. The master in that couple admitted that his slave was actually better at sniffing out bullshit than he was, and agreed that a team approach would be a good thing, even if the actual decision was his.

✦ Not abandoning the slave to their own insecurities. At this level, the slave's only recourse is to demand to scale down the intensity of the dynamic (assuming that their master/mistress will go along with that) or to walk out, which will be a painful and difficult choice if they are deeply committed to the relationship and the dynamic. This puts them in a very vulnerable position, and if they begin to feel insecure it is the M-type's job to work on that and find ways to reassure them.

✦ Openness about other partners. I personally believe that even if the M-type has this level (or higher) of authority over someone's life, it's important for them to be honest about what other people they may be playing with, including casual one-nighters. It's also important that they be clear about safe sex limits, and what precautions they took with each person. This is not because the slave has the *right* to know at this level; it's because being open and honest about such things, and clearly showing the slave that they are making every effort to guard the physical safety of themselves and the person they are responsible for, builds trust ... and the opposite behavior tears down trust. To be dishonest about these things is to shoot themselves in the foot. It's always better to build trust and trustworthiness, because it binds the slave closer to you. For a deeper discussion of this issue, see the section on *Putting On The Dominant Panties*.

Everything Is Owned: No Recourse

At the fifth level of intensity, the slave is property, chattel. They have agreed to this, hopefully not only willingly but enthusiastically. In some cases, the slave has given up their ability to enforce any rights and decisions, and they are so fully committed to this life, this owner, and this vow that no matter what happened they would stay on and try to make it work. Only the worst and most dangerous circumstances could drive them away. In other cases, the slave is internally enslaved, which means that the owner has (with the slave's permission and usually collusion) slowly and deliberately induced conditioning so that the slave is psychologically unable to disobey. In either case, the slave has no card to play (like "I'll leave or make your life miserable if you do X") in the event that the relationship goes in a direction that is difficult for them. There is no recourse, and they must trust their owner with every part of their existence, including their sanity.

The big issue at this level is the slave's ability to find a way to have a good attitude about emotionally difficult processes ... and the owner's ability to help them find it. An owned slave whose owner is doing something that bothers them should be able to go to their owner and say, essentially, "Sir/Ma'am, I want to be able to do this and be happy about it. I just need some help getting there, because I can't see my way clearly, or I can't quite get there on my own." The price that the owner pays for this much power is that they are obligated to do whatever is necessary to help their slave find a point of comfort with the process. You can't just command them into being emotionally fine with something. They are human, and should be able to ask for help and get it.

Any s-type can benefit by working on their ability to find a good attitude about hard situations, but the more intense the power dynamic, the more it becomes a real survival skill. The following section contains useful ways in which the dominant can help them to get there, but submissives should study the list as well as a self-help tool. For further help for those on the submissive side, I suggest the various essays by slaves later in this book.

How To Help With Attitude

When a slave has trouble being anything but unhappy and miserable about something, far too often a beginning owner will simply expect them to figure out a way to get right with it. Sometimes they can manage that, but sometimes they will need help. It's the owner's job to figure out ways to help them, because the slave is usually in this position due to the owner's wishes. With privilege comes responsibility.

My slaveboy reminded me that during the process of intense-level enslavement, there is often a period of time (sometimes years) where many of the slave's independence and coping mechanisms are dismantled in order to be rebuilt. As my houseboy so succinctly put it, "It's like when you're reorganizing the pantry. For a while, everything is a mess and nothing is in order, but it has to be that way for a few hours before it can get lined up in its new configuration." He also points out that while a compassionate dominant might feel that it's not such a good idea to introduce potentially emotionally difficult concepts to a slave during this time, such refraining is not actually a good idea. If the slave knows that a challenging activity is coming as soon as they get themselves mentally reorganized, it's not exactly an impetus to help speed the process along. Do it anyway, he suggests, and just be aware that they will need a lot of assistance from their owner in making themselves all right with the situation. On the other hand, this can reinforce the concept that the owner will be there for them, no matter the difficulty of the process.

Some methods we've found useful:

+ **It's Easier If I Have Something Of My Own Guaranteed.** Brainstorm ways that might make the situation easier for the slave, without abandoning the situation or compromising it to the point that others are unhappy. For example, if one slave feels insecure when the other slave sits at their mistress's feet and watches TV with her, perhaps they can sit somewhere else equally meaningful (assuming that the dominant invests it with meaning), or do a special job, or they get a certain number of nights where they get the floor space. The answer is not for the other slave to have to give up the floor space forever. It's more empowering for all involved if they can find a solution that works for everyone.

✦ **I'm Pleasing My Owner.** Remind the slave that the difficult situation pleases their master/mistress. Someone who is on the bottom side of a high-intensity power dynamic wouldn't be there unless pleasing their dominant was one of their motivations. They want to know that they are a good girl/boy/slave and that their master/mistress is made happy by their behavior. Find ways for them to concentrate on this, perhaps with a mantra. "This makes my owner happy. I want to see them happy."

✦ **Boy, Am I Owned.** One of the weird-but-great things about a power dynamic is that a slave can become both emotionally fulfilled and sexually turned on by not getting things their way. It's one of those things about the slave mindset that people who haven't been there just don't understand: "This isn't what I wanted, isn't what I would have chosen. That means I'm really not in control, that I'm really a slave. I can gauge how much of a slave I am by the fact that my preferences are not the priority here. Wow, I really am a slave ... that's wonderfully comforting to me." (Or, alternately, "...that's so hot.") If handled carefully, this can be a real enforcer of the dynamic, bringing home to them just how owned they are, and making them feel contented with that fact. However, it's best if they've reached and experienced this mindset in other less important areas of their life before trying to get them to that place with the challenge of polyamory.

✦ **Job Well Done.** My boy used to comfort himself about cleaning the catboxes (a job he hated because it reminded him of the cats he was allergic to) by doing a thorough, workmanlike job of it and telling himself that at least he did even the difficult things skillfully and well, without shirking. Relationship skills, including polyamory skills, can also be done meticulously and thoroughly. Have your slave research polyamory skills, mediation, anything about how polyamory can be done right. Make rules and protocols about how this is to be done; give your slave something to work on that they can achieve excellence in, and that is more achievable than changing one's emotions.

✦ **Positive Reinforcement.** As we mentioned in the above paragraphs, slaves like to know that they have pleased their owners. This means that their owners have a vested interest in letting them know when they've done the aforementioned good job. Slaves also tend to pretend (or tell themselves, and others) that they don't need compliments. It's not true. They not only love them (whether they admit it or not), but they need them, in the sense that they need a clear gauge of not only what they're doing wrong, but what they're doing right. The owner needs to remember to comment on that as often as they comment on the difficulties the slave may be having. For example: "That was great. You figured out when you were being triggered before it got out of control, you thought up a solution that would help you and wouldn't ruin the current situation, and you brought it to me calmly. You did great. This is exactly what I want. See, you're strong and smart and you can do this." Don't fake compliments, just let them know straight up when they do something right, and what you liked about it. You'd be surprised how well it works.

✦ **Peer Support.** Finding another slave in a similar position—struggling through poly issues—and arranging for them to talk to each other can be a great help. There's nothing like peer support for realistic advice and real sympathy. The problem is that it has to be actual peer support. That means someone who is either on the bottom side of a power dynamic at least as intense as their own, or else is understanding or sympathetic to their position. The very last thing that a slave in this position needs is someone telling them, "Well, *I* wouldn't go along with that," or "Your master/mistress shouldn't even be asking such a thing of you! It's abusive!" or "You should threaten to walk out if your master/mistress doesn't back down." Those things are the opposite of helpful. Help your slave find someone who can discuss the situation usefully and sympathetically.

+ **Remind Them Of Their Place.** Make sure that your slave's job is not threatened. Give them "territory", tasks and activities and behaviors that are theirs alone, and don't give them away to future partners. (This means choosing those activities carefully; can you be certain that you'll never want another slave to vacuum the floors or bring you drinks or provide anal sex?) Seeing that the practical aspects of their place with you does not change in the least, even when polyamory happens, can be a big reassurance.

+ **Distress Tolerance Skills.** While we're not suggesting that slaves are mentally ill or mentally challenged, there are resources out there for both these populations that can help anyone with figuring out ways to tolerate a minimally-to-moderately distressing situation without going all to pieces. If your slave lacks good distress tolerance skills, it might be worth it to check those resources out and help them to work on it.

Communication, Communication ... Transparency

"Communication, communication, communication" is one of the polyamorous rallying cries. We're all tired of hearing it, but it's entirely true. The majority of problems in a polyamorous relationship come from ineffective communication, and can often be solved by the application of effective talking with all parties involved. But in a power dynamic, what does that look like? In these relationships, the word that comes up the most is transparency. This is the concept that the more open the s-type is about his or her thoughts, feelings, and motivations, the more the dominant has to work with in creating the right space for the s-type to flourish, and the better the dynamic works.

My slaveboy and I started doing M/s before there was much in the way of available references for us to look at. Or rather, I should say, *useful* references. There was plenty of porn, and none of it was realistic enough for daily life, or referencing the sort of life that we wanted to lead. We felt our way through the dark trying to use common sense, and wrote up what may be one of the most boring contracts around.[8] It had nothing in it about "slave positions" or sexual fetishes. It did, however, have a clause that I considered the most important piece in the entire document.

> **Absolute access to mind.** Joshua has no right to privacy of word, thought, or deed from his master. Raven can demand and expect to get immediate and truthful information on any part of Joshua's life, including dreams, thoughts, fantasies, information, knowledge, and words and deeds past and present. Anything that Joshua knows, thinks, or writes will be at Raven's disposal.

---

[8] For those who are interested in seeing the entire contract, it's online at http://paganbdsm.org/joshcontract.html and also can be found in our book Dear Raven and Joshua: Questions and Answers About Master/Slave Relationships, available at Alfred Press, http://www.alfredpress.com.

This piece was my biggest deal-breaker, because without it I couldn't do my part of the relationship. Let's say it yet again: *Responsibility works best on maximum information.* If it was all going to be on my head, I needed to know everything possible about what was going on, in order to make the right decisions for all parties involved. If you have total responsibility for maintaining and repairing a vehicle, you'd better learn how that vehicle works, inside and out. You can't take that kind of responsibility if the hood periodically refuses to open and allow you to find out why it's making that suspicious noise.

We didn't have the word *transparency* then, but I knew instinctively that the key to my being able to run Joshua's life in a way that would, ideally, be even better for him than the way he might have run it himself depended on knowing everything that was going on with him. If polyamory requires a deeper level of communication than monogamous relationships in order even to survive, power dynamic relationships require a deeper level still. In each case, you're upping the required trust on everyone's part, and openness must be increased relative to that trust.

Power dynamics are difficult enough when there are only two people's worth of secrets to deal with. When you bring in others, it's extra important that the dominant(s) in question enforce as much transparency as the subs/slaves in question are willing to give. It's appropriate to let the degree of transparency vary with the level of power-dynamic intensity—for example, a slave who is property and has turned over all their decisions to their owner requires fairly complete transparency in order to make it work, whereas a submissive who only turns over authority for specific areas may only need to be entirely transparent on subjects that pertain to those areas and their satisfaction with them. How much is too little? Try this for a standard: Even for a non-owned submissive, if the standard of openness falls below that expected in an intimate, long-term egalitarian polyamorous relationship, it's not enough. In order to know what that looks like, it's worth it to read about and observe actual egalitarian poly dynamics. They set the minimum standard, below which you do not want to fall.

Some dominants claim that they don't want transparency, because they don't necessarily want to know every tiny little thought in the submissive's head. Either one of two things is going on in this case: the dominant may actually believe that they can run someone else's life without bothering to find out what that person thinks, which is a recipe for one of those disasters ... or, more likely, they associate "transparency" with "running off at the mouth". To this second group, I assure you that transparency does not mean that the submissive has to keep up a running dialogue at all times. You, the One In Charge, can decide how much information you want at any given time, but they can't hide anything. If you want it, it's on tap. If you don't want it, you can turn the tap off. Transparency is, as we said in our contract, is "absolute access to mind". (To the first group, I simply shake my head and wait for your "slave" to show up on an online list complaining of your breakup.)

I would also mention, here, the issue of job-related secrecy. For some jobs, there is confidential information that the individual is not supposed to reveal to others, and in some limited cases could actually be legally prosecuted for doing so. Being as client confidentiality often happens in service jobs (for example, social workers, counselors, ministers) and the more service-oriented among s-types have a strong tendency to end up in such jobs, this sometimes means that there is one area of their lives which they cannot ethically share with their dominants. Rather than making this a place where a slave must "hold their boundaries" against their master/mistress, which can hinder the process of transparency, it's better for the master/mistress to tell the slave that they must be open to them in all things, no exceptions ... and they give their solemn word that they will never ask these things, because they understand that it would be ethically wrong to do so. This builds trust and removes boundaries rather than keeping the slave in a state of vigilance and fear over this issue.

What about the dominant figure(s) in all this? It's true that in an unequal power relationship the master/mistress is not generally required to be as transparent to their slave as their slave is to them. It's also true that there is a lot of pressure on dominants to "create a mystique"; slaves often enjoy the fantasy of the implacable master who never cries, breaks down, has problems, or explains anything. We'll go into the other dangers of these fantasy expectations later; for now I'll just say that this sort of "mask" isn't really sustainable past a part-time, non-live-in situation. It's also a serious barrier to real intimacy ... and to sustainable polyamory.

So how much is the dominant required to communicate? Must they also be transparent, or can they hold back some privacy? Where is the line drawn? I can tell you for the record that polyamory does increase the necessary amount of transparency for everyone, including the dominant. One's private feelings have to be carefully scrutinized, and so do one's motivations in keeping them back. Wanting to preserve a false front of perfect dominance for purposes of mystique is the first thing that must be thrown out the window. First, it doesn't work with even one live-in slave. He/she will be constantly watching you anyway—or he/she *should* be, in order to notice your needs and desires—and no façade is going to stand up under someone who's that far into your business, much less two people. Second, masks (meaning artificial roles that no one acknowledges as such and everyone pretends are what's really going on) are detrimental to intimate polyamory practice, power dynamic or not. They can work with casual, non-intimate nonmonogamy, but if you go further than that, you need to be willing to show yourself warts and all. As I said, they'll figure it out anyway.

When Joshua and I worked out the communication in our dynamic, we built it around the concept of "radical honesty". This is the practice of holding back nothing, including one's feelings around a given subject, and possibly jettisoning verbal niceties if they are getting in the way of one's emotional expression. We see radical honesty in a somewhat different light than many of its proponents (some of whom seem to merely want to use it as an excuse to be a public asshole and never bother to take anyone else's feelings into consideration), because we are BDSM practitioners. For us, radical honesty is something that, like BDSM, can hurt—but you do it anyway because the results are so good. And, like BDSM, it should only be engaged in with the full and verbal consent of all parties involved. If your wife or the checkout boy didn't consent to engage in it with you, don't inflict it on them. Similarly, radical honesty can be turned on and off in the same way that an egalitarian couple who like to play with power exchange flick their dynamic on and off with the addition or removal of a decorative collar. It works because there are pre-negotiated rules in place as to what is expected.

Joshua has agreed to give me full radical honesty in everything, when I ask for it. I have agreed to transparency in anything that concerns my feelings toward him, our relationship, our dynamic, and anything else that I realistically think is something that could cause possible problems. If he asks me for personal information that I am not comfortable giving out, I first shove my initial reaction aside and carefully judge whether holding back this information could negatively impact our dynamic. I might ask him his opinion on that—after all, he may have information I didn't think of, and his perspective is a resource for me to use. If it looks like it needs to be laid out in order to make things work better between us, I'll do it.

I'll also grit my teeth and try to decide whether *I* would be emotionally better off for sharing that information. Just because we've agreed on rules that say that I *can* hide something doesn't mean that I always should. My slaveboy has permission, if it seems like I am struggling with something, to gently offer himself as a sounding board should I need it. He also has strict orders to leave it alone, and not take it personally, should I refuse. He knows me well enough to be sure that I am experienced in my own emotional maintenance, and that if I need to open up to someone about something, I will come to that point in my own time. On my end, if a subject is too sore for me to talk about, I've learned to make a commitment to work it through until it can be shared, and not to put that off. Sometimes I'll even set a date for myself to have dealt with it. Knowing that I am capable of this kind of self-knowledge process is part of why my partners can be all right when I say, "Not yet. I'll talk about it later." Because they know that I actually will.

If it is something that I judge to be none of anyone's concern, and that neither myself nor anyone in any of my relationships will be directly worse off by not knowing, I'll make a statement to that effect. I've found that it's best to be very clear about where the "black boxes" are where my slave is concerned, so that at least he won't be uncertain as to whether a given subject is none of his concern or fair game for discussion. Of course, in practice I share a lot of nonessential (or painfully intimate) things, because we *are* emotionally intimate. With my egalitarian partner, we both have the right to "black box" what we want from each other, and as she has chosen not to consent to radical honesty—which is her right—we simply trust each other to bring things up when they are ready.

As an example of my honesty process with my slave: Let's say that Joshua has made an error earlier in the day that angered me. We've dealt with it, but hours later he finds me glowering in front of the computer. Worried, he asks me if I am still angry with him. If the answer is yes, I'll tell him so. This is in both our best interests. It's important that he knows, at all times, the full consequences of his actions with regard to me. If I hide that he is the source of my disgruntlement, he'll probably assume it to be true anyway in the absence of another explanation, which he won't get because I've given my word not to lie to him. The discussion might then turn to how he could further repair things, or I may tell him to leave me and go do his chores, with the understanding that I will either get over it myself or I will come up with a way he can ameliorate my emotions. Either way, he is apprised of the truth and assured that I am handling it in an adult way.

If, on the other hand, the error was long forgotten and I was disgruntled over an annoying email in my inbox, I'd at least let him know that it has nothing to do with him. I am not required to share that it's about someone else's email (although I probably would because there's no reason not to), nor what that email says (although I probably would because I vent to him about such things). If I say it's not about him, he will believe me because I have a track record of speaking truth to him.

Let's say, instead, that my black mood was not quite so easily summed up. Let's say that I've been weighing my own possible responsibility for his error—did I give clear enough instructions? Was this something that he's failed at in the past and I'm setting him up to fail with no aid on my part, and a scolding when he inevitably does it? Perhaps I've been staring blackly at the computer screen trying to figure out if any part of it is on me, and if so, is it enough that I need to apologize for blaming the entirety of the problem on him? (He doesn't *need* me to apologize in these situations in order to salve his feelings, by the way. Were I to do so, it would be for myself in that I am holding myself to Right Doing, and secondarily for him in that it builds trust for him to see me holding myself to Right Doing.) When he asks, my first reaction is to tell him to go away, because this is embarrassing and difficult internal processing. I shove that aside and look realistically at the subject. Does this fall into the categories of him/our relationship/our dynamic? Damn straight it does. Am I obligated to tell him about it? Absolutely.

Am I obligated to tell him that moment? Not if I feel that I have not finished processing it to the point where it can be usefully discussed—e.g. I haven't figured out how much, if any, of the error was my fault. So I could theoretically just tell him to go away, but I know from experience that's counterproductive. Telling him instead that he is part of the problem, but only part, and I will discuss the situation with him as soon as I've finished working it through, is much more effective in terms of trust-building and making him feel less insecure. However, I am obligated (again, not to him, but to my own integrity and effectiveness as a master) to work it through in good time and not put off discussing it just because it's uncomfortable.

When it comes to a slave with a transparency agreement, what happens when the M-type is demanding information and they haven't gotten it straight in their heads yet? One assumes that the M-type knows their s-type well enough to figure out if they're the sort who tries to put this off and ignore things, or the sort who has more trouble than most in getting their emotions into a verbal state. If the M-type has the first sort, it's good to be firm and give them a deadline—"I'll leave this for the moment, but by tomorrow when you get home from work you have to be able to discuss it. Write in your journal tonight if it will help you get your thoughts together. I won't look at it until after our discussion." (With the implication that yes, I have the right to look at it, but I will give you temporary privacy because I know that it will help you to get me the information that I want.) If the M-type has the second sort, then the couple needs to work together—and perhaps experiment—to give the M-type clear information on how long the slave reasonably needs to verbalize their thoughts.

Transparency is not an easy request. It will probably take a submissive months and perhaps years to get to the point of being able to manage it. There needs to be a huge amount of trust which cannot be demanded and must be earned steadily over time. There needs to be complete assurance on the part of the submissive that their dominant will not penalize them for saying unacceptable, displeasing, or angry things. This means that the best thing the dominant can do to support the growth of transparency in the early stages is to remain calm and not become defensive when the submissive says unpleasant things. This takes a lot of self-control, but it's crucial to getting an honest submissive. (On occasion, a would-be dominant asks me, "What if I just can't do that? What if the things she says just set me off and I can't stop it?" I have to take a hard line on that one: to be in control of another human being, you need to have better-than-average control over yourself. Perhaps one might even say "exceptional". Sorry. Work on yourself and try again when you're better at it.) If the submissive has a lot of trust issues, it's going to take even longer. It's also good to reward the submissive in some way for speaking truth rather than hiding it. For some, the acceptance is reward enough. Knowing that one is in a space that is safe enough to be truthful without negative consequences can be a huge gift, and one that can bind a sub to a thoughtful, self-controlled dominant.

The other process that has to happen is that the submissive needs to become self-aware enough to give the dominant accurate information about their own headspace, what can be reasonably expected of them in that space, and ideally the roots and cause of any problems that occur. Some s-types are better at this than others. Some dominants are better at guiding them into that process than others. (One master that I know repeatedly tells would-be owners that if they want an intense level of power dynamic, they should prepare for it by studying psychology and learning what makes people tick, before they're responsible for one.) At any rate, neither this process of transparency nor any other is something inflicted on the s-type, or that the s-type must struggle with alone. It's a mutual process engaged in as a partnership, a slow and mindful dance with each other.

Both parties need to be committed to that dance before it starts, and they need to remind each other of that commitment during the hard parts. There will be days when the sub doesn't want to be transparent, and the dominant has to push or coax them through their barriers. There will be days when the dominant doesn't want to bother with an inconvenient activity on which hangs gain or loss of trust. There will be days when the sub is tongue-tied and inarticulate, and days when the dominant is defensive and angry. They need to remind each other, "Remember? We decided, together, that this was a good thing for our dynamic and we were going to work to get there. Let's try to get back on track."

Bringing this into polyamory: Transparency is especially important when there is more than one s-type in the picture, because the dominant may well need to mediate between them, or at least facilitate them working things out, and he/she will need every ounce of information possible in order to do that effectively. With high levels of transparency, a dominant can prevent the poly disaster of one s-type burying his/her feelings about something the other one has done in order to keep the peace (being non-confrontational is a common trait of submissives, and it can be exacerbated by wanting to please), until it finally erupts in resentment. I've found that one of the most telling questions a master/mistress can ask a slave who is accustomed to transparency is, "What are you thinking about (with regard to X) that you are hoping I won't find out?" If there is something going on, even before they speak there will be a particular look that will communicate volumes.

If there are egalitarian relationships involved—egalitarian partners or other dominants—the poly rules run for those bonds like they would in any egalitarian poly family. Sometimes, for the dominant who ends up doing a lot of facilitation in a mixed-status family, it can be a bit tricky to switch back and forth during discussions between someone who is required to reveal everything to you, and who you can order to stay and process until things are resolved, and someone who can claim their privacy and walk out when they like. As I've said repeatedly, polyamorous dominants need to learn a lot of conflict resolution skills.

One tricky area is the interview process—finding out whether a new person is good for this particular family. While I can understand that there may be areas that the interviewers might want to remain private, the more information you can give a prospect, the better they can make their decision—and the more information they are likely to give the interviewers in order to make *their* decision. It's a matter of honor and courtesy, not to mention common sense. As slave gypsie put it in a letter to us:

> I am slave. I identify with the Wolf, I am a pack animal. I am also Native American. I love the feeling and security of familial tribal relationships. Being both, the need for a hierarchical plane, is mandatory for me within the poly and/or Leather family.
>
> The Master is the Alpha Wolf of the pack; we are here to serve him (or her). We are chosen for them or they choose us, dependent on our wants, needs and desires as negotiated prior to joining that pack. To be a Master is to know one's inner self, inner demons, inner weaknesses and inner strengths. To be slave is to know the same. If the negotiation included being part of a poly relationship and the slave has surrendered herself to the Master under the dictates of that agreement, she is bound by her integrity to honor that agreement or leave. The same holds true of the Master.
>
> For myself, I do not believe the slave can place conditions on the Master once she has truly surrendered herself to him. To place conditions on the Master takes

away his control and castrates his authority; which then neutralizes her slavehood and damages her slave heart.

Stating this, I believe that although privacy may be needed at times by the Master, it cannot be used as an excuse for nondisclosure. If a prior arrangement was made between the Master and his alpha slave, all of those arrangements and conditions must be—and I repeat this as I feel that strongly about it—*must* be not only revealed to any other individual being considered by the Master and their Family, but discussed in great detail to avoid further misunderstandings or manipulations of the original agreement between the original two.

One of the great things about polyamory in a well-run, mindful power dynamic is that it forces personal growth. The dominant must push the submissive(s) to become more self-aware and transparent, and must push themselves to be more self-controlled and self-aware as well, if it is going to work properly. It's a somewhat steeper learning curve, but one that is necessary to make it work smoothly. Yes, there's a little more responsibility laid on the dominant ... but that's the price of Being In Charge, and nearly every dominant will say that's not frightening to them or they wouldn't have sought out this job to begin with.

There is also a certain amount of responsibility laid on the s-type as well. Role-play aside, an adult sub or slave is not a child, and while he/she may need a certain amount of pushing and coaxing and dragging from their Person In Charge on bad days, they also have (or should have) a commitment to do their part and a need to hold to that. Very few masters will want a slave whose entire modus operandi is foot-dragging until they are forced bodily through something. While that can be fun for a scene, or in small amounts, when it comes to important things like learning to be open, that sort of behavior gets old very fast. Even subs who identify as "little girls" or "little boys" need to be adults when it's time for communication and honesty and the relationship is on the line.

Integrating The Egalitarian Partner

This is another of the subjects that people don't like to talk about, or think about. When people new to poly and power dynamics ask for advice about this, they don't get much, and the reason is vested in several layers of poisonous assumptions. The first assumption is that if you want a power dynamic relationship, you couldn't possibly want anything else. Surely, having once tasted being in a power dynamic, an ordinary egalitarian relationship where you have to argue everything out couldn't be interesting any more. This assumption is fed by the claims of all the happy power-dynamic couples talking about how they crave this, how they need it more than anything. That may well be true for them, but it is not an across-the-board reality that being in a power dynamic "ruins" every single person for an additional egalitarian relationship.

It's hard enough for some folks to imagine the contents of this book being about situations other than one master with several slaves; slaves with dual masters or who own slaves of their own is far enough beyond their imagining. Adding in people who are not part of the power dynamic is completely beyond their radar. That's why people get a funny look on my face when I say that I am part of a household, but it is not a M/s household, because more than half the people in it did not consent to be in any power dynamic with anyone. (On the other hand, I am part of a small poly-kink "clan", and I do not own everyone in it. Nor do I fuck everyone in it.) Most of all, they have a problem with the fact that I am legally married, and to an egalitarian partner.

Another assumption is that no one who would want to be in an egalitarian relationship would be able to put up with their lover either being a slave or owning one, or something on that spectrum. Part of this assumption is that the world is divided into two sorts of people: those who crave this and couldn't happily do anything else, and those who abhor it and think it's wrong. It is true that this does come up—one example of this problem is outlined in Interview With A Polyamorous Power Exchange Household, when Ian discusses his ex's moral qualms about his secondary service relationship. Certainly, there have been plenty of spouses whose limited understanding of "all this whips and chains stuff" was exacerbated into hysteria by their spouse announcing out of nowhere that they wanted to be a slave (or own one), but strangely enough, some egalitarian spouses end up finding equanimity with the whole thing. Karen, whose husband has a slave, says: "I'm just glad that he is getting those needs met somewhere else, and that I don't have to feel bad that I can't give that to him. Or, rather, I *could* feel bad about it, but I am experienced enough with poly to know that's silly—I'm not interested in sports games, either, and he doesn't need me to go with him to see the Orioles. The fact that your partner gets those needs met somewhere else is a good thing, so long as there's still enough between the two of you to make it work. I have a second partner who watches old movies with me—should I expect that of Will? No. Actually, it's good to make love with him and know that he's not frustrated and holding all that back. His slave's presence in his life gives him a place to have that. Better her than me."

Jamie, a gay man from Oregon, related: "Shasta is my life partner who I climb mountains with. I'll always love him—just looking at him is enough to put me into a trance. Kirby is my life partner whom I own. I love him in a different way. Owning Kirby means that I can beat someone, hurt someone, make someone crawl and obey, do anything I want ... and then I can go cleanly to Shasta's bed without dragging all that along with me, and inadvertently forcing it on him with my energy. Everyone gets what they want, everyone is happy. Especially Kirby, don't kid yourself about that. If I started getting all kissy-romantic with him ... well, he'd go along with it, because he wants to please me, but let's just say that it wouldn't be his first choice."

There are a few dangers to be aware of, of course. As I've said before, BDSM is very powerful for people who are "wired" to desire and/or need it, and power dynamics even more so. In polyamory, we talk a lot about NRE, or New Relationship Energy, which is that burst of brain-drugs that happens at the fireworks-and-whirlwinds early stages of a relationship. Sometimes people get so single-minded, especially if they're used to serial monogamy, that they end up acting pretty stupid. My poly friends and I call this Shiny New Lover Syndrome—NRE gone off the deep end. Instead of making an extra effort to pay attention to their senior partner, they throw all their emotional energy into the new nookie and eventually the senior partner (rightfully) gets upset, and all sorts of badnesses ensue.

What most people don't think about is that a power dynamic can exist as a source of NRE in its own right, especially for first-timers or for people who are really wired for it. By that, I mean that they can quite literally fall in love with the dynamic, and thus cast aside common-sense rules of polyamory that they wouldn't have ignored had the relationship been vanilla. In some cases the individual may actually be more in love with the dynamic than with the new lover they're doing it with, especially if they've been waiting a long time for this and there are years of fantasy built up in the anticipation. This means that a power dynamic relationship is more prone to Shiny New Lover Syndrome and all its pitfalls than an egalitarian one, and extra mindfulness has to be put in place. The individual in the middle would be wise to concentrate on the good things about having an egalitarian relationship when they are with that partner, so that fantasizing about the D/s dynamic doesn't overtake everything.

Moving from one sort of relationship to another can be a challenge because the expected behavior may be so different. Jade, a slave with a Mistress and an egalitarian wife, says: "Suzanne was good about the whole thing, considering, but she doesn't want to see me in 'slave mode' because it makes her uncomfortable. When I am relating to her, she wants me to act like a strong, independent, assertive woman. What this means is that Max and I have put boundaries and rituals together to 'transition' me from being Max's slave to being Suzanne's wife. That's helped to keep it from seeping over. Since part of what I'm doing in being a slave is focusing on having a 'following-the-rules' headspace at all times, the fact that Max has made it a rule—*I am not to act like Max's slave when I am being Suzanne's wife*—has helped a lot. Of course, what really makes it work is that Max is invested in not breaking us up. She likes Suzanne and wants it to work out with the three of us."

When the central partner is the s-type, the situation is probably more frightening for the egalitarian partner, unless clear and considerate negotiation is put in place immediately. For example, restrictions on sexual behavior is a common (and frequently eroticized) part of establishing a power dynamic. However, an egalitarian partner may not be amenable to restrictions that take away part of their sex life with their partner. Jay, a submissive man with a Mistress and a wife, wrote: "I fantasize about being kept in a chastity harness 24/7 while I'm away from my Mistress. (I see her once a week.) But it's not fair to rob Ellen of the use of my penis. I suggested that I could pleasure her in other ways, or use a dildo, but me having an orgasm is important to her. I suggested giving her a set of keys so that she could unlock me to have sex, but that was too much like what I do with my Mistress for her tastes. So we worked out a compromise. I have verbal restrictions on masturbating—Mistress set rules that I can only get off with my wife between sessions, and it has to be when she wants it—I can't pester her for sex just because I'm horny. It's a compromise I am willing to make because I want a relationship with both women where they each feel that they are getting enough of me."

Tirani Starpath wrote in depth about her situation with her master and her husband:

> My husband I have been together in a polyamorous relationship for 10 years; I have been with my master for a little over a year. My husband and I decided fairly early on that we would not engage in any kind of power dynamic because our relationship is built on a egalitarian basis, and we choose not to upset that balance and possibly threaten the foundation of our partnership. In contrast to this, my master and I came to our relationship with the full intention of establishing a power dynamic, and having a fairly clear idea of what we were seeking

from that dynamic. My master, while aware of the fundamentals of polyamory, had never participated in a relationship of that nature prior to our time together, but has taken to it (in my humble opinion) exceptionally well.

My husband is perfectly comfortable with my relationship with my master. This has not always been the case in the past, however, I think I can finally see what the difference between historical relationships and the current one is: my dynamic partner took the time to get to know, and earn the trust of, my egalitarian partner before we took the relationship to a more serious power exchange mode. My husband has enough academic understanding of the nature of the relationship between my master and I that he understands it is a need he cannot meet. One of the core principles of our polyamory is that no one person can meet every need of another person; allowing the ability to meet those needs outside of the relationship makes everyone involved happier and healthier, and strengthens all of the relationships a person is engaged in, platonic and romantic. My husband has also come to understand that my master's care for me rivals his own, giving him the ability to relax and know that I am cared for while he spends times with his other partners. Finally, not only does my husband understand my needs are being more fully met and I am in good care, he has discovered that my relationship with my master has given him more time to pursue other relationships and seek out individuals that meet needs he has that I cannot.

For me, the fact that I am submissive to my master is irrelevant to whether we can we can "pull off" the relationship structure that we have found ourselves in. The stability of the relationship is tied to the stability of the relationships individually, not the nature of the relationships. To wit, while my relationship with my husband is stable, my relationship with my master is stable, and the relationship between my master and my husband is stable, all of those relationships are stable because they balance against each other. If my master and I start having a problem, it throws the balance off, and my husband takes note, whether to intervene or simply provide support while we work to restore that balance. Were my master and my husband to have an issue with each other, I would encourage them to work it out, because their conflict would unbalance their relationships with me.

You might say the power dynamic of my relationship with my master is on a rheostat; it can get turned up and down pretty much at will. Sometimes it's strong and turned up high, sometimes it's weaker and turned down low. When we are around my husband, we make a conscious effort to keep it dialed back to a 1. When we are engaged in scene work together, it gets dialed up to 11 or so. There have been times when my husband has caught glimpses of what something higher than 1 looks like, but his comfort level with my master has prevented it from being much of a concern to him.

I have had very few problems going back and forth between the two of them (assuming the three of use aren't spending time together, which we do fairly often). This is mostly because the two of them make transitioning back and forth so easy. My master delights in seeing how much my husband and I love each other and the strength of our relationship; my husband take joys in knowing that I am with someone who cares for me as much as he does and that a very deep, persistent need of mine is being met in the power dynamic.

For me, my marriage is the central, stable point of my life. While I consider my husband and my master to be pretty close to co-primaries at this point, the fact remains that I live with my husband and I will likely not ever live with my master. My husband and I own our own home, have joint financial accounts, and generally have invested in a long view of a life together. Our home could theoretically provide enough space for all three of us to live together, but all three of us are introverted enough that doing so would probably drive us all crazy. My master is an intensely private person, and very much prefers his own space without others around at times. While we are on the verge of making a collaring commitment to each other that is akin to marriage, my master and I acknowledge that unless there are drastic changes to our lives, we will not live together. Finally, I'm also not entirely certain I could live in a situation where there is a 24/7 power dynamic for more than a few days without being consumed by it. While it is a nice fantasy to entertain at times, and indulge in over a long weekend or vacation together, the power of the dynamic that my master and I have could easily begin to erode my sense of self over a longer period of time. That is something none of us want to see happen.

I'll be completely honest, it's hard work. Harder than even "normal" poly relationships are to begin with, and it's definitely not for everyone. We have put an enormous amount of work to get to where we are now, and it's not been without its bumps along the way. We have had to deal with issues of my husband initially being concerned about (and perhaps a smidge jealous of) the strength of the bond between my master and I, issues of my master coming to terms with poly, and the things that come from being involved with someone who is already in a committed long term relationship, and issues I've had making sure I have enough "me" time while still making sure I meet the needs of my two men. It was by the slimmest of margins and a whole lot of care that we picked our way through the minefield to where we are now. That work is why I want to slap the dewy-eyed newbies who exclaim "You're so lucky!" No, I'm not lucky, I'm reaping the rewards of the one of hardest things I've ever done; we worked hard to make this into what it is today!

For my own relationship, my wife had some issues when I took on a slaveboy. First, she worried that I would use him to sit around and do nothing, which she felt would be wrong. Fortunately, I also felt that it would be wrong, and so I agreed that for purposes of the group household responsibilities, we would act as equals. I had my own duties (laundry, making salad, etc.) and I would not attempt to foist them all off on him. It comforted my wife to see me taking on household chores as if I was not someone with the option of slave labor, which felt unfair to her. She was also turned off by "slavey" behavior in the kitchen where she and others were forced to witness it, and since I value her (and the group house and my housemates) we choose to be discreet and act vanilla in public.

Our one argument was over authority. She made it clear to me that she wanted the option of being able to order Joshua around, not because she desired a power dynamic per se, but because she liked the idea of free labor on her own projects, and envied me the pair of willing hands to work on mine. I had to say no to that, because Joshua had not consented to be her servant as well; it had not been part of our negotiations, and while there came a point when I could have forced him, that would had been a huge breach of trust. Our agreement is based on him being a privately owned slave; while I may order him to do any activity for anyone else, no one else has actual authority over him and that's very important to his comfort. In addition, I knew that my wife and I have argued over the disposition of every other possession we've ever held in common—cars, money, property, pets—and I felt that the inevitable arguments over my slaveboy's time would not be good for anyone's comfort with the dynamic.

On the other hand, I do lend him to her occasionally—to give her a footrub, to help her with a project—and I have used him as a friendly prop in helping me to make love to her. As other dominants have mentioned, he is a place for me to put my dominance so that I can be patient and considerate with her; his presence in my life has made me significantly more courteous toward her. He supports me financially so that all her money is her own; he is my personal care attendant when I am ill, so she doesn't have to cope with that. We both feel that it would be bad for our relationship if she was forced into a caretaker role beyond what she might be willing to freely give, so the fact that I have a slave for that is extremely useful. So in many ways my slaveboy helps my marriage.

If it's handled correctly, it can enhance that of other people's as well. DK, a dominant with an egalitarian wife and a slave girl, reported that:

> We have two such relationships that we manage to make work. My wife and I met my slavegirl and her husband two years ago and we all became good friends, and had casual sex a couple of times. We were all kinky, but she and I were the ones who longed to be Master and slave. We'd both talked about it to our spouses. I had a couple of cyber-slaves online briefly, but that was a poor substitute for the real thing. Meanwhile, she was trolling for doms online, and we all know the kind of trash that accumulates. Her husband was actually quite worried about her because he would read their posts and say, "Who are these losers? I don't want my wife anywhere near them!" He was afraid that she would end up dead in a trash can, or dumped as soon as it got inconvenient and then he would have to clean up the mess.
>
> One day she asked him what they would have to be like for him to trust them with her. He said, "Someone like (my name)." She said, "Well, what about him, then?" They came together to our house and asked us both, me and my wife as well—it was really a wonderful moment. I was very honored and I collared her in front of both of them the next week, after a lot of negotiation. Then we went home to our respective spouses. We all thought

that it would be best to do that, to emphasize that we were both still married in spite of this. The weekend after—she wanted both of us to go to a hotel, but I sent my wife off to her sister's for the weekend and had my new slavegirl over for her first "training". When my wife came home, the house was sparkling clean. She's had no complaints ever since, and her husband knows that his wife is safe and won't get screwed over by some cyber-dom.

I think that us all being friends first helped a lot. In the absence of being friends already, I'd say that people should make an effort to all be friends if possible—spend time just hanging out as a group with everyone's significant other, or find an activity that you all like to do together—go camping or something. And getting your partner involved in helping you find a slave or dom, if they're into that, can help them feel better about it. Especially if your partner wants to be the slave. I would expect the partner of a would-be slave to seriously interview a potential dominant, and a dominant who wouldn't see their concern as valid would not be a good one for their partner.

Sometimes the partner isn't egalitarian, but the relationship is. Jules, a dominant with a slave and a wife who also has a dominant (not him) wrote about his and his wife's D/s relationships—which aren't with each other—and how they have improved things between them:

Cali and I started out polyamorous and wholly egalitarian—I didn't know that anyone, especially a woman, would ever want anything else. D/s was entirely outside of my mental locus. Cali got me into kinky sex, but we always switched—she is a fiery and rebellious woman, and I couldn't imagine her wanting to be dominated and told what to do. Certainly she didn't like it when *I* told her what to do. So imagine my surprise when she informed me that she was interested in a man she'd met at a local kink party who was a dominant, and wanted her to be his submissive? Not his bottom—his sub. Collar and all.

I couldn't believe it. Cali? Submissive? But it worked. I like John—he's calm, honorable, and most importantly he knows how to handle her. When she would start to scream at me, I would just walk away, but he physically dominates her in a way that she says she needs—he throws her down and controls her. She is still rebellious, still fiery, and he does a lot of punishing her, but they both seem to like that. He and I did a little negotiating—not a lot, just enough to set boundaries in a place that we were both comfortable with. If I need more of her time and attention, I call him and we work it out. We are both reasonable people, so it's never been a problem.

I am fine with him having charge of her, because making her behave is more effort for me that it's worth. I just let her do what she wants and I walk away when I've had enough. These days, I'm likely to call John on the phone and say, "She's in a mood again and behaving irrationally—can you make her calm down and see reason?" And usually he can. So I don't mind that another man is controlling my wife—better him than me, and when I ask for his help getting her to treat me better, he always gives it. He values our marriage—he travels and doesn't want to live with her, and he wants her to have someone to be with when he's not there. Cali is much nicer to me now, because he makes her be nicer.

I didn't think of myself as a dominant, because I didn't want a relationship that looked like theirs—punishment and takedowns are not my thing. Since I didn't know any other D/s people, I assumed that was what a D/s relationship looked like. Then I started exploring my bisexuality, and I met a gorgeous gay sub named West, and before I knew it I was in a D/s relationship myself. It doesn't look anything like my wife's relationship with John—West loves service and is very obedient. He doesn't live with us, although I'd like to see that in the future. I guess we're much quieter and I don't punish him—we just talk things through. Being West's master has made me calmer and more confident.

Strangely enough, my bringing home a slave threw Cali for a loop much more so than I felt when John picked her up. I think she believed that I couldn't be into that sort of thing because I couldn't do it with her, in the way she needed it. The fact that I brought home a gay slave also threw her a little, but she got over it. These days, our only difficulties are keeping our complicated schedule straight! Cali and I love each other and have a lot of fun together, but I'm not the sort of master she wants and she's not the sort of slave I want. I have to say, thank God for polyamory, because we'd both be pretty sad without it.

Introducing A Monogamous Submissive To Polyamory

This is that defusing-a-nuclear-bomb thing that I was telling you about.

First, I want to make the point that in some egalitarian polyamory circles, what I'm about to discuss is considered extremely unethical and probably downright wrong. It is most certainly a grey area morally. It could go well, or it could go terribly wrong and end up yet another poly disaster. What makes it other than a huge Wrongness? I'll tell you: the example of people who did it and made it work. That doesn't mean that it will work for everyone, but it has worked in at least some cases. It is, however, a tricky and uncertain process.

If a dominant decides that they want to explore polyamory, but their submissive is insecure, the temptation is to say, "Aren't I the one in charge here? Don't I get to say what happens? Who rules, me or their insecurities?" The answer is, *Yes, you are the one in charge, and as such the responsibility for minimizing damage is entirely on you.* First, you have to determine whether your slave is going to be able to emotionally handle your nonmonogamy. Some can't, especially if they have massive insecurity issues. In that case, you should be working on your slave's self-esteem first. Tools function better when they feel good about themselves.

There are some standard pieces of polyamorous wisdom that apply to everyone, even M/s couples, however. The first and biggest one is that you don't take on a new lover if your primary relationship is having problems. Ironically, it's an appallingly common reason to do so, but it's the worst thing you can do for either your old lover or a new one. It's actually a serial-monogamy custom ("My relationship isn't so good any more, I'll just go find a new one") rather than a polyamorous one. This means that if your submissive cannot handle a polyamorous relationship without severe emotional stress, you have only a few choices. You can remain monogamous, out of respect for their issues. You can dismiss them, and find someone more suitable to your poly needs. The only other option is that you can require them to work on the issue—something that an egalitarian partner does not have as an option—and find out if there's a way that they can be made content with the situation.

This last option is not guaranteed, and if it fails, you're back to the other two. It's also not something that they can do alone. In fact, the more help the dominant gives them, the more likely it is to succeed. That includes hour after hour of emotional processing, making small moves, constant reassurance, and a huge amount of communication between all parties, including the old slave and the new slave. If the two don't want to talk, it's up to the dominant to make them sit down and hash it out.

One of the few advantages to such a situation is that the master/mistress really can force the slaves to communicate ... but they have to put on their dominant panties and do it. (Check out my essay about just that in the next section.) One of the most common errors I've seen is a dominant who runs out, gets a second lover, and then sits around covertly hoping that the two will somehow miraculously start communicating and liking each other, but ducks and evades when the stresses start taking people in the opposite direction. All too often, it's done out of fear of confrontation ("...they'll outnumber me, and they'll both start crying, and then maybe one will threaten to leave!"), or fear of losing the new nookie, or a vain and cowardly hope that it will just all work itself out. Sometimes it does, miraculously, but it's just as likely to all go wrong. Dominants who are introducing polyamory to an existing M/s relationship have to be proactive and take both control and responsibility from the beginning.

In the end, it's about trust. Even a slave who thinks that they will be fine with polyamory sometimes ends up with issues and insecurities when faced with the real thing. In order for them to feel safe, they must trust the dominant to help them get through the rough parts with as little pain as possible. If the dominant does not act and do something constructive when problems arise, the slave's trust fails yet more. It's crucial to be in control of the situation, and that means being willing to make hard decisions and be a uniting force in the face of emotional divisions.

In the meantime, the first step might be to have the slave read books on how polyamory is done, and done right. The step that follows that should probably be to have them sit down and talk with a variety of long-term polyamorous families. The ideal would be families with D/s dynamics, or who are at least kinky, but if that's not available then vanilla polyamorous folks will still have useful things to say, especially about coping with jealousy, possessiveness, territoriality, envy, and all those monsters. The dominant also needs to read up on it and talk to people, because they need to have an even better idea of how a healthy polyamorous situation should go, being as they will have to successfully orchestrate a delicate situation. The submissive need only learn enough to be reassured, but the dominant will be making sure that the rest of the people involved do it right.

In egalitarian polyamory demographics, it is generally agreed that the hardest moment of all is when one member of a heretofore monogamous marriage decides that they really need to be polyamorous. There is discussion, or negotiation, or couples counseling, and both parties make hard decisions about how far they are willing to bend for the other one. If the monogamous party is entirely unwilling to bend, then either the other party has to give up their dreams of polyamory or the relationship has to go. The truth is that many (we don't know how many, but perhaps as many as half) of all such relationships break up after this pronouncement.

But what happens to the remainder? A study of monogamous partners of polyamorous people on a variety of Internet help lists was made by Elaine Cook in 2002.[9] (She points out that by definition the people on these lists are there because they are unsatisfied and need help; contented mono/poly couples are out living their lives, and not available to be surveyed.) She discovered that most of the couples who came to a positive feeling about the relationship were conscious that they were making a deliberate tradeoff. Their love for

---

[9] http://www.aphroweb.net/papers/poly-mono.htm

their partner and the emotional benefits that they received from the relationship were worth doing the internal work to adapt themselves to polyamory. They counseled each other to "focus on what you have that is good and works." Some pointed out that when monogamous couples divorce, no one blames it on monogamy—it isn't the relationship style, it's the people. Similarly, polyamory can be survived and can even be a place where a personally monogamous person can flourish, if everything else is done right.

So what does "done right" mean? In our anecdotal evidence from talking to egalitarian people who made it work, we found the following things happening:

+ There was a high level of honest communication already existing between both people.

+ There was a deep and foundational love and a long history of shared experiences. This implies couples who have been together for many years; "younger" relationships of less than five years are much more at risk for breakups in this kind of situation.

+ Each had a high level of trust in the integrity of the other person.

+ Neither party had problematically low self-esteem or pathological and unfounded mistrust of their partner.

+ Neither party was actively mentally ill.

+ Both members were able to talk about their sexual needs and be listened to, even if it was hard to understand the other party's needs on an emotional level.

+ Both people were aware of what activities made the other one feel loved, and tried hard to give them those behaviors regularly.

+ There was a commitment to make sure that activities with another lover did not take away time and attention from the existing lover to the point where the existing lover felt cheated and abandoned. Early poly exploits required extra attention and special activities with the existing partner.

✦ Both members were willing to read about and research the reality of polyamory, including written advice by various polyamorous people about the possible problems, instead of either one just acting from their (positive or negative) unrealistic assumptions on the matter.

✦ Clear boundaries were set in place as to behavior. In some cases it took negotiation and even mediation to find boundaries that both parties were even reasonably comfortable with, but all agreed that when starting out, any boundaries were better than no boundaries.

✦ The polyamorous partner agreed to start slowly, not rushing into things, and to keep the other partner informed.

✦ The monogamous partner had activities and friends in their life that did not depend entirely on the polyamorous partner, and was able to make satisfying plans when the poly partner was busy with their other partners.

✦ Both parties were open to the idea of "leaving normal", having a relationship that was "alternative". This means letting go of much early social programming, including the Cinderella story where the only "right" ending is "and they lived happily and monogamously ever after, like a pair of shoes or socks." A corollary to that was "What will other people (the children, my family and friends) think of this?" Leaving normal was one of the hugest obstacles to overcome, and the biggest aid in doing so was:

✦ Getting involved with poly friends and/or peer groups, especially ones where people could give support and advice for the various pitfalls involved, and—most important of all—be examples of long-term success. There's nothing like seeing it work in front of you to make you believe that it will work. This was one of the single biggest aids in getting a monogamous spouse more comfortable with polyamory—being able to talk to other monogamous spouses who were managing with equanimity.

✦ Being willing to be patient and wait the situation out, to the point where they could see that their place in the other person's life was not threatened, and that their partner's polyamorous lifestyle was not so bad after all. (This assumed that the polyamorous partner chose their other partners wisely and did not engage in immature behaviors that would prove the opposite to a monogamous partner.)

✦ The monogamous spouse was able to see emotional benefits in their partner from being polyamorous, and they could manage to come to a place where the happiness of their partner outweighed the pain of giving up their own dream of monogamy. This is a particularly important point for submissives, who we'll address specifically in a moment.

And what about moving this list to a power dynamic relationship? Frankly, there's nothing on it that shouldn't be seriously taken into consideration by an M-type and an s-type who are looking at opening these things up. This list is relevant for any dynamic. However, there are a few other points to add when it comes to dealing with a monogamous submissive.

Going back to the dynamic intensity-levels earlier in this book: If yours comes in at a level 3 or below, the dominant needs to assume that while the submissive may want to please them, the fact that there is a power dynamic in place is not necessarily going to be enough weight to make them agree to polyamory. Negotiate as equals in this area, go slowly, and understand that the polyamory may not work out. At higher levels, while there may be more ability to pressure the slave into going along with something, remember that their feelings are not necessarily going to be so different on this matter from an unowned person that you won't need to move carefully, slowly, and with attention paid to everything above. M-types should remember, again, that the more vulnerability the slave has with regard to lack of recourse, the more effort the M-type is obligated to put in to help them work their way to some measure of comfort, if it is possible.

If the dominant is normally a somewhat emotionally reserved person, it may behoove them to bother to really open up to the s-type about this matter and how emotionally important it is to them. Slaves especially are going to be more invested in learning to cope with polyamory if their master/mistress isn't just looking for another hole to casually fuck because it might be fun, but instead can say, "This is really important to who I am and what I need. I really want this to work for both of us, but in the end I will be very unhappy without it. It is that important to me. That means that I'm willing to help you get to a comfort point with everything I've got, but I want it to be that important to you, too." Good s-types want to please, and they can put more of their heart into pleasing in this difficult way if they understand just how happy their opposite number is going to be.

If the problem is the sub's lack of trust in their place in the dominant's life, this can be remedied by a written contract, or special rules, or the dominant having a good visible track record of keeping their word, or just plain old time. Don't be impatient. The intervening time can be used to acquaint the sub with poly people and poly skills.

If the problem is low self-esteem in the submissive, the dominant needs to prioritize working on that before leaping into polyamory. Therapy may help. If it is an intense-level dynamic, the dominant can force or convince the submissive to go into therapy specifically for this issue. In the meantime, there are a variety of ways that the dominants themselves can help the subs raise their feelings of self-worth.

As above, the issue of peer support is very important. If you can find s-types living in poly relationships who didn't initially expect or desire this, arranging for them to talk to the hesitant s-type can help. However, try to find s-types in relationships with dynamic levels roughly equal to one's own. A part-time sub may not be able to relate as well to a piece of owned property who is comfortable with having almost no rights and limits, and the owned property may not be able to relate to the "...or if you just can't handle it, you can leave..." of an s-type with a freer dynamic.

If the s-type is going to be home alone when the M-type is off with another partner, it's useful for the M-type to give the s-type special orders to accomplish in the meantime. Those could either be a more "free person" activity like "...get out with some friends and do some fun thing you don't normally get a chance to do!" or something more slavelike, such as specially designed chores that require a lot of attention and will make the s-type feel themselves still very much held in the grip of the M-type's will. Talk about what would work better for them.

Eroticizing the polyamory can help. While few slaves are going to respond to the kink that Shae L. writes about in her essay "The Pain Is The Point" later in this book, there may be many aspects of being a sub or slave in a nomonogamous situation that can be seen as sexy. Tell stories to each other and see if there's anything that can give a sexual kick to the situation. Some sexual kicks can even be stronger than negative emotions, or at least they can help get through the early scary points.

Some s-types do better if the poly starts with the M-type being sexual with others first. Some s-types (surprisingly) do better if *they* are sexual with others first, perhaps in a carefully controlled and arranged situation. Some s-types do better if the couple finds a third party that both of them like (admittedly the most difficult situation to arrange) and are sexual with them together as a team. While it may be difficult to discern which would be best while the submissive is in the throes of "No, please no!" being able to work toward figuring this first step out together is a good goal to strive for.

Be very careful who you choose for a first third-party experience. In a way, your submissive will lose a kind of virginity to this person. Just as the experience of losing one's physical sexual virginity can be positive or negative, and can leave repercussions on how the person views sex, the first polyamorous experience can do the same for polyamory. In a delicate situation like this, the submissive's comfort is more important, in the long run, than the dominant's fun, and intelligent dominants will understand this. Choosing someone who will be courteous, respectful, and ideally friendly toward the frightened existing partner will help. Choosing someone who is experienced in poly and perhaps even partnered elsewhere (and thus apparently safer) may also be a good move.

Dominants need to remember that some submissives are just never going to be happy with this, no matter what is done, and hard decisions may eventually need to be made. Submissives need to remember that over time, many formerly monogamous submissives have not only grown accustomed to their spouse's lifestyle, but come to love and trust other partners and see them as family in a way that they never would have believed possible when they took their first brave, trembling steps on this road.

Queer Templates: Polyamory And Power Dynamics In Nonheterosexual Communities

I. Gay Men And Nonmonogamy

Gay men have always been more prone to nonmonogamy than any relationship containing a woman. Scientists try to use this prevalence as proof that men are just "wired" to be nonmonogamous for reasons derived from primitive times and seeding one's genetics wherever possible. (Some scientists recently found that some women with regular sex partners spontaneously ovulate more when they spend days away from those partners, even if having an affair is not even on their mental radar. The theory derived from this is that while men may have evolved to be openly nonmonogamous, women evolved to be secretly nonmonogamous and pawn other men's children off on their own mate. Take it all on both sides with as many bags of salt as you like.)

Therapist Bruce Koff says that "Of the many questions gay men face in forming romantic relationships, two are most prominent: 'Can gay men be monogamous?' and 'Should they be?'" [10] In heterosexual or lesbian circles, seriously considering the idea *that the majority of people in relationships like mine might be wired to be nonmonogamous* would be unthinkable. However, the gay male community deals with that question on a regular basis. The arguments pro and con have gotten even louder and fiercer with the advent of HIV and monogamy being pushed as a preventative. The recent political push for gay marriage has also placed a heavier emphasis on looking like respectable couples. On the other hand, while claiming that there are no good studies on the matter, Koff does admit that "...they all report that varying degrees of non-monogamy are fairly common among male couples. Gay men seem more likely to explicitly address this question in their relationships than lesbian or heterosexual couples."

---

[10] http://www.windycitymediagroup.com/gay/lesbian/news/ARTICLE.php?
AID=19632

Gay leathermen also had models in the so-called "Old Guard" or "Old Leather" households, who might have several men in varying levels of hierarchy, based vaguely on a military model but with lots of hot gay leathersex. "Daddies" might have several "boys" that they would mentor; some would stay but others might go on to become daddies themselves. While masters generally had several slaves while slaves rarely if ever had more than one master, there was still a lot of playing around in the non-polarized interstices of the leathermen's communities. Things weren't quite as rigid as people pretend today.

In the book *Ask The Man Who Owns Him* by slave david stein and David Schacter, a groundbreaking series of interviews with 16 full-time male master/slave households, he notes that every relationship that they interviewed was polyamorous to some degree. Stein writes of his random selection of interviewees:

> An open relationship, at least for the Master, or outright polyamory is a feature of all these bonds. Over the long term, males seem to need multiple emotional or erotic outlets to avoid boredom. Although none of these relationships is strictly monogamous, in most cases the slaves have sex or play with others only with permission from their Masters. The Masters, of course, do whatever they want.

Of the 16 masters, all were nonmonogamous to one extent or another (or had been in the past and could be again), without consulting their slaves. Two had egalitarian primary partners; one was partnered with another man and the other was married to his wife. The slaves' situations varied from being exclusive with their masters, either by choice or on orders; being allowed to have casual sex; or having committed partnerships elsewhere. One M/s family of three seemed to stay pretty much within the family for their activities. While the interviews were necessarily short, none seemed to report too many problems with polyamory; a few mentioned past lovers who brought in drama, but the general feeling seemed to be that with the right people, it just wasn't a problem, and if someone proved to be not the right sort of person, they would simply be removed.

Since nonmonogamous relationships are so common and accepted in the gay leather community, when gay leathermen do come to monogamy, they find themselves there from a place of monogamy as a freely chosen option rather than a default social position. They find that they simply prefer it, rather than it being a matter of giving in to social pressure. (It may be the only place in Western society where this condition exists, even a little.) As an example, gay leatherman and master Patrick talks about his choices, and how he came to them:

> Monogamy's not a choice I ever pictured myself making—in fact, I don't remember making it. But it's how my relationship with my slave has worked for a couple of years now: it seems to be what I want. Not because of any rule or belief or still less any feeling that it's somehow morally superior, just because it seems to be the way I'm made. I'm not a multitasker. I can walk and chew gum at the same time, but that's about it. My gift is concentration, the deep focus on whatever I'm doing. The single connection I try to take deeper and deeper. That's where my searching and my curiosity lead. It's what satisfies me.
>
> I don't know if my slave knows we're monogamous. Is that comical? His sexual expression is subject to the usual slave strictures, but he's a lot like me, maybe even more so: those restrictions feel like freedom to him, he likes knowing where he belongs and to whom. He would absolutely say that I have the right to play around with whomever I please, and so would I. I just, well, don't. However, I absolutely would not, could not choose monogamy without M/s. The very foundation of it, for me, is having a dedicated sexual partner who is pledged never to say no.

I always say sex is like pancakes: you have to throw the first few tries away. With my slave, every time it's a magic carpet ride. Somebody off the street, no matter how hot he is, can't do that for me, and the prospect of breaking him in just feels like work. So I decline. It's been an occasion of friction with some of my leather friends. There's a hint of a "Poor guy, he's just not getting it" attitude at times, and I can find myself dealing with anger or somebody's feelings of rejection and not knowing how I got there.

The recent study *Beyond Monogamy: Lessons From Long-Term Male Couples In Non-Monogamous Relationships* interviewed a large number of gay couples whose non-primary relationships ranged from occasional unattached one-night stands to polyamorous families. While most were somewhere in the former range, and the research focused mostly on how casual sex was a positive addition to primary relationships, the researchers did comment on the 6% in poly families: "Although we only interviewed a small number of couples or families that fit this model, we talked with 2-3 times that many about participating. The model deserves its own study since the philosophy, dynamics, and issues are quite different from many of our study couples."[11] The results of the study do suggest that while gay men may be statistically quick to fall into bed with other men—to the point where there is a strong cultural acceptance of it in their communities—they are just as much fumbling pioneers as any other demographic when it comes to creating solid polyamorous families.

The exception may, ironically, be in the gay leather community. Patrick's point that he could not be monogamous without a master/slave relationship is telling and well taken. Gay leatherman Fish wrote to me: "In my local community, it's a combination of the gay acceptance of monogamy as not that important—some people do it, but it's a personal choice, not a social

---

[11] http://www.thecouplesstudy.com

norm—and the leather acceptance of the Top/Daddy/Master as the guy whose word gets respected. Gay boys aren't obsessed with monogamy like girls are, and it's almost expected these days that leathermen gather in households. Usually with a master and multiple slaves, but sometimes with a master couple and their slaves, or a master and his lover and slaves. It's part of our history, it's in our stories, so we don't see it as such a big hairy deal. If a gay leatherman doesn't want to get involved with that, he doesn't get involved. But the vanilla gay men are all so worried about copying respectable straight people that they get hung up about monogamy. The most stable gay poly-families I know are leather families."

II. Lesbians, Poly, and the Tyranny of Romance

Lesbians, on the other hand, tend to take less quickly to nonmonogamy of any sort. In a study done by Philip Blumstein and Pepper Schwartz that interviewed heterosexual, gay male, and lesbian couples, the statistical conclusion was that lesbians A) had less sex within their committed relationships than any of the other types, B) had outside nonmonogamy at about the same rate as heterosexuals but were much more likely to have love affairs rather than casual sex, C) had the highest rates of breaking up, and D) had breakups that were overwhelmingly due to outside nonmonogamy— having an affair, falling in love, breaking up.[12] Lesbian writer and therapist Margaret Nichols has seen these patterns in her work with clients, and describes them as:

> Two women couple, often very shortly after each has decoupled from a previous relationship, and frequently move in with each other after the briefest of courtships. The women pledge undying love for each other, feel perfectly matched, and enjoy ecstatic lovemaking. Two to four years later, the couple's frequency of sex has dropped off drastically. One partner

---

[12] Philip Blumstein and Pepper Schwarz, American Couples (New York: William Morrow, 1983)

may complain, but often neither really complains, and usually they claim that the rest of the relationship is "fine." They may rationalize the lack of sex in their relationship with political ideology about genital sex being patriarchal and so forth. They may make a conscious and overt decision to "open up" the relationship, because "monogamy is patriarchal," or nonmonogamy may "just happen." In either case, what ultimately happens is that one partner becomes sexually involved with a new woman, "falls in love" with the new person, and the couple breaks up, with the nonmonogamous partner forming a new couple with the third woman.[13]

Her explanation for this is a combination of social programming that conditions women to be sexually aroused only by intense romantic emotions, general sexual repression and mental detachment from the genitals, conflicting social messages about female sexuality, and greater expectation of intimacy and long-term excitement that is not always easily met. While she is uncomfortable with power dynamics (although not BDSM for sexual play), she does have suggestions for revamping female/female polyamorous relationships:

We need also to consider the possibility that the female tendency to fuse sex and love is not always an idealistic goal but rather a consequence of stereotypic role-conditioning. We are going to have to admit that very few of us are actually capable of negotiating prolonged emotional, sexual affairs with a new lover without damage to our primary relationships. Sex changes things, including friendships, and no matter where jealousy originated, it seems to be pervasive. If

---

[13] http://www.ipgcounseling.com/lesbian_theory_1.html Originally published in Lesbian Psychologies: Explorations and Challenges; Boston Lesbian Psychologies Collective, 1987

we are really interested in preserving, rather than jeopardizing, our primary relationships, we need to reconsider both monogamy as traditionally practiced or nonmonogamy as practiced by gay man. Gay male relationships are nonmonogamous more often than not, frequently without damage to the primary commitment, but the extramarital sexuality is almost always casual (even anonymous), brief, and recreational rather than emotionally intense. Moreover, gay male couples have rules for their nonmonogamy, rules that may seem to limit spontaneity but that surely serve also to limit the potential threat that outside sex poses to the relationship. These rules basically serve to prevent the partners from establishing precisely the kind of outside relationships that lesbians have hoped to achieve: relationships that combine both sex and love. The rules may be explicit or they may be nonverbal and merely understood, but they almost always exist. Most lesbians (as well as heterosexual women) reject this concept of nonmonogamy for the same reasons they reject all casual sex: It seems wrong, distasteful, immoral, and cheap. Many women who do not reject the notion of tricking on theoretical grounds are simply incapable of being turned on by sex without a relationship attached. If this is the case, we may have to live with monogamy until we can change our sexual preferences so that we are less romantic ...

What new ideas or techniques of handling relationships are involved in these modes of nonmonogamy? First, there is an acknowledgment that the feelings of infatuation that constitute what we call romance are feelings that are totally separate from committed love. In a sense, the gay men and a few lesbians who do this are able to take romance less seriously than others. That is, they see romantic feelings as a variation of sexual feelings and are able to enjoy them without seeing them as a reflection upon their primary relationship. Second, people who negotiate these kinds of nonmonogamous relationships are able to have intimacy that is intense but limited. Third, these individuals (and couples) see the function of a primary relationship as a good deal more circumscribed than do most lesbians (and most heterosexual women). Most people in this culture, and women more than men, are taught to view primary relationships as all or nothing. We expect that our main partners will fulfill all of our intimacy needs as well as sexual needs. We may recognize that we have intimacy needs that must get fulfilled by friends rather than lovers; we may know that we have sexual needs that must get met by people other than our primary lover. It is difficult to comprehend that we might have intimate sexual partners with whom we might want to be intensely involved in a limited way at the same time that we maintain a primary relationship. Our dualistic thinking leads us almost inevitably to compare and choose one or another relationship.

In addition, it takes a great deal of maturity to recognize that the intense passion of the initial stages of such an outside relationship is no indicator of what is to come, and to keep in mind that the apparent perfect fit of such new relationships is an illusion that will pass in time. To negotiate such multiple relationships takes an ability to circumscribe and compartmentalize one's life in a way that most women are unable or unwilling to do.

Ironically, in the 1970s which were the heyday of political ideology scrutinizing and colonizing every part of lesbian existence, some lesbian theorists decided that monogamy was part of the package of limited, constricting patriarchal marriage, and it was decided that lesbians should be nonmonogamous as a political act. Ideally, the theory went, "if we all lived in a healthy society we would be able to be sexual with all our friends without endangering our primary relationships." Many young and impressionable lesbians raced to try this new theory out.

That social experiment is widely considered, forty years later, to have been a complete disaster. With no models to follow and with all the baggage around sex, love, and intimacy that women end up with in this society, lesbian political nonmonogamy was not only nearly entirely unsuccessful, it created a huge amount of drama. This wasn't helped by the fact that a good many "lesbians" of that time were actually heterosexual or bisexual women who were disappointed in men and thought that relationships with women might give them a better deal. These "political lesbians" eventually left entirely, and the "ordinary" lesbians mostly settled into their continuing pattern of serial monogamy.

At the same time, SM dykes were struggling with these problems as well. As referenced earlier in this chapter, SM dykes took the brunt of early anti-SM rhetoric from their radical feminist sisters; the book *Coming to Power* was the gauntlet thrown down with the challenge to "own your illegitimate children". Fifteen years later, *The Second Coming* was published, and it openly discussed polyamory and nonmonogamous relationships. KJ, a self-professed "butch leatherdyke", told me, "Yeah, the older ones of us struggled a lot with whether it was abusive to do BDSM with each other, even when both parties loved it. We struggled even more with one woman having power over another woman, even when it was consensual. We didn't usually add nonmonogamy into it, though—it was as if these things were more acceptable if they were done in the context of two pair-bonded women who were madly in love with each other. Adding a third or fourth party, that was risky. But now you see the younger dykes, especially the young butch 'bois', they're as promiscuous as gay men. And you're seeing a lot more polyamory among all the young lesbians, but especially the kinky ones. However, I think that serious lifestyle power exchange is still comparatively rare, even among the younger kids."

Polyamory was another difficult cog in that machine, making things even more complicated. Leatherdyke femme Maggie wrote to me:

It's more about families for lesbians, including leatherwomen. I watched my gay friends fuck all over the city and then finally come to a place where they might like a more emotionally intimate network of lovers. For the women I know, we came to poly suspiciously. We weren't fooled, any more, by the decades-old idea that it was more politically correct because monogamy was patriarchal. We'd been there, done that, found out how emotionally dangerous it was, especially for those of us who still had yet to own our own sexuality wholly, or those of us with abuse histories. There's no drama like dyke drama, and poly meant drama.

But some of us made it work. I think that the most successful and stable long-term lesbian poly families I know didn't start out with screwing around and eventually add the new fuck to the family because they keep hanging around. It was more that they developed a heart connection with someone, added them to the "family" in an organic sort of way, and eventually it became sexual. We tend more toward close-knit romantic families than to a couple that has lots of outside adventures. Is that a female thing? Maybe. Women have always been hearthkeepers to one extent or another. I don't know. I don't think that leather necessarily makes this process easier or harder, although I think that leatherwomen may have a better grip on owning their own sexuality, and that makes poly easier because you're less insecure. If you really identify with leather, you've had to work through all those feelings of wrongness and come to some pride in who you are. Stepping outside what's normal, outside of the Cinderella fantasy, also helps you let go of the fantasy of monogamy.

For my own poly family, my leather family, we're polyfidelitous. Maybe my opinion has to do with my experience, I don't know. But our power exchange is built around love and family bonds, not always sex. Although the sex can be pretty hot.

Kai, who is much younger, reported something quite different from Maggie's experience: "I only hang out with people my own age. But I see a lot of free-form polyamory, a lot of promiscuous sex, a lot of families forming around lovers and ex-lovers and tricks. We're not afraid of poly, and we manage it pretty well considering. Maybe we grew up without so much of the girl programming. The problem for us is slave-owning. Fun power exchange is fine, like for a scene, but serious lifestyle power exchange is not OK for a lot of my peers. The more total-power-exchange it is, the worse it is, because our subculture is pretty radically egalitarian, young academic, politically aware. It's OK to play with power models and subvert them. It's not OK to invest in them. This has been hard for me, because I really love owning another woman. I've had two slaves and they left me because we couldn't really be out with our peers. We could be out in the leather community, but not if the word would get out to the vanilla bois."

Another younger woman agreed: "Most of the young dykes and queer boys that I hung out with when I lived in the city were very much into free relationships. Their attitude was, 'We can't know if we'll be together for very long, so we shouldn't promise anything we can't deliver.' Even monogamy was too much of a power dynamic for them—it was someone trying to lay chains on them. When I realized that I wanted a D/s relationship, I had to change communities."

The Bisexual Connection

Bisexuality is a funny thing. It's easy to hide ... unless you're polyamorous. Bisexuals who are only dating or committed to one person often complain that everyone assumes they're gay or straight. While it's not a reason that many like to admit, quite a few bisexuals have admitted to me that their bisexuality led them into polyamory both philosophically (if you can love more than one gender, you can love more than one person at a time) and practically (because if you want both male and female lovers in your life at once, you can't be monogamous). The two are so conflated that same-sex heterosexual members of poly families have to constantly combat assumptions that they are bisexual and involved with everyone in the poly group.

According to studies, there are fewer men than women in the middle of the Kinsey scale. Women's sexual preferences look like a bell-curve; men's look like a checkmark. That means that bisexual men tend to be mostly-straight or mostly-gay but will make exceptions, rather than being open to any gender. Transgendered individuals also anecdotally report that men tend to be less comfortable with them because they like their men manly and their women womanly (with a few notable exceptions). Researchers have theorized that this specificity of desire comes about because men are more prone to visual arousal than women, and the "look" of a person's body or genitals is more important to them.

However that works, it means that women are more likely to be "soft" bisexuals—meaning that they are more likely to fall "accidentally" into bisexual relationships, or make exceptions for a special person, or fall in love regardless of sexual attraction—than men. Poly families where the women are bisexual and the men aren't are more common than the other way around. Not surprisingly, there are more male owners with bisexual female slaves than female owners with bisexual male slaves. (I'm not counting "forced bi" situations or dynamics where the slave's sexual identity is considered irrelevant, just ones where the slave is allowed to have and defend a sexual identity.) Men tend to be "hard" bisexuals or else monosexuals—either they're into it or they aren't, and they're pretty clear about which it is, and it's rare that those preferences change.

The "forced bi" situation, however, needs to be mentioned, as it is generally found only in high-intensity power dynamic relationships. In this practice, monosexual slaves are ordered to have sexual relations with people outside their preference. Sometimes this is done to entertain the owner, either because they want to watch a sex show with a particular gender combination, or because they take sadistic pleasure in the slave's discomfort. Sometimes it is done as an act of hospitality; the slave is a sort of courtesan whose job is to pleasure whoever the owner indicates, regardless of their own attraction to the individual. Some owners feel that "true" slaves should have no gender preferences with regard to attraction, or that by getting into an ownership situation (at least with that owner) they are agreeing for any existing attraction to be completely irrelevant. When people with this dynamic collide with individuals for whom sexual preference is a powerful and sacrosanct factor in their identity, there are often horrified cries of "abuse!"

The practice of "forced bi" does seem, in 90% of cases, to be a heterosexual phenomenon. While many gay male masters will order their male slaves to service other men, it's very rare for them to force them to fuck women, and almost unheard-of for dominant lesbians to send their girls off to fuck men. In the former case the owner's reaction to the idea seems to be incredulity; in the latter revulsion. It seems that being straight and being forced to transgress via the taboo of "humiliating" queer acts is a very different psychological arena than being gay or lesbian and being forced to transgress via the taboo of "humiliating" heterosexual acts. It may be that a gay or lesbian identity is so much more hard-won, rather than being a default state handed to one by society, that it's just too high a taboo to jump over with any comfort on either side.

Politically, the bisexuals and the polyamory movement are beginning to encroach and overlap to the point where they are sharing a few conventions; bisexual conventions are loaded with poly workshops and poly conventions seem to have nearly as many bisexual people as heterosexuals, although no one is taking statistics yet that I've seen. There is at least one convention near me that is equally bi and poly, with some trans thrown in for good measure. Here we run into the division mentioned in the "Border Wars" chapter: the political differences between egalitarian and power-exchange poly families. It will be interesting to see how bisexual poly perverts manage to dance with that demographic, as they are the queers most likely to end up doing so.

Transgendered Boundaries

I'm not going to do a lot of writing to cover power dynamics among and with transgendered individuals specifically, because there's a whole chapter on it in my book *Double Edge: The Intersection Of BDSM And Transgender*. However, where those two intersect with polyamory lies a dangerous zone. Even more than the gay, lesbian, and bisexual demographics, transgendered people—and especially transsexuals—have been severely penalized for deviating from a strict standard of "normal" in their relationships. In order to get access to the medical procedures they need, for example, transsexuals have to go through "gatekeepers"—mental health professionals who judge whether they should be allowed to transition. For decades, gatekeepers laid their own social biases on their hapless clients in an effort to guarantee that they would be seen as the most socially normal of individuals after transition. Being nonheterosexual in one's new gender was not allowed until Lou Sullivan, a gay FTM, broke through that barrier in the 1980s. Dating or marrying another transsexual was frowned on in many areas until the 1990s—one's ability to land a "normal" man or woman as a partner was seen as a sign of success in the new gender.

Transgendered people who also took part in BDSM and/or power dynamic relationships were seen by most gatekeepers as fetishistic, and there was the possibility that their gender dysphoria would be dismissed as just another paraphilia; they weren't "real" transsexuals (who were presumably sexually normal except for their gender issues) and might be denied medical assistance. Polyamory was also not considered healthy, especially because of the association of MTF (male-to-female) transsexuals with prostitution, and both trans-sexes with promiscuity out of desperation and low self-esteem. Fear of being seen as abnormal was and still is rampant among in trans communities, including fear of some other transgendered person doing something that will be seen as abnormal and "ruining it" for their better-behaved brothers and sisters. There is a pervading terror that being less than visibly wholesome may cause gatekeepers to scrutinize transfolk more closely and be even less likely to give them access to medical care, and also that transfolk as a population will never be accepted in society if any of us get reputations for being perverts. This was clearly shown in the hostility that more conservative transfolk have shown to FTM (female-to-male) transsexuals who have chosen to stop testosterone and get pregnant after transition.

Recently, on a list for personal ads geared toward transfolk who were looking for partners, a telling argument broke out about whether polyamorous or BDSM-related personal ads should be allowed, being as they made the monogamous vanilla transfolk look bad—or at least that was the viewpoint of the complainers. While the list moderators chose not to ban anyone for their choice of sought relationship, it's an unsurprising conflict. There are many fissures in the transgender demographic, and "normal-appearing" versus "visibly socially abnormal" is one of the biggest ones.

At the same time, I know many transfolk—especially kinky ones—who have ended up in poly relationships literally because their desperation made them more open to unusual relationship structures. Being trans means that your dating pool shrinks to a tiny percentage of the population. Being trans and kinky ... well, it can look like a barren wilderness out there. During the writing of my book on transgender and BDSM, I interviewed several people who gave up and decided that it was better to be a secondary lover in a non-exclusive relationship than to be eternally lonely, even though polyamory was not their first choice. Interestingly, none of them regretted the choice, which is a different story from most monogamous people pushed into polyamory by their partners. A few had left their leather families for monogamous relationships, but the rest were still currently poly, if not cruising for other partners. Some related that belonging to a poly family where everyone accepted them was an unexpected joy, so much so that it made up for the difficulties of adapting to a poly lifestyle.

Part II
Essays From The Ones In Charge

Putting On The Dominant Panties: Responsibilities of the People in Charge

As I've said elsewhere in this book, if you are the dominant in a poly power dynamic with multiple s-types, whether the polyamory goes successfully is largely on your shoulders. If there are multiple dominants, they both (or all) need to take responsibility for the situation and do what needs to be done. (If there are egalitarian partners mixed in, things may go a little differently.) All too often I see dominants throwing new and old subs together, hoping everything will just work itself out, and then doing the equivalent of squeezing their eyes shut and crossing their fingers. When resentment begins, they attempt short-term containment rather than long-term maintenance and repair, or ignore it entirely until it blows up their faces. Part of this is because we as dominants are not trained in how to handle polyamory successfully. Actually, no one gets "trained" in how to handle polyamory successfully except for doing it, as it's still such a minority practice. We can perhaps be forgiven for getting it wrong. That doesn't, however, make the situation any less screwed up.

So what are our responsibilities? What are the crux-points of this relationship that fall entirely onto our shoulders? Which balls do we not dare to drop? I've tried to list the most important ones here, the ones whose violation is the most likely to eat the foundation out from under one's relationships.

Priorities. The more rights and limits that a slave has given up, and the less recourse they have, the more you are responsible for their mental well-being. The more responsible you are for them, the more important it is that their feelings are dealt with first when there is a poly crisis involving them. (This is especially true when it is them against an egalitarian partner or a partner with a much lower-intensity power dynamic.) When people in a poly group are having drama, your first responsibility is to the person under your care with the fewest limits and least recourse. If all the s-types are equal in stature, your first responsibility is to the one with the most seniority, unless that has been explicitly negotiated otherwise.

Can They Do This? You are responsible for realistically determining whether any s-type in your charge is emotionally capable of handling polyamory, theirs or yours. If you fail in this determination, the whole thing will go to hell, so you have to get that one right up front.

Code Of Honor. You are responsible for holding to the promises you make about how you will behave in these relationships. This is necessary for any sort of power dynamic, but it is especially important when you start adding more people to the mix. You are the fulcrum of trust and honor, and your s-types depend on you to be that fulcrum. If you find that you want to renegotiate and change your promises, you are responsible for getting your s-types to a place where they can handle the new changes emotionally.

We Function Better On More Information. You are responsible for finding out as much as possible about what is going on emotionally with everyone in your poly group. You can't be the decision-maker if you're working blind. Make it a priority to spend time with each group member, asking them how they're doing or if there are any problems. Don't let people get away with sandbagging ... stuffing down all their problems until they finally explode. Get everything onto the table, or at least onto your private desk. No one should be keeping anything from you that might jeopardize family harmony.

Owning And Operating ... Skillfully? You are responsible for learning the inside of your first s-type's head extremely well before you add another s-type. For example, do you know what all their emotional triggers are, especially ones about abandonment, self-worth, or attractiveness? More important, do you know how to bring them down from those triggers reliably every time? Do you know how to help them work through it until they can see things more objectively and get a handle on their feelings? Do you have a significant track record of accomplishing this, enough so that your s-type feels confident in your ability to give effective help when asked?

Are you aware of any tendency that your submissive might have to exaggerating their feelings, or having difficulty seeing things from another person's point of view? Are they passive-aggressive? Do you know how to effectively call them on that and get them past it? Do they have good distress tolerance skills? Do you understand how they best handle processing—can they sit in a meeting for three hours or do they get overwhelmed quickly and need such things in smaller bites?

We'll Make You Talk. It's up to the dominant to force people to communicate with each other as well as with you. If you have the negotiated right to make them sit down and discuss things openly and reasonably, with you as facilitator, do it. (I might suggest that a little training in mediation and/or facilitation and/or conflict resolution can be a real boon for a dominant in this position. Don't scorn outside training—it might be the best thing you've done for your relationship.) Show everyone in your poly family that the values of honesty and openness and commitment to working things through are not just lip service, but will be held to Or Else. Some dominants have resorted to Nobody Leaves This Room Until This Is Worked Out. Whether that draconian approach will work for you is your own judgment, but understand that you may have to teach your subs how to communicate with each other. You might think about setting up rules for how they should do it, rules designed to minimize problematic interactions.

Each Is Valued For Who They Are. If you have s-types in several different levels of power dynamic intensity, don't let them compare their own intensity level negatively with someone else's. Sometimes this manifests as a lower-intensity sub feeling bad in comparison to a high-intensity slave, not because they want a different deal—they don't particularly want to be a slave, deep down—but they fear that you will want them less because they are not comfortable going there. Alternately, a sub with a lower-intensity dynamic might honestly want to go there, but you want to go slowly and cautiously with them ... and they compare themselves negatively to an existing slave who has already spent a decade getting there with you. On the other hand, a high-intensity s-type may look at the closer-to-egalitarian partner as being more exciting than they are, because they are a more independent person with an outside life.

It's up to you to make it clear that the dynamic they're in is the dynamic you want them in, at least for right now. Make it clear to them that each person is valued for what they can give, fully and completely within the limits negotiated, not for what they might theoretically be able to give if they were someone they're not. Step on any attempts to compare themselves negatively to each other.

Never Encourage Competition. Encouraging s-types to compete with each other, even subtly, is destructive to a poly power dynamic. The overriding ideal should be that We Are A Team, working together. Competition, especially for your attention and approval, undermines everything. You may think it's fun and sexy, but it doesn't work as an everyday dynamic. If you sense competition, stamp it out and reemphasize teamwork. If each s-type has their own special place in the family, this can help things.

Avoid Silence. Finally, I'd like to further discuss the issue of withholding information. This is, in general, one of the ways in which a dominant can reinforce a power dynamic. For example, they can say, "Get in the car. No, you don't get to know where we're going." This reminds the submissive that they have given up the right to be an equal partner in deciding what happens to them, allows them to practice trust, and gives them the opportunity to relax and let themselves be carried along by the dominant's will instead of worrying about a situation. Saying, "We'll talk about that, but not today," reminds them that things will get done on the dominant's timetable and not theirs. (Of course, you do have to follow up and keep your word.) Restricting information can also be useful during training, when a submissive may try too hard to second-guess their dominant or the situation, or may use that information to attempt to win back some control, if only subtly. These are normal and expected parts of D/s and M/s, and have been used to advantage by most dominants in power dynamics.

However, the social baggage and triggers around nonmonogamy in our culture—baggage and triggers that every one of us has ingrained to one extent or another just from living here—do not lend themselves well to the act of withholding information. In fact, it's the opposite of useful. Withholding information about other sexual and romantic partners (and safe sex, and communication between partners) is, to be blunt, the sort of thing that egalitarian partners do when they are cheating and wish to deceive each other. Its association not only with cheating and deception, but with egalitarian relationship behavior, is so thorough that it is almost impossible for a dominant to deliberately withhold information about those things and not bring up those associations in the mind of an unhappy submissive. And as I stressed earlier in this book, behaviors that build trust in both the dominant and in the dynamic are money in the bank, while behaviors that lose trust in the dominant and/or the dynamic are shooting yourself in the foot. This is especially true for the early stages of a power dynamic (and by that I mean the first year or two) and for any period of significant change and uncertainty, which the early stages of polyamory can be.

While it's probably easy for readers to figure out why silence is associated with cheating and deception, it may take a bit of thinking to discern why it's so much an egalitarian practice in this case, especially given the aforementioned dominant use of restricting information for reinforcing the dynamic. Let's put it this way: The reason that an egalitarian partner hides their affairs from their unaccepting partner is because they do not want to face the confrontation that would ensue if they carried on the affair openly. Their partner could leave, or demand huge concessions in order to stay, or at the least throw a terrible emotional scene that the cheating partner would be overwhelmed by and unable to stop. They hide the affair because they know that *they* would have little recourse were it discovered.

In an intense-level power dynamic, things are entirely different. First, a slave in such a dynamic doesn't have the kind of ability to demand concessions that a more egalitarian partner (or, to be fair, a sub in a low-intensity power dynamic where polyamory isn't controlled) would have. They don't, for example, have the right to demand monogamy from their owner. If monogamy is what was explicitly negotiated at the beginning and they are counting on their owner keeping their word, that's a different problem, and one of violation of trust. However, it's up to the owner to be the one to actually decide to be monogamous, or else refer to other parts of this book. Hopefully they will make the best choice for the situation, whatever that is. Either way, to hide information is to imply that the slave has that kind of power.

Second, no dominant worth their salt should ever be afraid of their submissive or their submissive's emotional responses, period. You should never feel that you *have* to hide something from them. If the idea of revealing makes you hunch or wince, you are not in control of the situation. They are. This is the kind of real courage that it takes to be in charge. If you are doing something that you know will give your slave an extreme emotional response, you'd better figure out, before you start the triggering behavior, how to bring them out of that place and help them to work through it to a better headspace. Like I said above, learn one of them inside and out before adding new ones.

Just as hiding information is reminiscent of deception and cheating, and can trigger those feelings in a submissive, being completely honest not out of love but because you have no reason to do otherwise—*because you know that you have the power in the relationship*—is actually a much better reinforcement of the power dynamic. As an example, one heterosexual M/f/m triad that I know had some problems with insecurity on the part of the female slave. She was fine with the other full-time slave—they got along like brother and sister—but what she didn't like was her master's habit of picking up casual sex partners and having kinky one-night stands with them. He was completely open about this habit, and assured her that he always used safe sex, but was not inclined to share details with her. This made her worry that he was being dishonest in some way. She especially worried that he was dishonest about his statement that he was not forming long-term relationships with these individuals (he had made it clear that new subs to be added to the family would be brought home and introduced to the existing slaves before a decision was made) and would suddenly spring a new "slave" on them with no warning, as a former master of hers had done.

In this case, he had a number of options. He could have continued to do as he pleased and given no further information, but this might have brought his slave's insecurities to a peak of fear that might have exploded. He could have told her that he was the master and had the right to do as he pleased, and that she as the slave should not question him, but while this might be true, it would not have helped the problem any more than the last solution. He could have stopped his casual play, but that would not have reinforced the power dynamic in a positive way. He could have talked to her about whether she felt he could be trusted, and helped her come to trusting him in a subtler, more organic sense. This might have worked, but he felt that she needed a more direct lesson.

Instead, he told her that she was coming along on his next date, and informed her of what her behavior was to be. Her job was to smile, say little, and assist him. He had her stand by the motel room bed and hand him toys to play with the woman he'd met over the Internet. When it was time to fuck the new toy, he had her put a condom on his cock, lube him up, and insert him into her. Then she had to hand him more lube when necessary, and bring them wet towels afterwards to clean up. Afterwards, he said goodbye to the new toy and made it clear that they were done. (The new toy was fine with this, having expected nothing else.)

This was the exact opposite of the way that an egalitarian husband would have handled the situation, because an egalitarian husband could not have required that behavior of her and gotten it. By doing it this way, he clearly sent the following messages: "I am doing exactly what I said I was doing, and there is no deception. I will continue to do exactly what I say I will do, even if you aren't thrilled with it, because I am the one in charge here. You know without a doubt what you can expect of me. You know that I will be true to myself, and that while I am willing to show you who and what I am so that you will know me better and thus trust me more, it is not your whims that will rule the situation here. I can and will force you to confront your fears, even in ways that are not comfortable for you. And because you are really my slave, I have no need to hide anything from you ... and I'm not afraid of your reaction in the least."

On the way home, he asked her whether he had assuaged her fears, or whether he would need to bring her along on another date. She said, "No, sir. I believe you."

The Creation Of A M/s Household

Master James

I. Introduction

The Cast

It's 10:30 in the evening at miranda's house. We're tired; jaylynn is reading email and miranda has closed her laptop and has her head in my lap. She spontaneously moves from the couch to the floor and presses her cheek against my boot. Meanwhile, jaylynn is quiet, waiting for her to rise before she reads a funny note from a fetish group. My phone beeps and I gently shift miranda's head to pick it up.

I summarize the text. "Stephanie has landed safely and is headed home." Stephanie is my wife of seventeen years; jaylynn and miranda both ask me to tell her hello. The two of them are in service to me; my wife is not, though I act as dominant and top her sometimes. We have just been at a leather event, and Stephanie is flying back from the west coast where she attended a meeting of her esoteric order.

Not every evening is this ideal. There have been evenings with tears, loneliness, and some screaming and yelling … a collar thrown across the room in anger, eventually recovered and offered to me in outstretched hands. But there is a strong dynamic. There are expressions of love and mutual support. To say that things will always work would be hubris. Nobody can look into the future and pride goeth before a fall. Yet despite our initial worries, a year of adventures has strengthened our M/s dynamic. The reality of upsets, fights, and "another fucking opportunity for growth" has led to a chain of victories in terms of safety, stability, and getting along. There are bumps in the road ahead, but I feel like we, together, are in the driver's seat, and the happiness of this moment leaves me with a desire to share the steps we took to reach this calm place of strength.

No Such Thing As Happily Ever After

I'm known as a skeptic and a cynic. I don't believe fairy stories except the ones told by queer friends over mimosas at Sunday brunch. "Happily ever after" was purged from my vocabulary sometime between the age I lost faith in the tooth fairy and the time I learned to stop believing in "free sex" on the Internet. This makes it difficult to offer sound advice on how to run a successful polyamorous M/s household. Many guides I have found push unrealistic standards of behavior, discipline, or mental conformity that will not work for most people with a working lifestyle. I have made mistakes and I will make more. There is no "right way", and I think the only meaningful guide is to share the experiences of others who have already attempted the trip, gathering ideas from them that can make our own venture easier. My goal here is to suggest that "what we did worked", not "what you should do". I'll do this by looking at the reasons that people seek polyamory and slavery, my personal journey to M/s, the background of our household, and the challenges that we have overcome.

By focusing on the trials, I risk portraying a house of tears, continual crisis, and psychodrama, and that is not the case. Without all the positives—love, shared dinners, trips, play, bedtime stories, movies, and time spent talking with each other, what we do would not be worth the effort. It is my hope that you'll have your own positives, and that I can give some suggestions on how to hold them close and grow them, rather than being a victim of your own relationships.

II. M/s, Polyamory, and Social Structures—A Drama In One Unnatural Act

The Importance Of Polyamory In M/s

Both Master/slave (M/s) and polyamorous lifestyles are difficult. When it works, poly helps relationships last past frustrations and initial loss of new relationship energy. As a flexible model for relationships, it offers choices and safety valves that do not exist when "one on one" is the only option.

Aside from basic dishonesty, which damages all relationships equally, complexity and coordination are often cited as reasons why poly relationships fail. When *two* people cannot decide who is going to lead, they can take time to figure it out. When *three or more* become involved, paralysis can set in. Avoidance and paralysis makes the partners unwilling to confront problems and the relationship stagnates. M/s dynamics help sustain our poly relationships by providing structure and organization. M/s answers questions about "who is going to drive", and has allowed me the authority to force us to confront many issues that sabotage poly relationships.

Despite dubious romanticization, modern consensual slavery has little or nothing to do with historical slavery, which was typically economic in nature. Likewise, while I value the tradition of the "Old Guard" Leather Community highly, the fact is that most straight suburban boys and girls did not enter into M/s by saying, "I think I would like to imitate gay bikers." So why the drive to slavery in modern society?

Traditional Relationships—The Pre-Nuclear Family

Marriage from the Stone Age to the Victorian era was about personal survival. Period literature and modern drama tends to depict the wealthy few who had freedom of choice; most people lived a precarious existence as laborers or farmers. It is difficult to imagine how hard life was for farmer or factory worker even as recently as 1900. Until 1848, married women in the U.S. could not own property, make contracts, transfer or sell property, or bring a suit in court. Children were important sources of labor around the house, set to chores as soon as they could walk.

In contrast, in everything but lifestyle, modern society gives us vast choices ... we can pick from a hundred variations of latte. Years ago a friend who was a major in the U.S. Army told me that "relationships like that always fail in the end", and by "like that" he meant mine. He was being sincere, honest, and repeating the social mythology of his Catholic Baltimore childhood.

Mainstream media still tells us that there is safety in embracing the conservative traditions of yesteryear, preying on our fear of loneliness by teaching us that traditional behavior will make us happy while alternatives will bring us pain. We are told that sex before marriage is wrong, and that "in our heart" we know we want to love just one, marry them, and have children. But these traditions don't work for us because they were never about happiness. They were myths to get people to behave in ways that increased their chances of survival by making them feel it was noble to endure unhappy situations. "You must have only one love" made the sullen housewife stay put after she had bred with the first boy who made her pulse thrill. If she could not come to make herself stay in love with her husband, she was a failure as a woman and must stay on out of obligation and need. Either way, she and her children did not starve. Believing the lie and telling herself she loved her husband became important for her to justify the unhappiness of her life which she passed on to her children.

Today we come together with another person *by choice*, but our laws and traditions are still structured for us to make commitments as if we were choosing for survival. The labor-partnership nature of traditional marriage gave it a structure. The "breadwinner" made decisions and provided protection, while his spouse performed domestic services, granted a sexual outlet, and brought eventual helpers in the form of children. Modern marriage of equals by choice is a new creation. There are no bylaws, no *Robert's Rules of Marriage*, no guidelines for making it work. Sometimes newlyweds try to write down their rules in a set of vows, but it is too often considered gauche to write your own vows, especially if they are more than twenty lines. In selling the vision of an early marriage to the "one right partner", our mainstream media pushes our youth into the most profound responsibilities of life without preparation or a realistic outlook. Modern marriage is unstable because there is no survival reason to stay in an unsatisfying relationship. With no rules to create an agreement on expectations, the answer to problems is often to leave the marriage. This means that divorce rates among role models soar, and this creates a cultural feeling that marriage is unstable and insecure.

Is it any surprise that many people of both genders begin to crave a relationship with structure? Are they the outliers, or do they want what they believe that past generations got as a matter of course—something fixed in their life that they can count on?

Consensual slavery is one choice that offers structure along lines that are, realistically, often far less authoritarian than the average Victorian marriage. Despite M/s ideology, there is little reason to remain in a slave relationship that is going badly. What M/s *can* offer is a structure which has the *potential* to make the relationship more secure and fulfilling for the right people, so that there is less reason to want to leave it. Of course that depends heavily on a good Master, and that is a tough skillset to learn. Polyamory along *with* M/s is even tougher, a balance of individual choice and consensual structure.

III. My Personal Odyssey ... With Emphasis On The "Odd"

Becoming Poly and Kinky

Much of my personal understanding of M/s and poly is a product of my personal history. I knew that I was poly before I ever had my cock inside a girl. I got the basic idea from Robert Heinlein in *Stranger In A Strange Land*. If you actually love or care for someone, you want them to be happy, and tying that happiness to "you only" was selfish and narrow-minded. As time wore on, I also realized that it was a recipe for resentment and failed relationships.

In the early 1990s I married Stephanie, who came out of a failed marriage and had determined that she was poly by nature. Soft-core BDSM porn such as Anne Rice's *Sleeping Beauty* books was thriving in the late '80s, and the '90s saw a BDSM explosion. *Exit To Eden* went to the screen in 1994, followed by *Screw The Roses* being published in 1995. It was a given that polyamorous people were sexual experimenters, and as the '90s wore on we discovered kink already in progress at the local leather store. In terms of practice, I learned about kink largely from the Web.

Stephanie's Tale

Stephanie came from a deeply dysfunctional household largely dominated by her father. The smart but troubled scion of well-to-do parents, her father suffered from depression and had been kicked out of MIT for frat-boy drinking. Her bipolar mother, an adult child of alcoholic parents, vented frustrations on Stephanie. Home life was insecure and erratic, subject to the vagaries of both parents' emotional states and the tolls of her father's failed business enterprises. Bills went unpaid and utilities were disconnected without warning. Though she was not subjected to extreme physical abuse, her mother was intensely psychologically and emotionally abusive, teaching Stephanie indirectly that trust was a poor idea. One of Stephanie's memories is of a treasured collection of glass animals which her mother smashed in a fit of rage. She married young and briefly to get away from her parents for good. Despite her childhood traumas, Stephanie was sexually vivacious and adventurous, wanting more than her lackluster marriage had delivered. Talk about relationships was associated in her mind with being called on the carpet and abused by her parents, so the start of a "serious talk" put her on the defensive.

My own father was the adult child of an alcoholic. A distant and reserved man, he had a strong love of British culture. He avoided "unpleasant" things and eventually let his marriage die through emotional reserve, leaving me an aversion to confronting thorny issues. This worked for Stephanie, and represented a more stable refuge than her other options. Without any real discussion, we slouched into marriage with no long-term plan or purpose. While we both agreed on poly as an ideal, when we married the landmark poly guide *The Ethical Slut* had yet to be published. Without guidance, our "poly" rules were open to push and pull, which would become discord as Stephanie suffered from cyclic depression.

Entering The D/s World

By the time I came to power exchange I'd been married for nearly a decade and a half, and come out of a seven-year D/s relationship with a girl I'll call G, which had slowly ebbed away because I did not know how to meet her needs or sustain the energy. Eventually G left to marry a monogamous man who could provide for her. Despite an amicable parting, I found my overall attitude had become very bitter and jaded.

In the meantime, I'd met miranda, and in the grand tradition of "love at first sight" we instantly disliked each other. I saw her as a whiny girl and she saw me as a domineering jackass. We were thrown together at a friend's wedding. I was the most intelligent person to talk to, and she was clearly drawn to dominant males. I learned that she was a MIT graduate, and had a mind and personality. She was in a relationship-to-be-married with a handsome, decent, neurotic ex-athlete. Soon after that, miranda moved in with him and instantly wanted out. Over the next few months and several trips I collared miranda, and helped her through the process of moving out and moving down to stay with G until she could find an apartment.

Miranda's Tale

My slave miranda grew up in a wealthy upper-middle-class family. Her parents were conservative, though not fundamentalist, Christians, and she was overshadowed by a tantrumatic younger sister. She was the older "good girl" who stood by trying to be obedient while her parents ran in circles trying to please her sibling. She would get a pat on the head for being good, while her sister got the sun, moon, and at least half a dozen major stars to get her to shut up. In order to keep tantrums at bay, she was always given the same gifts as her sister, equally and together. Even if her sister had been a terrible brat and she'd been angelic, they would both get the same toy in the same color, or a very equivalent gift. She went through much of her childhood "on hold"; she could have a happy childhood real soon now, just as soon as her younger sister quieted down.

Around the time her sister began to become old enough to "know better", another child was born and suddenly miranda was expected to be a "young adult".

You'd think that was the perfect setup. I had, Svengali-like, lured a pretty young girl to drop her handsome boyfriend and move down just to be dominated by me. In fact, I was terrified. This was *real stuff.* Someone putting their life and future in my hands.

The Shift To "Master"

At the time, I was adamant that I was a Dom, not a Master. How could I be a Master? To act as a Master was to accept responsibility completely for someone else's life. But at about the time I began dating miranda, I made an online friend—a writer of profoundly powerful erotica who became a major catalyst in my shift from Dom to Master. She pushed me to admit to myself that I had been acting as a Master for years. I'd accepted responsibility for much of the relationship during Stephanie's depression, and had been the guiding partner and mentor in my relationship with G.

When miranda began to speak of deepening our D/s relationship, I responded by opening the potential of a trial period of slavery. Shortly after that, we attended our first Master/slave Conference (MsC) in Washington, D.C. Originally the vision of Master Taino, a leader in the D.C. gay male M/s community and the organizer of Master Taino's Training Academy, the MsC is the one major leather event that focuses primarily on dynamics and relationships, rather than learning how to beat people or poke holes in them. Master Taino and several of the other senior voices I heard raised were eloquent. I began to feel this was something I was actually *doing*, not extended roleplay. At the MsC I saw real relationships that had lasted twenty years or more. I saw proof that the M/s dynamic, and the poly dynamic, were no more inherently volatile than marriage. Most marriages end in divorce. But they *can* succeed and so could M/s.

IV. Towards An M/s Household

Head In The Sand

I still wasn't focused on the idea of building an M/s household and lifestyle. I was bitter about the failure of my relationship with G, and I talked a good line about the desire for freedom and casual play. I claimed miranda was an *accident*. I was going to "train" girls, not get emotionally involved in supporting them. I badly wanted to reject the responsibility of Mastery. Even as I was acting as a Master by assigning homework, agreeing to assume some control of life choices, and dipping my fingers into miranda's psyche, I upheld my freedom to *say* that my responsibility should end when I walked out the door. I did not want to restructure my priorities and play, and admit my own need to exert control, and take the required responsibility. I was afraid of failing again and I could think of a million reasons to dodge responsibility. Even as I considered bringing in another girl, I told myself that I could not *possibly* be responsible for two girls.

I undertook a new trainee, but my idea was that she would be my proof that I could simply train girls, not get emotionally invested, and let them go. I was fond of her but resolved to stay no more than fond. However, I had only barely started her training when her father required her to move to the Midwest if she was to stay in school at his expense.

My trainee had told her friend jaylynn something about my style as a Dom, and introduced us. I'd met jaylynn once before and thought she was pretty, although she struck me as quiet and moody. (At least we didn't hate each other.) She brought out a powerful dominant streak in me, and the second time we met I ended up hurting her in a stairwell with my hands around her throat. There was kissing too, though it seemed secondary.

Jaylynn's Tale

My slave jaylynn grew up the child of small business owners, who lived in the shadow of their own wealthy forbears on both sides.

Her parents lived beyond their means, yearning for material status symbols such as her maternal grandfather's elegant Baltimore mansion and shore house. In the meantime, the family business, a once prosperous hardware store inherited from a generation before, failed as the inner city encroached and what had been a suburban neighborhood fell to urban blight; jaylynn grew up feeling that there was one extra expense that her parents did not need in their life— her. Her father, who could be a textbook example for poor self-awareness, subjected her to a situation which was essentially non-consensual D/s. His dictatorial demands for quiet, thrift, and obedience were deeply inconsistent. No real disciplinarian, he expected his daughter to be a mind-reader and lashed out when her attempts to please him failed to measure up to what he expected but could not adequately communicate.

The Flying Fickle Finger Of Fate

Up until this time, the poly dynamic was fairly simple. My wife had her affairs, I had mine. Now the real juggling act began. I had added a third wheel, and it was my job to make a working tricycle. There is nothing like abhorrence of failure as a motivator. The easy conventional wisdom was that relationships of any kind are a matter of fate. Trite sayings like "women are crazy" and "you can't ever tell what will happen" seemed particularly common in the poly community, where the complex nature of relationships made them a tougher gamble. While nobody can predict perfectly, to disclaim any knowledge or ability to see what will probably happen is like saying that you cannot know tomorrow's weather because the meteorologist can only tell you that there is a 70% chance of rain. We know that in practice, this means "carry an umbrella".

This leads to the single thing about M/s which I believe to be a truth, not an opinion: *You, as a Master, are responsible for the success or failure of your relationships.*

This is the heart of where M/s differs from egalitarian poly or monogamy. Choosing to take the role of Master is a choice to *lead*, *guide*, and *direct*. The success of your relationship does not depend on the alignment of the stars, the craziness of whatever gender you have for a partner, or signs from on high. It depends on the actions that *you take today*. This means knowing when to lay down the law, and when doing so would make you a ham-fisted petty dictator.

V. The Care And Training Of The Female Slave

Training: Dominance And Submission

My identification as a Trainer came about as a secondary aspect of my shift to Master. When I initially researched slave training, I found that a lot of the written and online material was developed by the gay male community. This often seemed to focus on a military-style dehumanization akin to the depiction of Marine Corps basic training in Stanley Kubrick's classic movie *Full Metal Jacket*, where the individual ego is completely surrendered and replaced with an ideal such as service to the Master or the Corps. While I could see some merit in these doctrines, they did not suit my needs for training suburban girls.

Nonfiction literature provided some minor influences, but my first real spark came from Kink.com trainer James Mogul. Though clearly constrained by the need to produce marketable erotic video, Mogul created drama and story in his *Training Of O* video series with a personal angle of self-improvement and overcoming internal conflict that struck a chord with me. It is clear to me that over time I have expanded on the concept to the point where my idea of "training" may be different or unique. I feel a kinship to ego-replacement techniques, because I do seek to tear a girl down completely and rebuild her in a new image.

The difference is in the final goal. Many M/s dynamics rely heavily on service to the Master as a be-all and end-all. My ideal in training is to make the girl the best that she can be, along the lines of self-actualization described by psychologists Abraham Maslow and Carl Rogers. To that end, preserving elements of the girl's ego is not only important, but core to what I wish to accomplish.

Creating perfected girls is satisfying to my "will as a Master" because I like to build and create things. Preserving the ego of the girl is important to me because as a theatricist and dramatist, I am fascinated by interactivity in art. My artistic urges revolve around the collaborative fusion of audience and artist, so the final creation is a gestalt of my will and the will of my slave or submissive, each one different.

If the traditional model of building and teaching is to act upon an unshaped lump of clay and give it form, my model has always been the sculptor releasing the statue from stone. The sculptor put his mark on the statue, but the image was already in the stone and the sculptor is just freeing it. In the end, Michelangelo's *David* was the image in the stone, but only his hand could have produced a work so fine. I want to be judged by the quality of my slaves, and that means I want them to be proud, willful, and smart.

Every Slave Is Different

Everyone knows that there is a book of rules and discipline for the House. These rules, called Protocols, are inflexible, and everyone in the House can either learn to love them, or leave the House. Period.

The girls snicker when I read them that statement.

Many military or monastic-derived training protocols stress conformity. While I certainly embrace some degree of standardization, ritual, and routine, without the framing of a military-style environment and mindset, I feel that an extreme focus on conformation would be an exercise in driving square pegs through round holes. There is an additional danger of undermining the M/s dynamic by breeding resentment in the slave who could not "measure up" to the arbitrary standard of the day.

My slaves are very different and I want to keep them that way—jaylynn is an alpha personality with a switch side, and a strong sense of pride that spirals into her desire for humiliation play. Oddly enough, she needs different motivators than miranda, a strong submissive with a desire to serve who takes scolding very hard, and to whom humiliation is just "more of what my sister did to me". (We realize that the "oddly" is ironic, right?) In the end, I think that the degree of conformity stressed in many of the better-known training protocols would be very hard to apply usefully in small-scale domestic slavery where self-reliance in slaves is a must.

In many ways, I think this bears on the core motive of the Master or Trainer. In fiction, and with some larger organized training groups that publish material online, there is an assumption that the Masters train slaves, and whether an individual slave comes or goes is of no great concern. But since identifying as a Master, I have never set out to simply "train a slave". I have set out to train a *particular girl*, whom I cared for *individually* as a person. While some Masters might see this as a weakness, I think it is more often the case than not, and I think there needs to be training materials and programs that do not start from the assumption that actually *retaining* the slave is of little importance. Key to this is recognizing different individual needs.

My girls are very different in what they want and need—for example, jaylynn doesn't particularly like being called a "slave" in public. A pragmatist, she doesn't mind it as a generic (as in M/s), but in practice she prefers to be referred to as "in service to James" in front of others. The reason is simple. She's tired of the pained looks when she doesn't "act like a slave", even if we both agree that the stereotype of slaves as cringing doormats is hogwash. She is prone to anger, and has mantras which we have written which allow her to work through anger, worthlessness, and several other negative emotions. That's not as easy or Zenlike as it sounds. She asked me to laminate the cards "because sometimes I am going to want to rip them the fuck in half."

On the other hand, miranda has a token reward system because she cannot emotionally understand abstract praise. Saying "you did well" does not mean much to her. Handing her a token or a card means a great deal. Other examples: jaylynn has come to desire personal rituals with me, but may never want them as much as miranda does; miranda likes daily rituals in which she reminds herself of her devotion to me as a slave, and this is important to her inner life. One could construct an elaborate argument whereby I am actually acting as a service bottom by working to improve the girls in my house, and perhaps philosophically you would be correct. The artist is nothing if not a slave to his art. I can only say that the girls do not see it that way, nor do I.

With such different girls, what challenges did I face in creating an M/s household where my authority was not compromised?

VI. The Issues

"Last And Least" and "Most Special"

When jaylynn came to me, suddenly everyone needed more time and attention ... mostly spent telling me that they weren't getting enough time and attention. I wasn't surprised that it happened, but the intensity caught me off guard. First, jaylynn wanted to be a slave, and her initial reason was largely because miranda was a slave and that seemed *better*. Stephanie *didn't* want to be a slave, but worried that jaylynn and miranda being slaves made them more important to me. Being my slave had been what made miranda special; she feared being one of many and resented jaylynn being called a slave, while jaylynn had the sinking feeling that she would always be the last and least in the relationship, stuck by seniority at the back of the line. This was hard for me to understand. Private school, sports, and boys' organization had given me some of the male military mindset. Men are conditioned to accept "top-down" structures and I accepted that there should be a seniority-based hierarchy. To the girls, seniority seemed to be a value judgment. "Least senior" became "last and least".

I realized that for this group of girls, a healthy house needed an egalitarian basis between them. The problem was that being senior was what miranda felt made her *special*. I could say "everyone is special in their own way", or a hundred other patronizing truisms found in sappy pop songs, but it didn't help. There was no magic bullet to fix the problem, but I can identify many of the things that helped to defuse tensions.

Getting my shit in order. I needed more time to spend on the people who were important to me. that meant sorting out my life and priorities and organizing myself.

Building trust. This takes time; jaylynn needed that time to see that she was not going to constantly get the short end of the stick because she was newer than miranda.

Sticking to my guns. I needed to do this because jaylynn was naturally more dominant and pushy than miranda. She warned me that she would push to get time and attention even when she shouldn't. I had to learn to say No gently but firmly.

Making things special for miranda. She needed proof that even if I did special things with jaylynn, "everyone is special" still meant doing things with her as a focus.

Pushing the idea that I considered my girls to be the best of the best. My girls were a bright, shy MIT grad who could identify as a geek, and a smart, pragmatic party girl with a strong alpha personality. These were not typical girls. I had high standards in women and they measured up in different ways. Within bounds of dignity and decorum I identified our house's goal as being "among the best". That makes it hard to be "last and least". Both girls had problems taking pride in themselves, but a feeling of pride in "us together" could seep into them.

All these solutions just treated the symptoms. The core problem was two good girls who felt jealous of each other. Coming out of different backgrounds, they saw much to disrespect in each other. They needed to see the value in each other, and respect each other as much as I respected them. This meant understanding each other.

My own reserve meant I'd always made a point of not talking in detail about one girl in front of the other. It wasn't right to share details about someone's emotions with a potential rival, and to me, justifications for another girl felt like playing the beta male. How often had I seen supposedly dominant men spending hour after hour trying to justify one partner to the other? How often had I done it with Stephanie? I needed to remember that my girls were not rivals. So did they.

At the 2008 MsC, Master Taino had said "You don't talk badly about one slave to the other. But sometimes you have to talk. Sometimes I have had to say 'This is how Bobby is. You have to understand Bobby.'" The inference was clear. I had to speak respectfully. But I couldn't expect the fucking magical fairy of illumination to suddenly make one girl understand the other. I also could not lie to make things easier in the moment, or find myself conning a girl by saying, "Well, you know you should just tolerate this egregious behavior because ... you know ... it's easier than actually saying anything or me taking a stand."

Talking to each girl frankly still did not create a bond between *them*. They had no emotional guarantee that I was doing anything other than sweet-talking one so I could fuck the other. I needed to start talking to them together. There had been starts; miranda and jaylynn were already "friends" and had tried to talk about M/s issues on their own, with mixed success. Without someone to facilitate, they had talked *at* each other, but had always come away with jealousies and emotional jags. The girls did not want to fight, and they did not attack each other outright. There was awkward silence, and lying to save face and the other girl's feelings. Inevitably, this created resentment afterwards. When feelings did come out, they seemed harsh and bitter. Criticism was vented under the guise of "help".

My job was to moderate, and this went against all the reserve and distance of my upbringing. I had a streak of rebellion against my father's influence, but it had mostly manifested in writing. To make things work, I had to become the same person in flesh that I was behind a keyboard. I had to be self-assured and willing the say the awkward things while retaining enough poise and style not to seem like Mister Rogers while doing it.

It helped that on a lot of levels the girls liked each other. They just couldn't trust each other enough to really be supportive. In the end, each girl feared she was last and least, but there was no deep bias or hatred. Both got my time and attention when they really needed it, and they had very few real rivalries.

The First Breakthrough

It came on a Sunday afternoon when miranda and I were driving back from a weekend in Richmond, a special occasion with dining at interesting restaurants and a tour of Maymont House and its gardens. "It looks like we'll get back around seven," said miranda.

"Yeah," I replied.

"Can you text jaylynn ... and see if she wants to meet us when we get back, and do ice cream?" A short sentence. But Sunday night was miranda's time, and she was volunteering to give it up in order that we could all be together. It was reciprocated shortly. Of course, neither girl wanted to give up all or even most of their time. But shared time allowed being together as a House for long periods of time, which was a huge change of paradigm, giving everyone much more quality of relationship.

What else did we learn from the trials of our first few years?

Private talk. Shared time demands private time. We instinctively feel that it is impolite to have a private conversation in front of someone. In order to be together for long periods of time, each slave needs to feel free to ask for time alone or talk without getting sour looks from the other.

Resources. In plotting a course into uncharted waters, I made a point of consulting every authority and resource I could find: Dr. Robert Rubel's books on communication in M/s relationship, books on contemporary psychology by Berne and Rogers, articles online, and social networking through membership in the local chapter of Masters And slaves Together (MAsT)l, the national support organization for M/s relationships. These resources became invaluable guides in creating ideas to get beyond fail-points and crises.

Workload. We are a working household with external tasks in amateur entertainment. Both girls work to support this effort.

Workload must be balanced with "real life". If I work an 8-hour day and want to come home, relax, and watch Netflix, my slave is not going to be perversely eager to do menial tasks. Tasking a slave with real work needs to be done carefully, and slaves are often eager to overcommit. A ritual task may be better for extending a feeling of control and safety than a long menial chore that only breeds resentment.

The Almighty Dollar. A very sticky subject in M/s is money. Money is not referenced in our contract, but my slaves retain control of their personal finances, and I feel that changing the basis of our finances would call for renegotiation. It would violate our current contract to unilaterally impose such a change. I have a good job, but little in the way of savings. Three years ago, my mother's estate sold for a substantial loss. Theatre projects eat much of my excess income. I am not in a position to play the wealthy sugar daddy. Until my financial stability is absolute, I cannot jeopardize the girls' safety and security by combining their incomes with my own as Stephanie and I combine incomes. While it might produce a better situation, the current responsible choice seems to use their expertise to manage the theatre projects and my personal finances better, in order to improve the overall picture.

Meds And Therapy. A major element of my work as Master has been ensuring that jaylynn and miranda make the medical choices they need to be healthy. Our culture teaches us that a head cold is cause for sympathy, but that an episode of rage, anger, or anxiety is a moral weakness even when it comes from a chemical spike. We are taught that people who need to be medicated are broken or sick. While I am a believer in people taking responsibility for their own shit, that can't happen unless everyone has a level playing field, and sometimes "better living through chemistry" can help. My relationship with Stephanie included a point at which I threatened to leave in order to get her to consider medication for depression, and this gave me better perspective coming to jaylynn and miranda, who shared a bad track record with counseling experiences. Stephanie, like almost everyone who is well and successfully medicated by a competent doctor, had become a fan of meds. But

I'm not a doctor and cannot tell anyone if they should be medicated. I *have* ordered both jaylynn and miranda to go to a psychiatrist, describe their symptoms, and follow the doctor's orders. I also promised that if the doctor seemed ill-informed or accusatory, I would support them in choosing a different health professional.

I have little regard for Masters who restrict access to therapists. I think that's a sign that the Master is insecure, and feels that access to an outside counselor will weaken his or her hold. I have less regard for Masters who allow their hubris at being able to "fix" slaves to get in the way of making the best use of modern medicine. To me, therapy supports the M/s dynamic and vice versa.

Masters have a different role from counselors. On one particularly hard night, miranda asked me why I thought I could get her through this and be successful when professional counselors had failed. I shrugged. "They may have known about psychology, but they didn't know about you. They saw you for an hour every once in a while. I make a study of you. I know you well enough to know when something is wrong. They were experts in medicine, but I am an expert in you."

The Manse

I live in Hagerstown, Maryland, almost sixty miles from Washington D.C., in a large and somewhat decayed Edwardian house. My previous submissive, G, lived nearby and worked on theatrical projects with me, assisting me in setting up for dinners or parties, decorating, and keeping the "public areas" of the house clean. I never asked G to clean or work in the master bedroom, and when we stayed together we used an upstairs guestroom which she had decorated.

Neither jaylynn nor miranda are long-term live-in slaves, though we maintain a 24/7 power dynamic. I spend the night with one or the other at their home at least once a week, depending on need and scheduling. This allows them to have a sexual and social life outside of me, while keeping me close enough to provide constant support and check-ins. During a period when my wife's submissive moved into our house, he lived on the third floor suite and took ownership of that area. After he left, I had stayed there with miranda and jaylynn, but neither had ever felt any real entitlement or ownership. The house belonged to Stephanie and myself, and they felt like guests. If they were going to stay with me and allow themselves to become emotionally invested, that meant feeling a sense of ownership and investment in the house as well as the "household". I wanted them to feel that they had a place under my physical roof as well as in my affections. And this meant bringing them closer to my wife.

XII. The 800-Pound Gorilla In The Room

When I first began to look at how to integrate my slaves with my wife, I instinctively looked for examples. What I found was that there were none. Of Masters my age, all the examples I could find were either monogamous with children or once or more divorced. This was chilling, but brought out a certain pride. In reading about our struggle, it may be difficult to understand why we chose to stay together, but the problems are only half the story. Sharing them is meant to help others find ways to grow, but it is worth understanding that we like each other, get along well., and have a great deal of love. Shared in-jokes, pet names, and years of support did not prevent strains from occurring, but they were incentive to find solutions.

Stephanie's Story—Continued

So far this is a lovely story with a happy ending. Except what the hell happened to my wife? You remember, the one I married nearly twenty years ago? That's how she felt as well.

The late '90s and early 2000s had been rocky for Stephanie. A series of bitter clashes over our poly dynamic around the turn of the century left me feeling exhausted and burned. Both of us moved away from the other into the excitement of new relationships with others. It was a pattern that we'd repeat sequentially, never really addressing our own issues. There were resentments, but if life at home wasn't good, it wasn't bad, and we liked each other.

There was a gulf of distance, and much of it was frustration on my part. I saw Stephanie as having deep pain and trauma, but I had no real idea how to fix it, and settled for trying to be a comforting and stable presence. In doing so, my role became more domestic partner and husband, and less lover or dominant. Stephanie had a string of lovers who did not meet her needs. Some lasted longer, others a very short time.

In the push and pull of our poly dynamic, Stephanie had pushed more implied limits, but was also often the first to pull beyond them. She would become excited and ask if it was OK to do something. I would give my consent while mentally crossing out that limit. In the end, after years in which one of only a few stated "hard limits" was that we would not share our house with other lovers, she experimented with bringing a submissive into our house. He lasted less than a year, but that was more or less a "final limit" and left me feeling free to order my external affairs any way I pleased. By the time I had brought jaylynn and miranda into service, Stephanie's longtime relationship with a lover in Philadelphia was crumbling and she needed my attention and support. In the meantime, I had created a "household outside of the household" with my two slaves ... and I had no clear idea of how my wife was going to fit into that.

I may have been fair, but I had not been loving. I had drawn away from our relationship in the hurt and confusion over our clashes. I had not been emotionally honest with Stephanie, nor had she with me. Both of us sensed that the chemistry of our relationship had changed, and each felt guilty, but also found it easy to fault the other partner.

The Passive-Aggressive Dynamic In Marriage

While "passive-aggressive" sounds bad, let's remember that it is a way of exercising nonviolent aggression. It is the emotional and personal equivalent of Gandhi's "passive resistance". If it is immature, what would be more mature? Hitting each other with sticks? Screaming and yelling? Take two people who don't want to be mean to each other or hurt each other. Put them into a situation where they will, absolutely, have conflicts and disputes. Make sure that they understand they are both equal. Then give them *no structure or guidelines whatsoever* for resolving their disputes. The result is that they take the more "adult" course of passive-aggression rather than (usually) throwing the crockery.

Passive-aggression is cyclic and builds up. Ironically, the more we like our partner, the more dangerous it is; if we value the relationship and our investment in it, we are unwilling to threaten it by fighting over "little things" that jeopardize the relationship "for nothing". But the little things build up.

My situation with Stephanie wasn't a firm basis for an M/s relationship. Even though jaylynn and miranda were both friends with Stephanie, there was a strong emotional concern. What if Stephanie decided that my M/s relationships should end? I'd reached a point where I couldn't in conscience do that. Nor did I want to end my marriage. In the end, *everyone* feared they would be dropped. Stephanie even began to approach me again as a submissive, fearing I'd reached that point in life where men decide to "trade in on a new model", and that my marriage was no longer important. Both jaylynn and miranda feared that even though the situation was stable at the moment, they lived in a glass house where at any moment a chance word or misunderstanding with Stephanie could be a sledgehammer that shattered their world.

To Stephanie, my slaves were young and attractive rivals. And while Stephanie was strikingly prettier than a heavyset simian (and despite *Cabaret*, what girl wouldn't be flattered by *that* comparison), the old adage of the 800-pound gorilla we didn't talk about was apt. She was a powerful unknown that could break everything they valued. I needed to reassure everyone and figure out a point of stability. And that meant talking to my wife.

The Need For Integration

If I was to make good on my long-term commitment to Stephanie, and also to be a good Master to jaylynn and miranda, I needed to make our house a "household", and that meant including Stephanie. That required addressing what my long-term relationship was going to be with my wife. Was she going to be submissive to me? What would that mean in terms of my slaves?

There were a few ground rules—jaylynn and miranda both liked Stephanie and considered her a friend. They wanted it to stay that way. But they had signed on to be *my* slaves, and did not want to be put in a position of taking orders from my wife. I agreed. At the same time, even if she was presenting as my submissive, she was still mistress at the house which she and I owned jointly. This was ripe to create confrontations and awkwardness.

The solution seemed to be to talk ... but there was a problem. Whereas jaylynn and miranda were all about talking about relationships, Stephanie was as cool as most guys I know. Once again, there was no magic bullet, but a series of steps that culminated in limited success. I was able to take Stephanie with the household to the 2009 MsC in Washington, and have very frank, open discussions about the other girls' concerns. While Stephanie is often away, household evenings or trips that include her have been far more pleasant and less tense. In addition, jaylynn and miranda have come to care deeply for Stephanie and value her happiness, and she theirs.

What Went Right With Stephanie

Making it clear that being a slave was not a condition of being part of the Household. Stephanie feared and had come to believe that my attention and sexual interest was contingent on submission.

That she did not need to submit to me the "same as" anyone else. Stephanie has mixed feelings about submission. A part of her does want to submit, but another part of her is very independent. She needed permission to not feel this was wrong.

Validating Stephanie's emotions about her other partners.
Stephanie felt let down and betrayed by some of her other
relationships. As a mentor and Master, I had learned to offer support,
comfort, and validation to my girls first, then to try and address
things that I thought they could have done differently. With
Stephanie, my capacity for support and comfort had been worn
away through the cycle of passive-aggression. I needed to restore my
respect and tolerance to reach a point where I could offer comfort
before criticism.

**Recognizing Stephanie's right to pursue different courses
from the rest of the House without emotionally penalizing her.**
Stephanie, jaylynn, and miranda all work supporting me at
interactive theatre events. It can be thankless and grueling work.
However, Stephanie has grown in responsibility and activity with a
scholarly esoteric-fraternal organization which she jokingly calls her
"solar-phallic sex cult", and recently reaching a point where she
wished to back away from some of the theatre work. The
complication is that with elements of anger involved, I needed to be
able to tell her that she had permission not to continue to work at an
emotionally exhausting and draining task, without making her feel
like I was saying, "Well, fine, you can be replaced." In the end, I
pushed to get the message across that doing something that built up
resentment for me and for the House was not an act of loyalty.

Fighting passive-aggression and taking the lead. In dealing
with my M/s relationships I have learned to fight passive-aggression
by measured aggression, but in an egalitarian relationship that is
harder. What gives me the right to be the one to push, the one to
break the peace, the one to speak bluntly? In the end, I had to
consider that my dedication to the relationship gave me those rights,
and adopt many of the practices that had worked in M/s. Predictably,
there have been times when Stephanie saw this as high-handed or
dictatorial, and felt she was being treated like a submissive or slave.
But in the long run, it has begun to break many of the passive-
aggressive habits that we have become enmeshed in. Even though I
am not her Master, I must take responsibility for leading.

Opening a dialogue so that everyone feels they can ask questions and talk. I talk to Stephanie every day. Even then, there are subjects I dread bringing up. I know they are contentious or likely to bring about sharp remarks. If I feel that way after twenty years, how do miranda and jaylynn feel? The wisdom of a brain-damaged housecat suggests that simply telling them "Oh, she's really very approachable, go talk to her," is not the strategy for success, especially when Stephanie has been known to shoot the messenger who bore bad news. On the other hand, the answer is not for me to always be the one to go to her and play a constant game of Telephone where I try to negotiate between two states that aren't speaking. The answer is to take responsibility for bringing everyone together and making them talk, and be proactive in maintaining communications.

IX. Talking About Someone New

A few months ago, I was contacted by a girl who had once been a strong influence in my life, but dropped out of sight around the time I became involved with jaylynn. I let her know in the strongest terms that I'd be interested in bringing her into a D/s or M/s relationship. The offer led to some serious internal scrutiny on my part. Was I willing to take the time and "own up" to what I was offering? Whether she chose to join us as an occasional trainee, submissive, or slave, was it even possible for me to manage?

I realized that this was an area where I had to speak with profound clarity and care to jaylynn, miranda, and Stephanie. Obviously there was going to be fear. Would a new girl take time away from them? Would a new girl in my world mean a bright shiny that led me, in typical male fashion, to discard them? Would I treat a third girl as a third-class citizen, "last and least", causing the new girl to bitterly resent jaylynn and miranda? I rapidly came to a set of conclusions regarding what must be done if the introduction was to succeed:

Waiting and dropping a bomb would be the opposite of smart. It would ensure the very problems and resentments and problems I wanted to avoid.

While I did not want to compromise the privacy of the new girl, I needed to be frank about her and what I thought she would need. I could not say, "The person won't take any of my time and attention. You won't notice a thing." I had to be truthful and say that it would be a major time commitment, curtailing other activities to ensure I had enough time and energy for everyone who mattered to me.

I had to be emotionally honest about my feelings, and let each of the other girls know them. We are taught that it is wrong to tell one person you care strongly for another; that we should be hurt to hear it and that it hurts to say it. I had to be honest in expressing that I wanted this girl to be a part of my life.

Looking like an idiot was no excuse. While I feared looking like an idiot if she ultimately decided against training with me, I could not let my pride keep me from doing what was right. I could not drop a bomb on jaylynn and miranda, and I could not make the new girl miserable by dropping her into a situation where she was unwanted.

X. Challenges Going Forward

I will never wake up and say "I am a successful Master." I can only wake up and say "I was a successful Master yesterday," and " I will work to be a successful Master today." I don't say those things, of course; I usually say something like "fuuughh ... morning ... ten more minutes..." But you get the idea.

I've reached a point, though, where I do not wake up feeling like a refugee from a David Byrne song saying "This is not my beautiful life ... my God, how did I get here?" I feel a reasonable confidence that I am not at the whim of fate, but that I make my own choices and that I can live with the consequences.

Some Summary Lessons

Be willing to call your slaves on their shit. By this I mean, if they are doing something which is passive-aggressive, or unfair, be willing to make it an issue. Don't be daunted. When you back down from confrontation with your slave, you're not doing anyone any favors. You are failing to do what they are trusting you to do: to lead and take charge.

Be willing to call yourself on your shit. By this I mean, if you plan to take an action, search yourself for whether you are planning it because you are angry, jealous, irritable, or have an unresolved issue. If you do, then discipline *yourself*. If you have already erred, that means apologize, sincerely and honestly. If you have not, then bite down and *do not err*. You cannot expect your slaves to show discipline if you cannot discipline yourself.

Be polite. There are times to be a brutal bastard, or presumably a brutal bitch, and I realize that for some sceneplay extends into the 24/7. But to the extent that negotiated abuse is not part of the dynamic, act like a lady or gentleman. Most of my ideas on how to handle slaves came from how people with servants actually handle them; firmly and courteously.

Don't be a horse's arse. By this I mean don't be fuckwitted. Perhaps I can't define exactly what this means. Let's say that it means that no matter what your rules about confronting slaves on their shit, or them opening the door, the day that your slave is on her period, had a huge fight at work, and is dreading seeing her mother may be a time to say, "You need to relax and be off duty tonight. Sit down and let me get you a drink." For some slaves, this might be the time for strong discipline to fight off uncertainty and fear. But use common sense and don't assume that the M/s paradigm frees you from the need to deeply understand your fellow human beings.

Embrace failure. You *will* fail. You *will* make mistakes. The certain path to loss of respect is to sweep them under the carpet because "Master may not be right, but Master is never wrong." When you realize you have failed, accept it, apologize, explain, and move on. Nobody respects a liar, and your slaves cannot respect you if they watch you engage in self-deception. If you cannot admit your own mistakes, how can your slaves feel respect for you calling them on theirs? But do not let your own failure undermine the M/s dynamic. The fact that you have failed once does not excuse your slave from working to succeed.

Are They Real Slaves?

At some point someone will read this essay and conclude that miranda and jaylynn are not "real" slaves because of something in our M/s dynamic which they feel defines "true" slavery—probably that they are not docile doormats to my insecure manliness, kicked down daily to ensure that my ego is sufficiently large. Our relationship is what it is, and that is my strongest recommendation. Do not set out to "have an M/s relationship". Set out to have good healthy relationships in the pattern that works for you. Mine is to exert indisputable control over and receive sexual gratification from my slaves, while acting as a mentor and partner. But that doesn't make what we do right for you, and that is my final advice from our lessons learned: set out to find what is right and then build your own terms around it. Never let the words dictate the realities.

Thoughts On A Polyamorous Household

Sir Stephen

Initial Thoughts and Experiences

Polyamory. It was a term that I heard almost from the first day 13 years ago, when I gathered up my courage, left my computer, and walked into a TES (The Eulenspiegel Society) meeting in NYC. At that time, lacking a clear definition of what polyamorous relationships entailed, I imagined that this was really just code for those who wanted to incorporate swinging into their lifestyle activities. As I attended more meetings and joined other groups, I gained an awareness of the larger context of meaning behind the term polyamory. People in polyamorous relationships seemed to be committed to trying to form enduring relationships with multiple partners and not just get together on the weekend for sexual interludes (not that I am opposed to such, but it just seemed that there was an effort to achieve something more persistent in poly relationships). Such relationships did not necessarily include power exchange, but it seemed that many did. Of course, this could have been a reflection of the environment in which I was first exposed to the notion ... TES, MAsT (Masters And slaves Together) and similar organizations focused largely upon power exchange as exercised in BDSM pursuits or in pursuit of a Master/slave relationship.

At these meetings, individuals engaged in poly relationships shared their experiences ... their hopes, their failures, their successes. I observed that while many espoused the potential benefits of such relationships, many also struggled to find happiness within them. But I also observed that the powerful inducement of the potential within poly relationships drove many to engage in the struggle anyway. I observed people applying themselves with rigorous honor and integrity to the effort to succeed in the endeavor. As it is with all forms or relationships, some succeeded and some failed.

As a fledgling Master, how did the notion of polyamory impact my efforts to create a successful, enduring, productive, harmonious

Master/slave Household? Initially, I didn't really consider any of the issues associated with long-term goals or success. I was a new Master; I had left a vanilla marriage to take a submissive woman into my service, the submissive woman had left her vanilla marriage to come and serve me ... we weren't doing a lot of thinking; we were doing a lot of knee-jerk responses to hormonal impulses. Rather predictably, our focus was on escaping the restraints of our vanilla lives and embracing the hedonistic potential of the BDSM lifestyle. Polyamory seemed to be just the ticket for the ride we wanted. We both scanned our sexual radar screens for likely candidates and before long we found one. It was someone we both knew and had spent time with. It was someone we both found attractive. It was someone who had recently been uncollared. It was someone who we knew to have had experience as part of a poly household. She seemed to have the perfect profile for our needs.

A Moment of Clarity

Before we approached her, we sat down and discussed how best to integrate her into our relationship. As we talked we realized that our relationship was so new, so unformed, that we really could not offer this particular person any stability or any realistic guarantee of a relationship with us that would endure. We had little, if anything to offer, other than our self-centered hedonistic desires. As I said, we knew this woman, and we liked her, and we empathized with the emotionally distressing circumstance in which she now found herself. We had to own the fact that we would not likely be able to offer her any of the emotional stability and support that she needed at this moment in her life. This discussion, and this realization, hit us like a face full of cold water. We realized that for us, we would not be comfortable simply fulfilling our sexual fantasies, but that we wanted to form true, fully rounded relationships with additional compatible partners.

We were excited, perhaps over-stimulated, by our sudden immersion in the lifestyle, and in the release from the constraints of our vanilla lives. For a brief moment we stood in the eye of our emotional and hormonal storms and in that quiet moment we came to an understanding of what was right for us. We realized that bringing others into our relationship meant that we were accountable for their well-being. We realized that we would not be really be comfortable with anything less. There had to be enough stability, structure, strength, experience and knowledge within our relationship to provide a healthy and nurturing environment for those who joined us.

The Work Begins

As the Master the burden of articulating a philosophy, and a set of supporting policies and procedures, fell to me. It also fell to me to make it clear to those in service to me, and, in all honesty, to keep reminding myself, that we would not just talk the talk, but walk it as well. Although I had now realized that bringing additional people into my Household could not be an immediate goal, the structure that I was beginning to evolve incorporated the process for such to occur. But questions arose around this determination. How would I address the issue of gender, gender identification, and sexual orientation in applicants to my Household? As a heterosexual male Master, should I be willing to consider applicants who identified as male—straight or gay? Should I be willing to consider applicants who identified as female even if their sexual orientation was lesbian? In short ... what would I do about the BDSM and/or sexual needs of anyone other than a straight or bisexual genetic female? Was I obligated, as a Master, to even consider such needs, or should I steadfastly consider only my needs, sexual or otherwise?

Poly: from the dictionary—many, several, much, containing an indefinite number more than one.

OK ... my household was to be poly ... but, was it to be polyamorous?

Amorous: from the dictionary—strongly moved by love and especially sexual love.

I am a heterosexual male Dominant. I knew that I was comfortable with bringing additional female slaves into my

Household. My first slave, slave catherine, is bisexual, making the inclusion of other slaves to whom I was sexually attracted less threatening to her. But I was, from early on, likewise committed to having a Household that was harmonious and safe. To fulfill the goal of harmony I determined that I would not bring another female slave into the Household for sexual or play purposes unless slave catherine was sufficiently comfortable with that individual. I had seen far too many instances of Masters forcing a new slave into an existing Household despite resistance for the slave(s) already in service. Invariably, the results were bad feelings and a serious disruption of the relationship. Sometimes ... rarely ... these rough waters could be navigated and everyone would come out happy in the end. But more often than not the outcomes were disastrous.

I decided to make the process of application and admission to my Household an extended process, as I felt that this would assist in preserving the goal of a harmonious Household. Applicants who, by word or deed, produced an on-going disruption to the smooth functioning of my Household would not be allowed to proceed to the next stage of acceptance into my Household. Further, I decided that I would consider sexual and/or play activities only after the potential slave had progressed past the stage of applicant.

By the time I finalized these policies and procedures, I had the opportunity to observe in others and experience first-hand that the introduction of someone new into an existing Household was *always* disruptive. Sometimes the disruption was minimal and could be easily managed. Sometimes the disruption was much more serious and required much more time and attention to resolve ... if possible. I felt that the policies and procedures I had enacted would provide the best chance of preserving harmony within my Household while expanding it.

These same policies and procedures addressed my responsibility as Master for the safety and well-being of those in service to me (as well as for me). The process of application and admission gave me time to learn the details of the sexual and medical histories of applicants and provided time for all parties to obtain a set of current medical tests results to establish the risk, if any, of the transmission of any STDs or other conditions. Rather predictably, as a result of these rather stringent barriers, I had few applicants at all, let alone applicants for sex and play.

Poly Experiences

Few, but not none. Over the years I have had a number of individuals in service to me for varying purposes and for varying lengths of time, including straight, bisexual, straight, gay, and transgendered individuals. As of this writing I have, in addition to slave catherine, two other individuals in part-time service to me and one individual who is considering applying to my Household.

Of all the individuals who have served me I have had an interest in sex and play with only a few of them, and of that few only one has both shared that interest and met the criteria for a play/sex partner as detailed above. That individual, still a dear friend, only served briefly in my Household as ours was a long-distance relationship and her needs required a Master within her immediate geography.

So, in reviewing my history I am forced to ask ... was I building a Household that is, as I have referred to it over the years, an extended Household, or was it polyamorous ... or both? Clearly it is an extended Household ... extended in that the only slave currently in full-time service to me is slave catherine, but other slaves serve part-time either by visiting my home or by providing service at a distance, generally involving assistance with the planning and execution of lifestyle events with which I am involved or by assistance with the maintenance of various lifestyle lists and websites that I own.

But is it polyamorous? Well, I think it clearly fulfills the poly part ... my Household exceeds the simple structure of a single, primary, binary pairing. Is it amorous? In order for me to lay claim to being poly-*amorous* I need to provide a definition of amorous that is non-sexual in nature. I think it is clear that there are many forms of love. As I said, I have only had a sexual relationship with one slave other than slave catherine, and yet I have cared about all those who ever provided me service. In every instance I tried to express my affection for those in service to me. I set aside time for each of them in an attempt to come to know them better and to provide them with such emotional comfort, guidance and advice as I could. I held the desire to see them experience personal growth as a result of their time with me. To me, this is caring, an expression of love. I cared for each slave differently. I cannot say that I loved them equally or that my expressions of caring were given with equal affection. I cared for them each to the best of my ability. (And, of course, I remain open to the possibility of finding those who wish to provide me with sexual and/or BDSM service and who fulfill my Household criteria.)

I think that by my history of care and affection for multiple members within my Household, my willingness to accept their signs of affection in return, and my willingness to accept sexual service offered within the parameters of my criteria I can lay claim to the designation of polyamorous for my Household. So with the definitional elements of this essay out of the way I can speak a bit about what mechanisms I have put in place to try and ensure the best possible outcomes from the inclusion of additional individuals in service to me.

Trying to Make it Work: The Mechanisms

Roles and Responsibilities

I felt that one of the impediments to the successful integration of multiple individuals in service was that many Households seemed to treat all the servants as a common pool with no uniquely defined roles and responsibilities for those in service. I felt that I stood the best chance of success if I only invited additional potential slaves into the Household based on their ability to provide skills and abilities not already available from those currently in service. My home is not very large, so initially I did not require two slaves both assigned to cleaning. Likewise, I needed only one cook, one laundress, etc. I determined that each new slave was to be assigned unique responsibilities that they could call their own. This provides each slave with a sense of security (their jobs are their own); the knowledge that they are doing meaningful work; and it reduces the friction that can occur between slaves who are competing to provide identical forms of service to the Master. This meant that I had to be willing to turn down applicants, even otherwise attractive applicants, who could not provide service currently lacking in my Household— and I have done so. My commitment to the well-being of those in service to me also means that if someone applies with a skill set that duplicates the skills of a slave currently in my Household that I do not replace the current slave to enjoy the excitement of someone new. Such behavior is, in my opinion, unethical and undermines all my efforts to create stability and harmony. How can slaves attain the level of trust in a Master that is essential for their ability to fully dedicate themselves to his service if they are plagued by the fear of replacement, not for failure in their service, but for the fun the Master might derive from a new face?

Again, these kinds of concerns evolve out of my personal philosophy. I believe that this philosophy represents the truest calling of a Master. I am sure that others may feel differently. My philosophy does not apply to those Masters who regard slaves as disposable objects taken on for their pleasure and released as it pleases them. Such philosophies and such Masters exist, and there are slaves who willingly take up the call to serve in such Households. It suits them … it does not suit me.

I came to the conclusion early on that I did not enter into this lifestyle to abandon my personal code of ethics. To do so would be very uncomfortable for me. I had been uncomfortable for years in my vanilla life because I compromised who I truly was inside. I was determined to be as true to myself as possible in my newly adopted life. So I was stuck with creating a Household that would be built upon a code of ethics that would limit my range of options. But I also knew that if I adhered to that code, when I looked back over my history in the lifestyle that I would be comfortable and perhaps even proud of myself. This was important to me.

The initial structure that I laid out worked well for a Household with a paired relationship in which I was the sole source of income, and slave catherine was a stay-at-home slave. We joined groups and began to attend events. We educated ourselves about the lifestyle and I began to evolve a much clearer image of what I wanted to be as a Master and how I wanted my Household to be structured.

Funny thing about life … it changes on you. I made service to my community a goal of my Household. I gradually took on numerous lifestyle commitments, and enlisted slave catherine's assistance with them. As a result, she began to require periodic assistance with her household chores (cooking, cleaning, laundry, etc.). As another result, I have frequently made use of my part-time slaves to support her in those areas. In these instances they do not assume the full role of cook or laundress, but rather function as assistants to slave catherine. So I found that duplication of service could be of value when properly applied. On the other hand, whatever duplication may exist, I still try to provide some unique areas of responsibility for each servant.

Experience began to convince me that it is important to provide a context in which the service provided is seen to be as meaningful as possible. Yes, cleaning the house is important in and of itself. But a part-time slave supporting slave catherine in these areas might derive greater satisfaction if they are given a full understanding of the positive impact of what appears to be a rather mundane task that is not directly associated with me.

Examine what happens when a slave assists slave catherine by cleaning my home. First, they relieve slave catherine of the stress she is experiencing by virtue of the priority that I have assigned to community work which has resulted in less time for housekeeping. This contributes to the overall emotional well-being of my Household. Second, in assisting slave catherine they provide a service directly to me in that they free up more of slave catherine's time so that she may fulfill her primary role of companion to me. Third, they provide a service to the community by allowing slave catherine to devote her time and attention to the needs created by our lifestyle commitments. Finally, the trickle-down effect of the service provided by both slaves is that it frees up some of my time and I will have more time available to spend in personal interactions with each of them.

This sharing of responsibilities has become even more important as slave catherine has had to return to work this past year. It is explained to each slave how important the completion of these simple tasks is to the overall harmonious and productive functioning of the Household. Further, it is explained that the different slaves, unique in their own skills, abilities, and emotional needs, should not compare themselves to one another. While I do my best to treat all the slaves with equal care and consideration, I interact with each of them differently and express my concern for them in different ways. For example, slave catherine is both my slave and my wife, and has a continuous 13-year history of service to me. A slave new to my Household looking at my interaction with slave catherine and expecting that my interaction with them will be the same is setting themselves up for disappointment. I explain this to each new slave in an effort to manage expectations. I have observed that unrealistic expectations are a primary source of disappointments and it is best to try and bring expectations into alignment with the realities of the Household as quickly as possible.

Conflict Resolution

Despite all these efforts, disagreements and bad feelings will arise. It is important to establish effective methods for communication and dispute resolution. In my Household I encourage discussion and devote considerable time to it with servants individually and together as a Household. The following section of my Household Manual devoted to Code of Conduct speaks to this issue:

> *Members of the Household should not speak ill of one another either within or outside of the Household. In the event that issues arise that lead to the disruption of*

personal or Household harmony, the affected member(s)
should bring this to the attention of the Master and/or the
other Household members in as positive a manner as
possible.

It is understood that some issues may arise that
require guidance or support from outside the Household
in order to be resolved. All members of the Household
should feel free to seek out counsel and support as needed,
but should not view this as an excuse to indiscriminately
discuss Household concerns.

I explain to those in service that if there is a dispute between two or more of the servants that their first effort should be to attempt to resolve it directly, without involving me. I encourage this for several reasons, the first being that my time is valuable and coming to me before making an earnest attempt to resolve the issue indicates an abdication of responsibility and a disregard for the value of my time. If a sincere effort has been made and the issue cannot be resolved, then by all means it should be brought to me. I try to inculcate those in service to me with the knowledge that issues should not be left to fester and grow larger and more toxic, and that there will be no negative repercussions from bringing issues to my attention in an appropriate manner. Further, I expect to be informed of issues that have arisen and been resolved without my intervention. I do this so that I remain aware of such issues should they resurface again. In addition, by being made aware I can offer praise and positive reinforcement for having successfully resolved the issue. On the other hand, if the issue directly involves me then I have instructed the servant(s) to bring it directly to me in a timely fashion.

Termination

As noted above, things change. Some slaves have joined my Household for limited periods of time for various reasons and have left when their agreed-upon term of service ended. Others have left for reasons of their own, and still others have been dismissed.

Termination is a predictable part of M/s relationships and should be considered. Ending such relationships is generally an emotional process for everyone involved. Of course, it is to be hoped that such terminations are for mutually agreed-upon reasons that are positive in nature and are seen as contributing to the growth of the slave as their journey progresses. Again, in my Household Manual I provide anyone interested in joining my Household the following information:

> *Circumstances may arise which require a servant to request an unscheduled release from service. In such circumstances the servant will make a formal verbal request to be released. At the discretion of the Master, the servant may be requested to supply a written request. At the discretion of the Master, the request may be approved or denied. At the discretion of the Master, a formal process of gradual dissolution of the bonds of service may be initiated. Such a process may include written materials, discussions, and possibly outside counseling to insure a satisfactory, honorable conclusion to the term of service, and a smooth transition for both Master and servant.*
>
> *If the Master deems that there is a need to terminate a servant, he will so inform the servant. The Master will supply the servant with a complete understanding of the reasons behind his decision, as needed. The servant may request a formal conclusion to the term of service, including a transitional phase, as outlined above. The Master's decision in regard to that request will be final.*
>
> *Terminated servants may request a written reference to be shown to potential future Masters. Such a reference will be supplied at the Master's discretion.*

Unfortunately, circumstances may arise which require the Master to terminate a slave for gross violations of the Household

Code of Conduct (should such a code exist within the Household). In my own Code I indicate the following:

> *All members of the Household will adhere to rigorous standards of honesty and honor. All forms of dishonesty including lying, withholding of information, misdirection, manipulation, etc. will be justification for punishment and may be cause for dismissal.*
>
> *Theft will not be tolerated and will be cause for dismissal.*
>
> *Violation of the rules governing fluid bonding as detailed below will be cause for dismissal.*

The Final Arrangements

Life is about change, and one of the changes that comes to us all is illness and eventually death. Masters and slaves, in my opinion, take on the responsibility for seeing to the needs of one another within a specifically defined set of policies and procedures. It is the final proof of the quality of both Masters and slaves that they have made arrangements to ensure the well-being of the Household members even in direst circumstances.

Such arrangements consist of having all necessary medical and legal paperwork done (Last Will and Testament, Living Will, Power of Attorney, Medical Proxy, etc.). The location of such documents should be known to those who are in the Household.

The Master may consider that if he falls ill, an arrangement with another Master to assist his slave(s) during such a time would relieve some of the stress felt by both the Master and the slave(s). Should the Master be permanently disabled by an illness, it is hoped that the slave(s) would continue to serve the Master, but having a previously designated Master pro-tem (as it were) would make sense. A similar arrangement following the Master's demise would be an act of great compassion.

Slaves should likewise have all appropriate medical and legal documents completed. In the event of a slave falling ill, the Master should direct all members of the Household to do all that is possible to comfort the slave and assist in the slave's recovery. Should the slave suffer irreversible damage from illness or accident, I believe that the Master should retain the slave in service without regard for their diminished capacity. In such circumstances the slave should be treated by the entire Household with honor and respect. In the event of the death of a slave ... well, what can be said? I would mourn the loss of anyone who is currently in service to me, or who has ever been in service to me, but the depth of despair I feel at even the thought of the loss of slave catherine is immeasurable and threatens to overwhelm me entirely.

I believe that it is the Master's responsibility to ensure that all the necessary mechanisms are in place. One advantage of a poly household is that the members should have learned to support one another in the good times and it is to be hoped that they will continue to fulfill their roles even in the direst of circumstances.

Pinning Smoke To The Wall

Andrea Zanin

I was going to try and write an essay about the details. About the technical aspects of how I've learned to navigate non-monogamous D/s relationships. About the communication strategies, the scheduling, the judicious use of power, about jurisdiction and rules and vocabulary and alternating weekends. But every time I started getting into the particulars, it started to feel pointless, as though it were just so much droning on about this and that practical matter, rather than engaging with the real questions. It felt like trying to teach good spanking technique without addressing the relationship that makes spanking sexy in the first place. Like lecturing about latex gloves and lube and dental dams without talking about passion.

So instead I'm going to talk about framework, and approach, and mindset, and values. I'm going to try, as hard as I can, to do this well. Sometimes it feels like finding the words to talk about power and love is like trying to pin smoke to the wall or take a photograph of a dream—not because it's all that complicated, but because it's so intensely personal that I'm never sure that my vocabulary will be meaningful to anyone other than me and mine. Because in a world of concrete practice, with leather dress codes and safewords and datebooks and precise figure-8 flogging, it often feels like we are still lacking words to talk about the essence of what it is that we do.

A Bit Of Background

Let me start by telling you where I'm coming from. Actually, I'll back up even further than that just to mention that I usually don't write essays with this much "I" and "me" in them, but there's something about the topic at hand—the intersections of D/s and non-monogamy—that makes it really difficult to do anything but speak from a deeply personal perspective, and hope that pieces of it might resonate with others.

Okay. For starters, I'm a queer woman of many genders. That means a number of things when it comes to my politics, my way of thinking, and my experience of the world. Practically speaking, it also means that most of my friends and acquaintances are some sort of queer, and a fairly large proportion of them identify as women or as somewhere along the trans spectrum, and I like it that way.

I've been non-monogamous for about ten years now, after spending the prior decade in monogamous relationships. I've been kinky for my whole life, and came out into the leather and kink community around the same time I started being actively poly.

When it comes to non-monogamy, I've experienced a variety of configurations including fairly classic pair-based open relationships, multiple non-domestic partners, fun sexual escapades as a non-partnered person, and most recently, two consecutive full equilateral triads. At the time of this writing I am partnered with two people in a triad, one of whom is my collared boy of three years, the other of whom is submissive to me within an ongoing exploration of power that hasn't yet coalesced into a specific form. The two of them have been friends for several years, and are now partners and lovers to each other as well as to me.

When it comes to kink, from a physical point of view, I'm a sensation junkie and I love to bottom, just as much as I am a multi-skilled top who loves doing terrible things to people. But that's all hedonism. I like to play in much the same way as I like to both fuck and get fucked, cook and eat, dance lead or follow, make art or appreciate others' artwork, give gifts or receive gifts. As in, bring it on, any which way! But when it comes to power dynamics, I'm a dominant through and through. My turn-on—physical, sexual, relational, spiritual—lies exclusively in dominance. That said, I don't have a strong need to be in charge of everyone or everything all the time (that would just be obnoxious), and am perfectly capable of following someone else's lead when appropriate. I'm a firm believer in knowing your jurisdiction and acting within it.

I've spent the better part of the past decade engaged in one form or another of ongoing, explicitly acknowledged power relationship—from "we don't know what the hell this is but let's try to figure it out" all the way to solid, long-term ownership-based relationships involving extensive degrees of authority, protocol and structure. I haven't done dozens of these, but the ones I've done have lasted—I go for quality, not quantity. They have run the gamut from totally platonic to intensely erotic, and from domestic to long-distance. Some have ended; most have simply morphed from their original form into something else. Among other things I am blessed to have my two former long-term submissives as members of an amazing and supportive leather family, and others as friends and members of my extended leather community.

The leather community has provided me with language and concepts to help me make better sense of the things that have consistently happened in my relationships since before I really knew what to call them. People make themselves vulnerable to me, place enormous trust in me, tend to follow my direction, and try hard to please me. I haven't always known how to manage that well, but I've put many years of thought and intense personal work into learning how to take up that dominance in ways that are responsible, ethical, spiritually aware, beneficial to the people who choose to grant me that power in their lives, and that serve a greater purpose than simply satisfying my own personal preferences about how things get done.

Listen Up

My approach to both non-monogamy and D/s is rooted in my spirituality. That's true for pretty much everything I do, but it comes out in specific ways within my approach to relationships. I believe that my chief job in this world is to listen—not to other people per se, although that often comes as part of the package. No, what I'm talking about is a deep sort of listening to the universe, to the flow of what's supposed to be happening around me, to what's needful and right; and from there, my job is to act in accordance with what I'm hearing, whether I like it or not. I usually experience the "answer" as to what needs to be done in the form of strong gut feelings, but sometimes it's more explicit, or it becomes clear thanks to the way events transpire. I live in constant dialogue with the universe—power, flow, God, whatever you want to call it. Unlike many spiritually inclined leatherfolk, I don't ascribe to a specific spiritual or religious tradition, although I've found insight in the texts of many religions. But for me they all end up just feeling like a middleman between me and the source of it all. So I just engage in an ongoing one-on-one conversation with the flow of things. Sounds diffuse, but it works for me.

My approach to non-monogamy is a principle-based one. That is to say, I'm not non-monogamous because I met two different people and fell in love with them, or because I wanted to spice up a previously monogamous relationship (situational non-monogamy). I'm not non-monogamous because it's the progressive thing to do (political non-monogamy); and I'm not non-monogamous because it's the only workable solution to my desire to get laid a lot (practical non-monogamy)—although I do desire to get laid a lot. No, I'm non-monogamous as a way of life, regardless of the specific contours of the relationships I am in at a given moment. My non-monogamy works in keeping with a personal ethic and philosophy that has a lot to do with generosity, openness, transparency, and a firm belief in embracing the reality that I am not personally in control of love—my own or anyone else's—but I am very much in control over what actions I take. You might almost go so far as to call it an orientation; I am non-monogamous whether I'm single or partnered, alone or in a pile of naked bodies. It's not actually about my relationships to other people per se. It's about my values and how I move through the world.

My concept of non-monogamy is based on the firm conviction that we can't control love, and so we're much better off learning how to navigate our lack of control than investing in futile measures to clamp down. In other words: there is no such thing as forever, because you can't possibly know today how you will feel in twenty years. There is no such thing as "the one" because we are all evolving and changing at every moment, and we all have infinite potential to meet others with whom we could share a few steps or many leagues on our journey. There *are such things* as love, and as now, and as trust.

I believe that when the universe sends us someone who we click with, it's very arrogant to think that we are within our rights to say "no thanks." The proper thing to do, spiritually speaking, is to accept the gifts placed in front of us, to honour connection when it arises, and to act in ways that hold the feelings and desires of everyone involved to be equally valid. I don't believe in "primaries" and "secondaries" because I can't conceive of treating someone I care about as though their feelings were somehow less important than another's. I do believe in letting each relationship take the importance it's meant to.

As such, I practice a form of non-monogamy that's based on deep trust and strong, rich, constant communication, but not on strict rules. The rule is simple: listen, and always follow what the universe brings.

When I enter a D/s relationship with someone, that means they're essentially choosing to align themselves with the universe through me. That may sound grandiose and pretentious, but in fact it's a very humbling place to be. It means that I hold no illusions about being the one who's truly in charge; I'm a follower as much as anyone else, I'm just holding a different position in the authority structure within a given relationship. Essentially, I submit to the universe, and I dominate others on her behalf. If ever I should begin to think I was the true source of that power, that somehow I knew better than the universe what needed to happen, I have not a shred of doubt I'd start to make stupid mistakes, and that any power or credibility I hold in the eyes of the people who submit to me would crumble very quickly.

This doesn't mean I refuse personal responsibility for what I do ("...the universe made me do it!"). Rather, it means I act on a long history of built trust in my conversations with the universe, and I act on that trust as a fully flawed individual. I'm not perfect; I still make very human mistakes and have my own personal quirks and foibles. I still misread cues and misunderstand messages. Still, consistently, if I do what my gut feeling tells me to do, things turn out right.

Consistently, if I try to force a course of action that goes against that gut feeling, things go badly.

This kind of dominance isn't necessarily kinky, although it likes to hang out there often enough. It's not bounded by the limits of a scene, it doesn't show up only when I'm wearing a certain outfit (though I like my leather pants as much as the next perv). It's more like a way of being, and the contexts of specific relationships allow me the freedom to express that being to more or less explicit degrees. Sex and S/M play are convenient ways to channel that being or express the resulting dynamics, as the body is a useful tool—in many ways the most powerful and easily accessible one—for getting into the spirit and soul. But sex and play are by no means the only ways to go there.

These days, I'm finally accepting that even though I'm not crazy about the terms "master" and "slave" for various political and definitional reasons, what I do is M/s. Dominance and submission, for me, are not about role-play or about an escape from my everyday life; this is how I live. I don't move in and out of "dominant headspace"; I am what I am all the time. I have what I like to call a fetish for constant improvement—both my own and that of the people who choose to place themselves under my authority. What I do is an art that I'm constantly trying to perfect, a spiritual calling that I have no choice but to follow, a sexual draw that I couldn't turn off if I tried, a way of loving that feels more true and real to me than any other I've ever known.

Ownership

Despite what you might read about the Old Guard or the New Guard or the four archetypes or the ten basic protocols or any other supposedly "right" way to do things, trust me on this one: everyone who does D/s or M/s does it differently. With that in mind, all I can tell you is what I've figured out works for me and mine.

I generally function on the basis of an ownership model—essentially, I gravitate toward relationships with submissives in which I take ownership of them. They conceive of themselves as my property, and they are very precious property indeed; I hold them to high standards of self-care, emotional and physical health, self-presentation, good behaviour and ethical choices, and I designate them as responsible for meeting my standards in those areas. I hold broad authority in their lives and provide them with challenge and guidance, and they are trusted with great responsibility in my life and provide me with care and often with service. We essentially provide each other with intense forms of care that may appear quite polarized and unidirectional to the outside viewer but that are actually in a fine and ever-evolving balance, a delicate dance in which we take great mutual joy. This dynamic is framed by a clear set of principles, guided by certain rules and often, though not always, expressed through a range of behavioural protocols.

For me, personally, what draws me to D/s is the opportunity to crack someone open, get deeply inside them, gain their trust. The more trust they have in me, the greater my influence in their world, and the more potential they have to grow under my hand; I want to see them in all their depth, including the ugly parts. I want people in D/s relationships with me to become more authentic, more grounded, healthier, happier, more beautiful, kinder, softer, to have less struggle in their souls and more joy in their hearts. That requires enormous dedication and work on all parts, and you know what? It's fucking hard. Paradoxically, choosing happiness and health can be an enormously painful process—both for the person who's choosing it and for the person who's supporting them. I've gone through it myself (and continue to), and I know just how much it can cost, but because of that I also know just how much it's worth.

In turn, I want to be seen and loved for all that I am rather than just the palatable bits. I don't want to be feared; I want to be respected. I don't want to be depended on; I want to be trusted.

This might all sound very high-minded, but the practical side is hardly something to sniff at. Power dynamics turn me on. I figure it's the universe's way of convincing me to do this—make it dead sexy and how could I say no? Nothing gives me a bigger hard-on than seeing someone kneel for me or push past a boundary in order to please me, and nothing melts my heart more than that look of openness and willingness to please on a submissive's face. The grace and beauty of well-executed protocol gives me the shivers, and I still feel a catch in my throat when I see my collar snugly fitted around my boy's neck. It never fails to get me wet when I take up my entitlement to torture someone, to know that it's my privilege to give them pleasure and my right to inflict pain. I grin every time someone presents themselves wearing an outfit they know will please me, or possibly selected by me—I'm an unabashed aesthete and love to showcase the beauty of the people who submit to me. And let me acknowledge that it's awfully nice to have people dedicate time and energy to making my life easier—cooking mouthwatering meals for me, polishing my boots, cleaning the bathroom, running errands and so forth. The responsibility, discipline and attunement of providing quality service and of receiving that service well provides a constant reinforcement of the chosen framework of a D/s relationship, but let's face it, the practical value of it is also huge.

Strictness Within Fluidity

So how does a fluid concept of non-monogamy line up with the idea of ownership? It might seem incompatible, but it actually works pretty well.

First, I want my submissives to follow what the universe brings, up to and including connections with others that may eventually lead them away from me. Mind you, that has yet to ever happen. In my experience people don't sign up to be someone's property if they want to be able to flit away as soon as someone shiny comes along. But is it on the table? Absolutely. My ownership is as good as another person's desire to be owned. If that desire disappears, I have zero interest in holding them to a form of relationship that no longer fits. I don't believe in contracts for the same reason I don't believe in marriage: I'm not interested in being in a relationship with someone just because we signed a paper that represented what we wanted at some point in the past. To me, the worst reason to do something is because you made a promise you now wish you hadn't. That violates all the principles of authenticity and sincerity I believe in, not to mention all but the most technical definition of consent.

Second, I expect them to follow certain specific safer sex practices that we discuss in detail based on our specific concerns and health situations. If a situation with a new person becomes ongoing rather than occasional, we include them in a new discussion of those same concerns, and take their situation into account too.

Third, I require constant communication—preferably before they get into a sexual or emotional situation with a new person, but as soon as possible afterward if not, and consistently within any ongoing relationship they have. And I provide that same transparency in return. It's not because I'm a big bad dominant that somehow I feel entitled to withhold my own information. When it comes to communication, double standards aren't a sign of dominance, they're a sign of hypocrisy.

Fourth, to maintain the touch of my ownership and ensure that the submissive feels appropriately held, I place certain specific restrictions on sexual behaviour. Of course, my ownership and its ramifications apply to my property, but not to the other person who might come along, so outside safer sex precautions, I don't try to place restrictions on the new person's actions; rather, I place them on the actions of my property. That's my jurisdiction.

Last but not least, my property can be tied up and beaten and fucked by other people to their heart's content, but my property wears nobody's collar but mine. I suppose that technically this limits the potential new partner's ability to do what they please— what if their kink involves collars? Or naked necks for that matter?—but anyone who can't wrap their head around this restriction is probably not a great choice as a sexual partner for my property anyway.

Two Kinds Of Rules

In my world, rules and protocols fall into two categories. The first category is those that are in place because of my specific personal preferences. So, for example, in my home and in the homes of the people who serve me, I like the toilet paper placed on its holder in such a way that the paper rolls from the top rather than from underneath. It's easier to grab that way. This has nothing to do with the well-being of my submissive; it has to do with the ways in which, within my own domain of influence, I like to set things up for my own greatest enjoyment and comfort. For the most part they're pretty trivial things, but if someone wants to enter my service and follow my lead, then these preferences provide a consistent framework within which they can experience the touch of my authority. For someone who strives to serve and to please, having a clear sense of what's useful and what's pleasing is extremely valuable. For someone who craves to be held to high standards of performance, having those standards laid out in no uncertain terms and down to the last detail is a welcome relief.

Now, most D/s dynamics of which I have been a part have involved a fairly high degree of service. But if service is not part of a D/s dynamic, I wouldn't try to impose this stuff. Really, if I have to fumble for the toilet paper, it's not going to kill me; I'm not that much of a princess. And not every D/s dynamic looks alike. Some D/s relationships look like mentorship rather than like service dynamics; many D/s relationships start out being primarily sexual before they shift into a broader place where the details of my toilet paper preferences would be of any relevance; and so on. My service preferences are ready and waiting if a relationship goes in a direction where they become relevant, but that's not necessarily where D/s starts. When they are relevant, though, they're consistent across D/s dynamics because they're all about me and not specific to a given person.

The second kind of rule is the kind that's particular to the guidance and shaping of a submissive along their journey of growth. That, of course, means these rules are entirely dependent on the context of what's going on with that individual and what goals we have set for their development. Does a submissive want to improve their health? Perhaps I'll require them to see a fitness trainer, keep a food journal, and stop eating potato chips. Are they a sloppy dresser?

I may create a rule that says they can't wear sweatsuits when they're not at the gym, or that their shoes must always be polished, or that they may only wear shirts that have buttons. On the flip side, if a submissive is obsessive about their weight to a point I believe is unhealthy, I might require the opposite—gym visits no more than four times a week, no scales in the house, and dessert at least twice a week. Or if a submissive suffers from excessive vanity or is uptight about their looks, I might ban the wearing of neckties on weeknights, or forbid them from ironing their jeans. Essentially, whatever it takes to bring balance.

Practically speaking, either set of rules can bring two submissives into conflict. In the first instance, if my preferences are not extremely clear-cut, then two different approaches to meeting them may net different results. A good example was when my boy and my former boi were tasked with making dinner together for the first time. My boy is a creative cook with a flair for finding new ways to please my taste buds and a knack for whipping up something delicious even when the fridge only contains half a jar of peanut butter and a week-old broccoli. My former boi is a rule-follower, with a fetish for precision and a knack for replicating exact results by adhering strictly to formulae that work. Tossing them both in the kitchen with a chili recipe and a bunch of ingredients produced quite a heated situation, with one insisting that I would appreciate a new variation and all the better that it would use up the leftover zucchini, and the other insisting that I wanted exactly what I'd asked for, and that if I wanted zucchini in the stew I'd have said so and it certainly wasn't their job to question my orders. There's nothing like having two submissives with radically different personalities to help a dominant figure out what they want and get really good at communicating it!

In those relationships, it became crucial for me to set out my expectations with clear indications of where creativity and initiative were welcome and where they were not. Some basic tasks were equally appropriate for either one, but I also learned to assign tasks based on their differing strengths; re-alphabetizing my CD collection versus decorating for a party, say. On the flip side, it was equally helpful to cross-assign tasks in order to develop their respective capacities. Telling the rule-follower to come up with meals that would please me, with no further direction, might have caused a bit of panic the first time but eventually provided opportunities for her to experiment with creative cooking and experience my encouragement and approval at the results. It also required that she pay more active attention to my likes and dislikes rather than placing the onus on me to lay them all out. In parallel, insisting that the flighty boy follow certain rigid organizational systems has provided him with a stronger sense of structure than he'd been able to create for himself to that point, and gives him a feeling of security and groundedness. It also gives him the triumphant sense of having "done it right" when faced with detailed expectations and prevents him from going overboard and investing too much time or energy into embellishing things where I really just want the job done quick and simple.

In the second instance, that of personal growth, differing rules can also lead to both positive and negative results. On the positive side, it's always a good thing to show a submissive that you're really taking their individual paths seriously; part of what's so intimate and powerful about D/s is that it's a way of seeing someone with a degree of depth and clarity that's hard to achieve in other relationship forms. But when multiple submissives can clearly see the distinctions in how they are each being held and guided, that can lead to insecurity. "Does she care about the other one's health more than mine, and that's why she's insisting on that diet or exercise program?" "Why do those two have a written calendar for managing their projects, whereas with us it's informal and verbal?" Once again, clarity of communication is key—not only in terms of laying out what's happening, but also in terms of the ability to explain why I make certain choices, why they are different, and when that's an indication of a problem versus simply being an indication of different situations.

Giving Only What's Yours To Give...

For all that I gravitate toward an ownership model, full ownership of another human being is not generally the sort of thing that one can just take up overnight. It requires time and energy to build the kind of trust that full ownership requires. In my experience, ownership is also something that often comes in bits and pieces—I sometimes speak of it in terms of gradually taking someone piece by piece until eventually I become a majority shareholder, and perhaps eventually a full owner.

That piece-by-piece process becomes all the more relevant in poly situations. If a person is involved in an existing relationship when I come along, for example, some pieces of them may already be spoken for, whether explicitly or implicitly. Let's say I wanted to own someone's cock, and they want me to own it. That's well and good, but if they're married, their spouse might have some vested interest in having access to and use of that body part, and might justifiably resent it if I were to come along and take that away. So no matter how much that person might want to give me ownership of their cock, I can't in good conscience take it up unless I discuss it openly with anyone else who might be affected, or at the very least take their needs into account.

You can find creative ways around most situations like this—perhaps my ownership would include a blanket access provision with regard to the spouse, but would place the cock otherwise off limits, so no masturbation without my permission. Perhaps it would be about presence, as in, "When you're in my presence, your cock is mine," or "The only time your cock is not mine is when your spouse is present." Perhaps it would be about time—as in, "You have four hours of free use of your cock every week, and you are tasked with fulfilling your spouse's needs in that time, but I don't care when it happens." Limitations can actually lead to innovative ways of relating that might never otherwise have been possible.

It's relatively easy to think of ways to work within most limitations; after all, most people in this world hold down some sort of day job as well as other responsibilities that must be considered when tailoring the shape of a D/s relationship. You can't very well decide that you own a person's hands, say, if that person needs to spend their days typing in order to earn a living—unless you're willing to assign them to do their typing work for pay as part of your ownership, or you provide them with an equivalent salary to what they'd make doing the typing work. Both of these options, and many more, are most certainly available, but my point is that ownership doesn't exist in a vacuum. You don't get to pick pieces of someone the way you'd pluck cherries off a tree, and simply walk away with them in your hand. No, if you own the cherries and actually want to enjoy them, you need to think about watering and fertilizing and pruning the tree, too. If you can think of poly navigation in a similar vein, it's not terribly complicated, but it can require a certain amount of creativity.

...And Taking Only What You Can Hold

The counterpoint to giving only what you've got to give, as a submissive, is the importance for a dominant of taking only what you're capable of holding. For all that I might like to own five or six submissives who would cater to my every whim (can you just imagine the blinding sparkle of my bathroom tiles and the extinction of dust bunnies for all time? The mind boggles!); thus far, I have personally hit my limit at full ownership of two people. These relationships take enormous time, energy and focus—and that's when everything's going smoothly, never mind if conflict or other challenges come into play. And while reclining in a velvet chaise and being fed grapes is lovely and all, in real life I'm also a writer with deadlines to meet, an educator who spends a considerable amount of time on the road, and a grad student with a towering stack of scholarly books to read.

For me, it's important not to overextend myself. The last thing I want to do is to fumble and drop someone who's counting on me because I'm too busy concocting elaborate protocols for the third cute slaveboy of the month. That doesn't go far in the trust-building department, and if what I feed on is trust, it's incumbent upon me to be worthy of that trust and to act according to it. And that means that, dominant or no, sometimes I don't get what I want. Or rather, I get exactly what I want, I just don't get all of it all the time, because that would be enough to wear out a football team. Hey, I'm still having exquisitely intense and pleasurable relationships with people who worship me, pleasure me, and make me dinner and iron my shirts to boot. I can suck it up.

Practically speaking, it can be really hard to let someone slip away when you'd like to engage with them. But non-monogamy makes many things possible, and circumstance can create beautiful new forms that fit well into existing situations. I currently enjoy a wonderful relationship with someone whom I had to turn down as a play partner and potential submissive because I simply couldn't create enough time to engage at the depth that full-time D/s would have involved and I couldn't stand the idea of doing a half-assed job of it. The relationship we created instead is one of mentorship, devoted friendship, on-and-off living together, occasional service and sweet flirtatious banter, and I wouldn't give it up for the world. Love and power can take many forms, and part of being the one who calls the shots is listening for clarity about what's realistic, and acting accordingly whether you like it or not.

The Jealousy Question

Yup, perverts get jealous too. It's a totally human thing. It's just that pervs wear black leather while feeling insecure. It makes us feel tougher.

What can I say about jealousy that hasn't already been said a thousand times? Jealousy is the classic question in polyamory. This is hardly groundbreaking, but I find that it helps to understand jealousy as a blaring neon sign pointing to an area of insecurity that needs to be addressed. What you do about it is entirely dependent on what's actually going on in that place.

For some reason we seem to think that it's a good idea to change the behaviour that provoked the jealous reaction. I think that for the most part it's precisely the opposite—as soon as a behaviour results in a jealous reaction, displacing the responsibility for healing onto an artificial grab for control over the situation that exposed that need for healing is the least healthy thing you can do. It's one thing for a submissive to experience that; a susceptible dominant may find themselves trying to soothe a submissive's feelings by promising to change a behaviour that's actually perfectly reasonable, and then who's really in charge? This sort of reaction undermines the entire dynamic. But it's even worse when a dominant feels jealous, and makes up for their own insecurity by clamping down on the submissive and calling it "control" when in truth it's simply fear operating through a D/s paradigm. Dominants need to be especially careful to analyze their motives and actions when feeling jealous. It's not always easy to differentiate the powerful possessiveness that one can feel with regard to a piece of valued property from a plain old whiny need for reassurance that's not very dominant at all. But that differentiation is crucial so that you're not just using the authority of dominance to build an artificial situation in which you never have to face your own fears. Spiritually speaking, if you're gifted with power and authority, guess what? You're also tasked with using it honestly.

D/s dynamics can be used beneficially to deal with jealousy. A collar might provide a submissive with the assurance they need that they have a place, that they are desired. The heightened focus of service can demonstrate devotion to a self-doubting dominant. Further along the continuum, a dominant's influence might push an insecure submissive to work on repairing their insecurities through therapy, self-help reading, or other emotional work; a submissive's care might inspire a dominant to figure their shit out in order to become more solidly grounded. But when done with less bracing insistence on health, D/s can foster terribly messy codependent relationship patterns. The choice is entirely in your hands.

DIY D/s And Personal-Pan-Poly

The joy and the curse of both D/s and non-monogamy is that ultimately, we get to make each of them exactly what we want.

There's no set of guidelines, no officially approved format. The whole point is that we're operating outside the conventional understandings of how relationships work—y'know, the ones that prescribe unspoken, un-analyzed heterosexual gender-based power dynamics, insist on monogamous marriage despite the towering statistics showing that it doesn't work for most of the population, and make it entirely acceptable to live in a relationship for years without ever actually talking about things like sex or values or feelings.

In D/s, you pick the power dynamics that work for you, and you tailor them so that your most intimate desires slip into them as snugly as your fingers might slide into a kid leather glove. In non-monogamy, you opt out of the traditional stream and swim against the current, which means there are few examples to follow and no prescribed destination. For better or for worse, there are no rules. We all make it up based on what works for us. The bad news is that means we really have to think hard about what we want and what's right, and work hard to get it. The good news is that we get to really know what we want and what's right, and we just might get it.

PART III
ESSAYS FROM THE ONES WHO SURRENDER

Two Slaves, Two Wives

Renee

(Renee says about herself: "I'm a 50 year old bi female slave. Although I still identify as bisexual, I am only allowed sexual contact with my male Master.")

I'm an owned slave. My master is 68 and straight. He's both my Master/Owner and husband. We've been together for 16 years. Our relationship is very vanilla and very extreme M/s at the same time. It isn't high protocol and there aren't a lot of rules, rituals, or any of that. He is, however, very strict and requires absolute obedience.

I was never poly. I'm still not. He is. When I met him, he was married to another woman and so was I. His wife knew what he was doing and I was introduced to her right away. She was also his slave. Me, I was cheating on the woman I had been with for more than 10 years. It's not something I'm proud of but it's the honest answer. The relationship had been lacking, and after 2 years of trying to rebuild things, I just decided to get what I needed elsewhere. I had no intention of leaving her at the time as she was dependent on me. In the end, I left her for my Master, but I still support my ex financially after 15 years because I did do her wrong.

I lived as his sub for the next few years with him taking more and more control over my daily life. When his first wife died, he married me and made me his slave. A few years later he took another sub and started having those "I want her for life" feelings about her too, so he made her a wife and slave as well (although not a legal wife, she is every bit as much a wife as I am).

When he decided that we were going to be poly again, I fell apart. It had been just the two of us for a few years and I grew comfortable and found security in that. When he mentioned he wanted to start taking others, I felt insecure, jealous, and worried. I also felt a lot of self-doubt, feeling like I wasn't good enough or wasn't serving very well. It made me really feel worthless. It was a hard time, to say the least.

It was my Master who helped me to cope with it, then accept it, then embrace it. He made me realize that what he felt for her had nothing to do with his feelings for me, and that loving her didn't mean he loved me less. He told me it would take time for me to feel comfortable again, but that I would. He said it would come when I realized that he wasn't going anywhere, I was safe, he loved me, and he was never letting me get away. He was right, but it also came with getting to know her, understanding her and how she loves him, and knowing that she is just asking me to respect that the way she respects my life with him. I learned to breathe again once I realized she wasn't a threat to what I had with him.

He keeps us both to himself. We don't play (or have sexual contact) with anyone but him. We don't even have sexual contact with each other. Communication is what holds it all together and why it still works. I don't think his being poly facilitates greater communication; I think it's the other way around. I don't see how poly can work successfully for any amount of time without communication. There isn't anything either of us can't say to him so long as it's respectful. He's a good listener. But the key to the poly working is really in how she and I communicate.

What makes our lives different than a lot of folks who live a poly lifestyle is that he keeps us in separate homes. While both of us have been trained to put him first always, he knows that we'd clash eventually and it would make things less pleasant. We are such different women with different ways, tastes, habits, desires, etc. that if we lived in the same house we'd have killed each other by now.

Instead he's made us two women (neighbors really since we live across the street from each other) who just happen to have the same man as a husband and Master. That's where the communication comes in. Since we aren't all doing everything together, it's up to her and I to coordinate our work schedules, vacation schedules, and family schedules to keep things working smoothly.

We don't really have a lot of rules or protocol any more. He leaves it up to the two of us to figure the schedule out. He's home with me every other night and with her on alternating nights. That changes when one of us has a vacation, is sick, or has some other need for a change or skip in beat. She and I actually work very well together in keeping things coordinated; we both tend to take the other into consideration very well because it's good to get the same in return. Being selfish with him won't get us anywhere because he won't allow himself to be manipulated and won't put up with foolishness. We like to keep the relationship between us slaves a good one. After all, we both want the same thing, and that is to be what makes him happy. Together we do that.

With polyamory, I think the first thing is to know what you're getting into. It's not easy. It can be a lot of work. It takes a lot of time and effort on the M-type's part to keep things running smoothly. My Master says he's got big shoulders and can handle it, but I know that sometimes we're a lot of trouble.

Just recently, she and I both had that "emergency" need for more attention. My dad died on a Tuesday morning and she fell in the parking lot at work and broke her leg that same afternoon. He had to drive the 60 miles back and forth between the hospital and the funeral home for the next 4 days trying to take care of both of us. It's that sort of thing, watching him (at 68) go through so much stress to take care of us when we have need of it, that makes his being poly so easy to accept and even embrace. He never makes either of us feel left out or neglected.

It's important for a slave in this situation to know that it's OK to feel special in your own way, but not entitled to more. Being selfish about your Master will destroy the relationship. My Master's other and I are both special in his life, but we serve entirely different purposes. I'm the one who has adventures with him. I get on his bike and ride with him, I get involved in sports activities with him. He'll come and pick me up at work and take me to the gun range and we'll practice shooting during my lunch hour. She is less adventurous, but enjoys being the one involved in his church activities with him. She won't go near a gun or a motorcycle, but we're each special because we serve him in different ways. We each have that "special purpose" in his life, but that doesn't mean either of us is better or more important or entitled to him more than the other in any way.

He's getting old now, but he has taken other women as lovers or playmates over the years. He's even taken a sub or two, but no other slaves. (He says two is enough for any man.) She and I never really concerned ourselves with his other women unless they tried to cause some kind of trouble for us, which did happen a few times. He's always very upfront and honest with women in letting them know where they stand before starting anything with them. Most of them understand it's a "play arrangement" with no ties, but every once in a while you get that one who wants to stay and intends to push one of us out. I think it's important for those outside of the dynamic to realize that there are people the M-type has a dynamic with and respect that.

We don't really go around advertising our dynamic. Those who know us, know he's the boss. They know he has two of us. They asked a lot of questions, and now just think we're "different". I do still get a lot of "I don't know why you put up with it all" statements from friends, but I'm used to that. We don't associate with the local polyamory or BDSM community. My entire exposure is limited to Fetlife and a Yahoo group.

If I knew back then what I know now, I would have saved myself a lot of stress, heartbreak, and possibly a wrinkle or two. I would have been more accepting right away, but I guess I had to deal with those jealousy and self-worth issues. The most important thing I've learned from being poly in a power dynamic is that love isn't limited, and that love is sometimes strict, sometimes cruel, but always worth it.

Malleable

Cecilia

It's how she wants me to be. It's how a slave ought to be.

You're not supposed to say "ought to"s among M/s people these days, so maybe I shouldn't phrase it that way. Yes, you can be a slave and be totally rigid. At least I assume that you can, because anything's possible. You can also theoretically play basketball when you're four feet tall and have bad knees, and you can also theoretically be a cop if you're terrified of guns, or a nurse when body fluids make you vomit, or be able to touch your toes if you weigh 400 pounds ... but it's going to be a long, hard trip. It's going to be much more difficult if you're not malleable, not adaptable, not able to find ways to change yourself and your emotions at will, or at least with a little effort. I won't say that you can't do it, but it will be like fighting through a wall of thorns every time. With malleability, that's not necessary.

I was always malleable. I was the kid who wanted to do whatever the kid I was with wanted to do. But it's a skill that can be learned, unless your personality is so rigid that you just can't let go. My Lady Antonia sets me exercises to help me with that. Here's a hobby—learn about it, find a way to like it. Here's a new hairstyle that you would never choose for yourself, find a way to see it as "you". This is something that even a single slave who is still looking for an owner can do.

Being malleable is sexy. The hardest part was when my Lady Antonia would change my appearance. My look was important to me then. It was how I expressed myself. I feared that if I let her change it, she would change that self. I was right and wrong. It did change me. And it didn't. Some core things remained the same. But one day I looked in the mirror when she'd dressed me up in yet another different way and she was looking over my shoulder. She called me her doll, her toy, her blank canvas to draw on and then erase and draw on again. That was so sexy to me! I'm proud of how she can change me—butch(ish) one day, femme(ish) the next.

Student punk. Elegant arm candy. Cute geek. Trashy slut. Being adaptable has become my "look", my "self".

Being malleable is good for more than just obeying as a slave. It's good for all the times when situations change on you, when you were counting on one thing but something else happens, or when stuff just doesn't work out the way you were hoping. It's especially good when it's big things that you couldn't stop anyway—it rains on parade day, someone gets hit by a truck, someone comes down with cancer. People who aren't malleable have a hard time then. Like them, I feel pain ... but unlike them, if I'm managing to be as adaptable as I strive to be, I don't get stuck mourning what could have been and wasn't over and over. I can pass more quickly to "What can I do now?" or "Is there something I can help with?" or even "Next!" I can let go of the rigid ideas I had about how things were supposed to be, and ask myself, "OK, so this is how things are actually going to be. Is there any way I can find happiness here?"

So why am I talking about this here? Because malleability is also very useful in polyamory, especially polyamory when you're on the bottom of a power exchange. In fact, it's the most important thing to cultivate. I'm not talking about being brainless and unthinking here. To be truly gracefully adaptable is the opposite of brainless and unthinking. In fact, I believe that being rigid is the true unthinking-ness. People who just react from their assumptions about how things ought to be are the ones who don't question ... themselves, their upbringing, their ideas. They don't ask questions like, "Where did this feeling come from? Does it have to be this way? Do other people always react like this? Is there a way to be happy in this situation? Would I have to become a different sort of person to be OK with this? Is that such a bad thing?"

To be malleable requires a great deal of mindfulness. You have to keep telling yourself, "I am not that feeling. That feeling is not the core of who I am, even if it lies to me and tells me that it is." You have to keep looking for ways to reroute the negative thoughts, to implant positive ones, to look for ways to find small joys. (Many small joys add up to big joy. I'm serious.) You have to brainstorm new ways to retrain your mind. A smart owner can help you with that, but it works best and quickest and most strongly if you hold up your end of the deal. I may be passive in other areas of my life where my Lady controls me, but I have to be active in my own process of adapting to her will.

I am slave to my Lady Antonia. I knew that she was poly when she collared me. It was kind of hard to miss her other girl, Marie. I had no illusions that she was going to give up Marie and live in happy monogamy with her forever, da de da de da. Cue swirly music. Now bring it to a screeching halt. I had to make the decision myself. Do I want monogamy that badly? Or do I want this lifestyle that I love with this person that I love? Maybe I could get the first with monogamy, but I couldn't get the second one. I was open to poly, I'd tried poly at least once before with another lover, but being a slave makes you so vulnerable! I had to think about it for a long time. It wasn't going to be me and Antonia. It was going to be Antonia, me, and Marie. In that order. That's how I would prioritize things, forever. Now I get to cue different music. Is it going to be dark and ominous, or a triumphant march, because I faced the challenge and wrestled it down and I won? That, I realized, is my choice.

Since I was collared, Antonia (I'm going to just refer to her by her first name because it's not like we have formal protocol all the time, mostly she is just Antonia for me and the Lady is implied) has had not only Marie, but J, C, and D. I won't list their names, because they came and went. J lasted for almost a year; D only for a few months. I allow myself to have a lousy attitude about them because they pissed my Lady off and she dismissed them. But at the time, it was part of my job to find something good about them, and about them being in our house, sharing our Mistress's time and attention. It was part of my job to work on my attitude, and to bring her my feelings in a respectful and not nasty way when I needed attention or reassurance, before it got to any point of explosion. That was mindfulness, too.

Being a slave has been one long training in mindfulness for me, and that mindfulness has spread out into serenity in the rest of my life. When my co-workers eat all the donuts and don't leave any for me, I can ruin my own day by thinking about how selfish and lousy they are, or I can think, "I have a happy life and I can afford to let them have all the donuts. What would I want them to think if I ate the last donut? There will be more donuts. There are enough donuts in the world that I can trust in this fact." When I am feeling insecure about Antonia being with Marie or another person, I can concentrate on all the bad thoughts that pop up (which I'm not going to list, because you can all figure them out anyway, you've heard them in your own heads) or I can adapt and think positive things. I can think, "Antonia is having a good time, and I want her to be happy. I like Marie, and I want her to be happy too. I know that Antonia can walk out of the bedroom after having sex with Marie, and come spend time with me and not want me any less, and isn't that a terrific trait in an owner? I know that my turn will come around, because there is enough room in Antonia's heart for both of us. There will be more love for me. There is enough love for me here that I can trust in that fact."

Being malleable is what makes poly not only tolerable, but a joy. Seeing new challenges as yet another opportunity for love, for friendship, for camaraderie, for seeing my Mistress made happy. And for having more hands to do things around here! Maybe even things I hate doing. Marie and I kid about how our reward for having a good attitude about the new slave novices is that we get to foist off our most-hated chores on them! Especially floors. When we're doing floors, we speculate about where to get another slave as soon as possible. We have both joked with Antonia that maybe "likes doing floors" should be on the "must have" side of the list.

But all jokes aside, polyamory more than anything else has stretched my ability to be malleable. It has been my biggest challenge and the one that I'm the most proud of. Anyone can conquer fears, but conquering fears that then bring more love into the world? That's pretty great. After that, I think there's not a lot that I can't handle. Poly has shown me my own strength, and given me my biggest victory ... over myself and my own selfishness, my own rigidity. It's mind over ... um, mind. I did it. You can do it too. It's a little piece of the big road to happiness.

Being In A Leather Family

kelRat

Our leather family has eight people in it—my Master C, his three boys robbie, stephen, and myself; robbie's boy ferrar; Master C's leather sister Sasha, and her girl leesa. (None of these are our real names, but it's not the names that matter, it's the story.)

I've heard a lot of different definitions of what a leather family is, and a lot of arguments about what definition is right and who fits into it. The most broad and general one is that it is a chosen family of people who like each other, are kinky, and at least some of them are having sex with each other. The most specific is that it is a household where everyone is in a Master/slave relationship with each other, usually live-in, and who all subscribe to the tenets of Leather. There are people all along the continuum between those points. I don't know if I agree that every one of those points should be called a leather family, but I'm willing to be open-minded and let people convince me otherwise.

What's Leather? Leather, as a life philosophy, grew out of the gay leather scene. Leather is about forming tribes and families of your own because your own families wouldn't speak to you (or even if they did, because there are rites of passage and acceptance that only a gay leatherman can give a gay leatherman). Leather is about integrity and honesty, about being role models for each other. Leather was an antidote to the "fuck everything you can get your hands on, do every drug you can find" lifestyle that was so prevalent in the gay male community for so long. Leather had a code of honor—form your family, your tribe, and defend them with your life—and we were role models. We are role models. In a way we're reinventing the morally strict but loving upbringing that most of us didn't get because we were queer, only we're doing it with a queer slant. In Leather, you earn your position, and you are judged by others in the community. Leather means that you have a heritage, an inheritance to pass down to others. Leather gives us pride in ourselves and our lifestyle.

I have to say, that worked a lot better when there was actually a small, closeknit community to do that. Now things are different, people are spread out, many of the older ones are dead, and "leather" can mean whatever anyone wants. I'm not whining for the old days here, I'm just saying that we are now faced with a time of reinventing what Leather means in a way that works for what we have to work with today, without diluting the integrity of the original philosophy. We surely still need family today, maybe more than ever.

The way the history of our leather family was told to me, it started with Master C and robbie. They weren't exactly monogamous, but they weren't really what you'd call polyamorous either. Actually, I don't think they'd ever heard of that word at that point in their history. They tricked with other sub boys, because that was the way it was done among leathermen at that point. They promised to keep the casual flings casual, and that robbie would be the only permanent slave. He tells me that he was very insecure at that point, afraid that Master C would take a fancy to some hot guy and then he'd be yesterday's meat, and eventually out the door. His insecurities came from having been in that position more than once before, and from watching the guys at the bars swap each other around like Kleenex. He's old-fashioned, he told me, and he wanted commitment. He grew up kind of conservative, and commitment to him was monogamy, or at least the emotional and lifestyle version that gay guys practiced.

Then, somewhere along the line, robbie got to like playing with one of the sub boys, and he started wondering what it would be like to have him as a boy. That seemed kind of crazy to him—could he be Master C's slave and someone else's Master? The boy was amenable to it, because he trusted Master C as well. They talked about it, and Master C gave permission ... so long as he knew that he could step in with final authority over both of them if need be (which he promised only to do in serious circumstances) and that he was going to be looking for other boys as well. He also promised robbie that he would be the alpha slave and help break in the new boys. Being a Master had given robbie confidence that he didn't have before, and it cleared up a lot of his insecurities. Of course, the fact that they'd been together for almost ten years helped too.

The first boy that robbie played with didn't last, but a few boys down the line came ferrar. It's not easy being the boy of an owned slave. A lot of guys weren't comfortable with the chain of command, but ferrar fell in love with robbie, and with Master C too. By this time, Master C had acquired me as well. I served him for a year and a half from outside, traveling to see Master C and robbie three to five days a week. Eventually it got to the point where all my belongings were at their house, except for my bed and the stuff I didn't need, and I gave it all up and moved in as a full-time slave. Why did I wait so long? I wanted to be absolutely sure, and there was that last bit of paranoia—was I going to give up my life for this only to be kicked out years later, having wasted all that commitment? (That was how I thought of it.) I had to ease into it, or maybe a better way to put it is that I grew into it. The family eventually sucked me in completely.

There was also the problem of love. I wasn't in love with Master C, although I think he is one of the greatest men on earth. I'd been in love before, in relationships with equals before I got into leather and found my slave heart. Since then, no. I look up to Master C, I respect him, I would take a bullet for him, but I don't feel about him like robbie does, or like farrar does with robbie. I guess I'm strange that way—I like the Master/slave relationship best when the Master is a little distant. I can give service more cleanly that way. Signing on to Master C's household meant that either I would never have the experience of being in love again, or I'd have to have it with a leather brother or someone outside the family. I was afraid that no man outside our family would want to have a romantic relationship with a man who was someone else's slave, so I was really giving something up when I took that leap.

I didn't fall in love with robbie, either, or with farrar when he came along, or with stephen when he came along, although I love them all like brothers. Actually, right now I want to talk about how great it is to have leather brothers. Yeah, sometimes we get jealous of each other for Master C's time and attention, but the rest of the time we really care about each other. We've all fucked and played with each other at least some. I've topped robbie (with Master C right there telling me what it was all right to do) and farrar (with robbie right there telling me what it was all right to do) and robbie has topped me (ditto) and we all fuck occasionally when we are allowed by Master C to do so. It was a little difficult to integrate stephen into the family, because it was all new to him and he had trouble getting along for the first year. But we eventually had a breakthrough with him, too. We cry on each other's shoulders, we hug each other, we play-wrestle. I never had brothers growing up and I really love it. I'm still looking for the right man to fall in love with, one who could love me as Master C's slave or who could come into our family, and I haven't given up, but in the meantime I have three other men with true slave hearts who understand me.

Two years ago, things changed. Sasha was an old friend of Master C's, and he called her his sister. Eventually that became his leather sister, and then they started talking about adding her and her girl to the family. Up until this point, entrance into our leather family had been a rite of sexual initiation. There wasn't one of us who hadn't done it with all the rest of us, or who wasn't in service in some way to Master C, and here Master C wanted to bring in two people who weren't going to have a sexual bond. It completely changed the tone of the leather family, and I can tell you that the four of us boys weren't sure that it was going to be a good change. You'll probably think that it was all about the fact that they were women and we were men, but that wasn't the case. We were all thinking: how will they fit in? It really brought home to us how much of our bonding was about sex, was about being gay men together.

I think this is one of the biggest differences from polyamory ... and by that time, two years ago, we had learned that word. We didn't use it so much because if someone asked us what kind of relationship we had, we'd say that we were in a leather family and that was that. But by that time, leather families were starting to look like all kinds of things. We'd seen leather families where a Master would take on a slave who they didn't fuck—it was pure service only. We could respect that. We even saw gay men who took on women, and straight women who took on straight women, and so forth. Unlike vanilla polyamory, people could be added to a family without sex, because the role of Master and slave was more important than sex in its own way. But this was going one step further. What would Sasha and leesa be to us?

Well, it ended up that Sasha became my dirty, nasty leather Auntie. The kind who makes nasty comments about you, but you can stay up all night with her when you've got a problem and she'll give you good advice. It took a while for leesa to be comfortable around us, and us to be comfortable around her. Part of that was because while Sasha is a dyke all the way, leesa is hot for gay men and she had wistfully hoped that becoming part of Master C's leather family meant that eventually one of us might bend and end up fucking her. It didn't happen, not because she's not a great person, but because we're all just on the really gay end of the Kinsey scale. So there was some tension until she figured out her place as our leather sister—our little leather sister, we call her. At first she resented us treating her like a little sister, but then she figured out that it was our way of helping her to find a role that we could all live with.

I went onto a polyamory email list recently, just because I was curious, and I asked a question about who they let into their family. I was interested in whether their practices still clung close to what ours had been like, or if they were more what ours had evolved into. It was full of straight vanilla people, and they took me by surprise when they reacted pretty badly to the word "family". To them, "family" was their blood relatives—often, the people who they had to hide their relationships from. The idea that you could create a "family" through polyamory was not even on the radar for most of them. It was just too queer.

You could say that being in a leather family has nothing to do with polyamory, but then you wouldn't understand how queerness and power exchange come into polyamory and alter it. The power dynamic is more important than anything else for us, except for one part of the queerness ... and the part of that queerness that is most important, more even than the power exchange, is not who we fuck or who we desire, or what parade we march in. Listen close, I'm trying to bring it home to you. It's the part of queerness that created the leather family—the part that says, "They'll never accept me out there, because they don't understand me, so I will create my own family designed around affirming my sexuality and my lifestyle." That's queerness, even when it's a leather family full of straight people. That, not sex, is what binds us together.

You could call it love, because there are a lot more kinds of love than there are kinds of sex. That's another secret that my leather family has taught me. It may look like there are a million kinds of sex, but there are really only a few ... good sex and bad sex being the main division, sex that does you good and sex that messes you up. There are many, many kinds of love. And correct me if I'm wrong, but isn't that the second half of that "polyamory" word anyway?

Working Our Way There:
Polyamorous Household Integration

Eala

I'm a 28-year-old biological female; I'm pansexual, polyamorous, and kinky, among other things. In kinky terms, I'm a submissive with the occasional urge to switch. I'm a bondage junkie and a masochist. I'm also the parent of an almost-seven-year-old boy. I like to keep life interesting.

When I was a teenager, I heard about bisexuality and was delighted that some girls played with both girls and boys. I had always thought just one would be somewhat boring. Later in life, I learned about non-binary gender, and found all new playgrounds to explore. Essentially, I discovered that I don't really care what shape someone's body takes, as long as they can converse fairly well and have an engaging personality. Try explaining that to the other moms at the birthday party.

I have found there are two types of people I tend to enter into relationships with: dominant personalities, and anybody who I find interesting. The dominant people that I typically get involved with are not playing a role—they are strong, dominating personalities, and expect obedience 24/7. This is something I've realized in hindsight, not something I sought out intentionally. Everyone else is, well, anybody I click with. In the past, my relationships have usually involved one dominant person as a primary relationship, and two to four less-involved (read, "less time-consuming") relationships with people who are either vanilla or submissive, and who are either on equal ground with me (regardless of their overall kink-orientation) or submissive to me. (A note—I use "Dom" as a general term to refer to anyone of any gender who considers themselves more Top-ish than bottom-ish. It's just easier to type that way. I also use "sub" in the same manner, only reversed, for the same reason.)

DG is a 38-year-old biological male, straight, kinky, and was monogamous when we met. Luckily for me, he was open to trying polyamory. He has a background in the Vampire subculture, which he has integrated into how he runs our family.

O is a 33-year-old biological female; she's bisexual, kinky, and polyamorous (although this is her first poly relationship).

DG is the Head of Household, and my Owner. I am the Alpha slave; O is household property. As a fairly recent addition, O has very little say in the workings of the house (though we try never to disregard a good idea). After a year and a day of service as house property, she will become a full member of our family. She is doing very well as a domestic servant, and seems to be flourishing personally in that position. I have two other long-standing relationships with people who are not within our household. One is another biomale dom, who has his own household, and the other is a biofemale switch. They are both long-distance, for now.

DG and I are also married. Of all the reasons that poly people get married (to one partner), ours was particularly based in the kink aspect of our relationship. I have never had any desire to allow the government to authorize or recognize my relationships. I have never felt the need to have my vows to my loved ones presided over by an officiant; my vows would be just as binding with no witnesses at all. However, when DG and I started dating, I was also dating the other male dom and female switch, both of whom I love and am still dating today; marrying DG was my way of giving him, incontrovertibly, the "final say" in my own power schematic. It is a concrete symbol, for him, that I am owned by him. I may play with other doms, but it is at his discretion. In the case of the dom I have a relationship with, that entire relationship has received a sort of "blanket authorization" —DG does not micromanage the other dom. The same is true for my relationship with the switch. However, other people who wish to play with me, but do not have an established ongoing relationship, are subject to DG's scrutiny. ("Play" means, for us, any BDSM or sexual play.)

In the past, O and I have both been shared with DG's former roommate, who was a straight vanilla male; he was given a moderate level of leeway with O and I, due to his proximity and his long friendship with DG.

I was poly when DG and I met; I knew I wanted to be part of a multi-relationship household. Although I was not new to BDSM, I was new on the Leather scene, so being a part of a Leather Family also had appeal. So for me, the polyamory came first; I was already in two other relationships when we met, and I was not actually looking for another dom.

DG had never heard of polyamory when he and I met. I remember feeling like I was doing a terrible job trying to explain it, because he kept saying things like, "So, how many playmates do you have again?" The BDSM thing he understood, though. It wasn't that far, as a subculture, from his experience in the Vampire subculture. It also didn't hurt that we had a mutual friend who, before introducing us, warned DG that I was "into that crazy whips and chains stuff." Having been to large fetish events, such as FetCon, in the past, DG did not need that part of my "craziness" explained. So he entered our relationship expecting some level of BDSM to be involved, and knowing himself as a dom. He also knew I was poly, but he expected to remain monogamous himself. He always had been, and didn't see a reason to change at that time.

Our relationship began in a very casual and vanilla way (though there was BDSM play, there was no power exchanged outside of sex). We both dated other people, without needing each other's permission. As we explored our fantasies, though, we began to develop a Daddy/girl relationship. This was a first for both of us, and led to a great deal of introspection and negotiation. It actually took us weeks to realize we had completely different ideas of what a Daddy/girl relationship should look like (that was a revelation). I'd like to say that we talked it all out at every step, but we are human, after all. Often, it seemed that we simply were using the same words in different ways—and so we were each assigning different meanings to the other's words without realizing it. The power of vocabulary should not be underestimated.

Our D/s relationship has always been fairly stable. There was never any question that he was the Dom and I was the sub. Our poly relationship has undergone several incarnations, though. When we first decided to enter a less casual relationship (one with a defined power structure outside of play), DG saw no reason for him to stray from his monogamous background, but neither did he see a reason to change my polyamorous ways. So I dated him and a few others, and he dated me. I felt that was unfair, but accepted his choice. Eventually he started to feel like it was a little unfair, too.

So, although he enjoyed his "alone time", when he stumbled across another female sub who was interested in joining us, he allowed himself to become interested in her, also. Unfortunately things did not work out with that female, due to errors by each of the three of us. DG and I had not worked out exactly what we expected from each other, or from a new family member, before entering the relationship with her. To be honest, I don't think we knew what our concerns, expectations, and responsibilities would be with an additional person in the relationship. When those concerns came up, the other girl took those concerns as personal attacks, and became defensive. For her, defensive meant manipulative. DG took her manipulation as an assault on his control of the house and family, and things spiraled swiftly downward from there.

My error in this situation, as I see it, was in how I reacted to the conflict from the beginning. I was unsure of what either person expected of me, so I stayed completely out of it ... or at least I tried to. In hindsight, I don't believe it's possible for one person to be completely exempt from a conflict in a triad. Certainly there were parts of it that did not involve me. DG does not switch under any circumstances, and this girl attempted to force him to at one point. That went quite poorly. The aftermath still affected me, though, as each person attempted to ask my opinion about what should be done. In the end, the three of us did talk about the issues together. DG and I took responsibility for our errors; the other girl agreed that DG and I were at fault, but could not see that she shared any responsibility for the conflict. DG and I chose to end the relationship with her, lessons learned. It would have gone far better for everyone involved if we had either planned ahead more, or taken things much more slowly in order to feel things out before diving in.

Despite the bad ending, that experience introduced DG to the idea of having a triad, and introduced us both to the nuances we would have to consider before entering such a relationship. By the time we became involved with O, we were much better prepared to add a third person to our inner relationship. The second time (with O), we took our time and had a much clearer idea what we wanted and what we expected from each other before entering a relationship with O. Essentially, we just improved our communication (in fact, we are still working to improve it, and probably always will be).

Negotiations have gotten decidedly more effective with copious practice and an ever-clearer idea of what we each want in our lives. I had to learn not to mix negotiation with sarcasm. It was never as funny out loud (during a negotiation) as it was in my head. My sense of humor has always been rather caustic, which can be a problem in sensitive situations. Learning to negotiate with DG has done more to teach me to temper the harshness of my humor than any other life experience I have had.

I am (currently) the only one in our family with lovers outside our family's power dynamic. One is another Dom, who is far more experienced in these lifestyles than the rest of us. He has been a wonderful source of advice and mentorship for both DG and me. DG had some difficulty adjusting to the presence of another Dom in my life, but was able to move past that obstacle fairly easily once he developed a friendship with the other Dom.

My other relationship is with a mostly-vanilla, kinda-switchy woman. Where the other Dom is somewhat integrated with our family's power dynamic, this woman is completely outside of it. My relationship with her is not a power exchange, though we do play power games in bed.

Both of my other lovers were aware of my preferences before we started dating, and they have never had an issue with the development of my relationships with DG and O. There has been extensive negotiation between DG and the other Dom, which led to their friendship and avoided their potential conflicts.

As I write this, we are changing our circumstances.

Five months ago, I moved from the home I shared with DG in Texas, to Arizona. At that time, O was a friend who we cared for, and who DG had played with a few times. Before I left, DG had expressed a desire for he and I both to be marginally monogamous during our separation. I say 'marginally' because he did not expect me to end my two long-standing relationships (which would become long-distance as well), but he did ask that I not start any new relationships during that time. He did not intend to enter any new relationships, either. I agreed, although I was honestly expecting him to need a play partner of some caliber. A few weeks after I moved, he did ask that we renegotiate; he wanted to take O on as a service submissive. I was happy with that idea, knowing that he is happier when he has company (both companionship and sex) and help around the house. She proved to be an excellent domestic servant, and was fun for him to play with as well. We already knew from our friendship with her that she would be a good fit for our family, so when she asked to be considered for ownership, there was very little negotiation needed.

So O moved in with DG as a full-time domestic servant and slave. In the meantime, DG and I had some rough bumps between the two of us; stress over the financial stress of maintaining two separate households led to anger being expressed as jealousy or suspicion. As my owner and husband, the distance between us led to DG feeling like he was no longer in control of my actions. Discipline, which is an integral part of our D/s relationship, was problematic. The difficulty was greater than usual because I was unable to set up the Internet in the house in Arizona. I became afraid that I wasn't "submissive enough" for DG, and he became concerned that I was blowing him off and would replace him with a local Dom. Text messages became our primary means of communication, so everything we said was devoid of inflection or body language, and often got taken out of context. DG and I had to learn a whole new level of communicating and listening to each other. We have learned to say, "This is what I think you mean ... is that right?" We also had to learn to better monitor our own moods. We are both prone to depression, and we didn't always notice when that was coloring our perspectives.

None of this was directly related to O. I was never concerned with her presence, and I don't recall her name even coming up as a subject of disagreement ... although I'm guessing their BDSM play sessions may have been a bit more intense after an argument between DG and me. Even though we lived separately, O automatically fit herself into a role that was submissive to mine. She did that on her own, but it pleased everyone in the house. The details of her position in the house have been negotiated as needed, with little to no conflict. So far, we have not come across issues that we did not foresee and prepare for, or were not able to adapt to quickly. O's biggest dilemma has been her concerns over pleasing me, sometimes to the exclusion of her service to DG. That is problematic, but not a cause for conflict. DG understands O's concerns, and is working with her (as am I). We take it one step at a time, and try not to get too excited about disagreements.

This week, DG and O are moving in with me.

We have worked out as much as we can work out in advance. I think the self-awareness and communication skills that we have learned so far on our journey will be put to the test over the next few months. So far, those two things have been the key to our negotiations. It's easy to say, as everyone does (correctly), that communication is the key to making poly work. But I believe that you can't properly communicate unless you are sufficiently self-aware. How do you express your needs if you don't really know what they are?

When it comes to communication: should there ever be things that can't be said in a relationship, no matter what the dynamic? I think that in the early stages of my relationship with DG, there were things that I would not have volunteered. However, DG has always been interested in learning all of my secrets, and was very persistent in his questioning. In light of his goals, I do think that his dominance helped me answer his questions, if only because of my desire to please him as a submissive.

We do communicate constantly, checking in with each other to make sure everyone is happy (or at least satisfied) with decisions that are made or situations that arise; this is necessary for the poly aspects of our relationship, our power dynamic, and even for the "normal" situations we all find ourselves in. I doubt any relationship could survive without that, least of all the more complicated poly/BDSM relationship set.

We have rules that we developed to make our particular arrangement work. We set up a hierarchy between O and I, and in effect laid the ground work for any future additions to our family when we did so. As part of my relationship with DG (as his wife), he allows me to have a measure of control over who he dates outside of our marriage. I suspect if that were public knowledge, DG would get more than a few sidelong glances from other Dom-types for allowing me veto-power over his partners. Perhaps his choice to allow that is a holdover from his recent conversion from monogamy, but it works well for us. I think his choice to allow that has led to a much greater degree of harmony in our family. (I might also be biased on that topic.)

The BDSM community we have spent time in (DFW, TX) was very poly-friendly. There was a pretty even mix of relationship types. I personally have never felt slighted for being poly. The only issue that has come up (and this seems to be common regardless of someone's kink-orientation) is when our polyfidelity comes into question. DG, O and I consider ourselves polyfidelitous. Yes, I have two other lovers; however we do not have an open relationship. We will not simply go out with anyone else who catches our eye. Any potential lover has to be accepted by the family as a whole; we are loyal to us, first, and have no plans to add any other partners in the foreseeable future.

So when one of us gets hit on by someone who knows that we are poly, the "sorry, I'm married" line simply doesn't work. I have been told by another Dom, after I stated my non-availability, that he knew I was available because, after all, my husband had a girlfriend so we must be poly. He became quite pushy, and I had to ask DG to have a talk with him. The idea that just because we are poly means we are always available is something I wish people would get out of their heads. I am a loyal member of my family, and being poly does not make me a slut.

I believe that in any D/s relationship, the Dom is responsible for the emotional well-being of their sub (although I'm sure someone could point out extenuating circumstances in which the Dom may not be responsible for a particular sub for this or that reason—I'm speaking in generalities). I think in poly families, the Dom(s) of the family are also responsible for the overall health of the family relationship as a whole. If we take that level of responsibility as a given, then multiple subs means greater responsibilities, while sharing a sub with the sub's other Dom/lover, or even another Dom within the family, may take a greater level of cooperation with another alpha personality than most Doms are accustomed to. That said, my personal advice to those newly entering this type of arrangement is to start slowly, one new partner at a time. The faster you add additional relationships, the more difficult it is for people to adapt to each other and their individual and group relationships. When people don't have time to fully adjust to each other before a new element is added to the mix, tensions and conflict can get out of control.

As in any D/s relationship, the sub is responsible for communicating their needs and their emotional state to their Dom. With our particular dynamic (in which there is more than one sub), I think it is equally important for subs to communicate with each other. For our house to be harmonious, we must know where the others stand, and take care of each other.

I think it is important for subs to know that it is OK for them to voice concerns, discomfort, or any other "negative" emotion when faced with moving from monogamy to polyamory. It does not make them a "bad sub". It makes them an honest communicator, and therefore an asset to their Dom. Also, a sub should know that if they do have doubts and hesitations, they are not the only one. It's likely that another sub in the family (or that they know) has felt the same way at some point in time. The best thing a sub can do for themselves is to know themselves, and communicate their needs honestly.

The most important thing I've learned from polyamory in a power dynamic is ... myself. Plain and simple, I have learned who I am and what I want. There has been a tremendous amount of introspection done on all our parts just because we have had to figure out what we wanted and needed from our relationships, as individuals. I served in the Army, and went overseas to experience things that most people consider the prime experiences that bare their soul and show them who they are; that taught me to survive, physically and emotionally, but nothing has made me more clear to myself than the introspection forced on me by walking these two paths.

Making Poly Look Tame

slave anneke

I'm slave anneke, and I belong to Mistress V. Seventeen years ago, I was collared by my Mistress, who has requested that I refer to her simply as Mistress V in this work. We met at a SM play party. As happens with many dominas, she was flooded with subs who were desperate for her attention. I felt lucky to be selected out of the crowd. It's not easy being a straight male submissive. You're one of a sea of faces, most of them only interested in getting their rocks off and their fantasy done, and it's obvious why the small number of female dominants in the scene will assume, at first, that you are one of *those*. Sometimes you feel desperate, and sometimes you end up eroticizing that desperation. Anyway, I felt really lucky when we hooked up, and even luckier when we began to pull a relationship out of our playdates.

One of the things that Mistress V loved about me, compared to so many of the other male subs that she knew, was that I was far less focused on my dick than they were. Oh, I had a libido, and fantasies, and sometimes that flood of hard, sharp, rough-edged desire would torment me. But I could always set it aside. That was something we had to do differently. She was used to controlling male slaves by keeping them in constant arousal, desperate to come. That didn't work for me. I love being controlled, but it's on a deep emotional level that the satisfaction comes. I love serving, I love doing a good job and knowing that I've pleased her. But my dick could only be pushed so far, and then I would just shut down sexually.

What she didn't know, at the time, was that I was keeping a deep and awful secret from her. To this day I am ashamed at how long I kept that secret from the woman to whom I'd sworn to tell everything. I was not transparent. I was too afraid, and ashamed. I had fantasized about being a woman and having a woman's body since I was a child. In fact, I believe that my veering off into BDSM when I was a teenager happened because I could not cope with how much I hated the idea of having sex as a "normal" man. I wasn't focused on my dick because I despised my dick. My genitals revolted me. Chastity was easier for me than for other men, because I was always dissociating from my genitals unless the awful wave of testosterone-fueled lust was washing over me.

So I became a slave. Oh, it wasn't a bad thing; I am definitely submissive, and I love the life. I love my Mistress, but although we have intimacy, I resisted becoming her "boyfriend", someone who could be her public vanilla partner as well as her domestic servant and kinky lover. I didn't want to be anyone's husband. I didn't want to get sucked into a public male role, outside of the job I worked. So when we became more and more serious, the question hovered there: would we be monogamous, if I was so unable to give her that? When we were first together, she played with other male subs, but after a while due to outside life circumstances (her job took an overtime turn) that fell by the wayside and we got used to it being just us. She had a couple of gay male friends who took her out to concerts with them, and I was basically her housewife and confidant, as well as her slave.

I've heard many (mostly female) slave-identified people talk about how they would never leave their masters no matter what ... unless he stopped being monogamous. That's the big deal-breaker. Well, there's a bigger deal-breaker that they don't think about. What if their master got sex reassignment? It can happen. Some of the transwomen I know were big macho guys once. It was a way of trying desperately to be normal. It's rare, but it happens. Sadly, I'll bet that if their master started taking hormones and growing breasts and dressing like a dominatrix (or in the reverse, if their mistresses started growing beards, smelling like a man, and having their breasts removed), their "slaves" would call a halt and go looking for someone more gender-normative. It is an unfortunately truth that very, very few relationships survive transition. This kind of change makes poly look tame.

I was not unaware of that, and it was part of the reason I waited so long. My Mistress knew that I had some transgender leanings, and once in a while she would ask me if I wanted to crossdress. I would tell her, respectfully, no. She would drop it for another few months. I knew that she was asking more for my sake than for hers. I also knew that if I started walking down that road, I would not be able to stop. The genie would be out of the bottle, and the pain of what I could and could not have would have torn my soul out. My Mistress is heterosexual, and while we had never discussed the issue, I was sure that she would have no choice but to leave me if I became who I truly am. And if she left me, where would I be then? If you think being a male submissive means that it's hard to find partners, try being transgendered. I'd heard just how hard that could be. They say that a transwoman has a statistically higher chance of getting murdered than getting married.

Well, obviously I did tell her, because here I am—a transitioned transwoman. And just as obviously, I stupidly underestimated my Mistress's generosity, flexibility, and all-around wonderfulness. When I finally, tearfully, told her everything, she reacted far better than I feared. First of all, she's not stupid and she figured that this might be the case—some of her queer friends had suggested it. She flew into action and got me therapy and herself information. She was upfront that she wasn't thrilled about the situation, but she likened it to that of some friends of ours who have to be on SSRI medications for depression—their partners have to put up with them either being miserably depressed or completely asexual from the side effects of the medication. One friend whose husband had cerebral palsy took her aside and talked to her—I don't know exactly what was said, but it affected her deeply. Sometimes people are "blessed" with certain medical conditions that put a heavy burden on the partner, she told me, and love and loyalty still ought to mean something.

I think it might have been tempting for her to use her authority over me to stop my transitioning, except that she saw how unhappy I was and she honestly wanted me to be better, and that's why I can trust her to have control over me. She can make the hardest decisions of all, and make them well. So I started hormones ... and then we had the Big Talk. The one where she said that there was no way that she could be monogamous with me if this was going where it was going. She wanted to bring in another male submissive, because she wasn't sure that she was going to be attracted to me after I transitioned. Not to mention that I would not be able to perform for her sexually in the way that she wanted.

She also had a problem with being seen as a lesbian, for a while. Then she met straight mistresses who had girl-slaves too, and gay men with dyke-boys, and that helped. They explained to her that owners could own all sorts of slaves, and it was about ownership, not about sexual preference. She passed this wisdom on to me, and told me that I was still her property, no matter what. She told me that it didn't matter how I was redecorated, so long as I was still hers. She promised me that even if she brought in another slave, I would be the alpha and take care of things. She had me contact some other slaves who were alphas, so that I could get an idea of what it was like and how I would be able to handle it.

I won't say that I wasn't insecure. I was, terribly, the more so because it was happening in the middle of my transition. I lay awake many nights afraid that I would be replaced in her affections. I believed my Mistress when she said that she would never throw me out for being transgendered. She had looked me in the eye and asked, "Do you really believe that I would break my word to you? Do you really believe that I am so shallow that I would throw you away for something you can't help?" No, I didn't believe that. I fought with that in myself and finally came up with a solid core of trust. She would keep her word. What I feared was that she would come to love someone else more than she cared about me. I feared that I would become a tolerated appendage, not a beloved slave and lover.

I acted pretty stupid when she interviewed the first couple of slave boys. I didn't make a scene or anything, but I hid in the kitchen and cried for hours. Finally she became exasperated with me. "If you're going to be the alpha slave," she told me, "you need to act like one. You're going to help me interview them. I expect you to get yourself to a point where you can be objective about them, and judge them by the criteria of my needs and desires, which you ought to be the resident expert on by this time." She set me to making a list of what qualities a new slave should have, but she only let me add one quality to the list per day. Then, at night, I was made to sit and meditate on that quality, on whether I had it (and if so, how I could be a good example) or didn't have it (and if so, how pleased Mistress would be to have it), and whether I was choosing that quality out of wanting her to have the best, or wanting to make the standard so high that no one would rate it. That was hard, because I really do want her to have the best. But I had to be humble and admit that another slave ought to be allowed at least as many faults as I have!

This went on for three months—it was quite a list!—and during that time Mistress did not interview other slaves. She worked hard on me, building up my self-esteem and letting me know that she loved and trusted me. In retrospect, I see how much hard work she put in preparing me for poly. She arranged email exchanges and in one case a meeting with other slaves in poly families for me to talk to. My head began to change—I went from insecure mouse to vigilant hawk, every time we went to a club I would watch the other male subs and think: Is this one good enough for her? Would she like that? I would see one of them serve in a particularly nice way and think, we should look for one who does that.

(At some point, I realized that I had stopped thinking and referring to them as the "other male subs" and started thinking of them as the "male subs", because I was a female sub, now and forever. At some point they became another category of humans. I realized that meant that I had really left that gender behind entirely, and become a woman.)

To make a long two years of hunting short, we eventually found slave bobby, who met almost every criteria on the list, and all the deal-breakers. There was one thing that I hadn't thought to put on my list, but it was on her list! She asked me, "Do you like him? Could you be friends with him?" And yes, I could. I am his big sister, his big lesbian sister. I taught him the ropes, I oversee his work, I prepare him for things. He was very much a beginner when we got him, so he depended on me to help him learn how to be a good slave, and how to please her. When I was laid up, he took care of me because Mistress had to work. He's become like a little brother to me. I was especially touched that he comes to me when things are hard—being a slave is not always easy, no matter how wonderful your owner is—and he wanted to know how to get through it.

By now you're probably all asking the Big Question: do I have sex with slave bobby? I have, because Mistress wanted to see it happen for her entertainment, although it was kind of a comedy of errors until she stepped in and started directing. That's something that we both do for her. In a way, we are both just her hands once removed, doing things to each other. By ourselves, we don't have sex with each other—we're both in chastity except for her will, and I don't have much of a libido now—and we are not attracted to each other. I'm not into men, and he's not into subs. But we care about each other. I knew that it was going to be all right when someone at a club said something mean to bobby, and hurt his feelings, and my Mistress and I were both indignant for him and talked all the way home about how we would like to beat up the person who hurt him. I was surprised at how angry I was to see him down like that. I guess that you can come to love someone over time, and it kind of sneaks up on you.

My fears about being replaced emotionally have not materialized. It was strange, but three of my Mistress's best friends went away about the time I was transitioning. One died, one had a fight with her and left, one drifted away with a new lover. I kind of stepped into the void left by their absence. I had always been her confidant on many things, but now I was her best girlfriend too. And still her housewife and lover. Yes, we still have sex, although it's different now—it's less selfish, it's more entirely about her and her pleasure. But I think that being able to create a new place in her life, one that fit me better and that I trusted would always be wanted and needed, helped me through the last of my worries.

Mistress V was there for me all the way through my transition. She assures me that we will be able to afford my vaginoplasty eventually. After estrogen, my genitals basically don't work anymore, so it will be nice to be able to have some kind of genital sex again after that. I've heard that it's a long time of recovery, so I figure that bobby will be taking care of me. I know that he will do a good job.

So now my Mistress is not a lesbian, but she has a girl-slave and a boy-slave. It was just really important for her to be seen as a particular preference. But then, it's important to me to be seen as a woman! So if she can be good about my need, I can be good about hers, and we can compromise. I've even been thinking about how it would be if we added another slave. If he was as good a man as bobby, I think it would be fine. What I'd want to tell people who are facing down poly is about honesty. We throw around the word "slave", but there is no definition of slave that I believe in that doesn't mean: your owner's needs are more important than yours. You have to be honest: what does that mean to you? Do you really understand what it means for their needs to be more important than yours? It's not that slaves have no needs, but it's still true. It can be the hardest part of slavery. But once you get past it, it is a wonderful place to be in. My Mistress's pleasure in her two slaves is like ambrosia to me. I could drink it in forever.

And The Pain Is The Point:
Being A Cuckquean Slave

Shae L.

Most people are going to look at that strange word in the title and not know what it is. In fact, some of you are going to run for your dictionaries. I'll head you off—*cuckquean* or *cucquean* in an old Elizabethan word which means basically a woman whose husband cheats on her. It's the feminine form of *cuckold*, which refers to a man whose wife cheats on him. So right away you're probably wondering, "What's cheating got to do with this? This is a book about polyamory. There's no cheating in polyamory, or at least there isn't supposed to be."

And you'd be right. My husband and I are polyamorous, and I am his slave. This essay isn't about dishonesty, or sneaking around while the other person happily thinks that you're monogamous. The words *cuckquean* and *cuckold* have taken on new terms in the modern fetish world, probably because they haven't been really used for their original meaning in centuries. In modern parlance, a cuckquean is a woman who gets a sexual thrill from her husband fucking someone else, and a cuckold is the male opposite number. It's more than the kind of warm fuzzies that you get from seeing your mate be made happy, or all those nice poly things. It's emotional edgeplay, with a big dollop of sexual fetish on the side.

Lots of lovers in the BDSM scene play with emotional edgeplay. They scare each other, or play with each other's triggers. They do humiliation scenes where the bottom is brought very close to their breaking point, and then brought back safely. I also know a lot of people who do this within a D/s context, because it's a long-term relationship where you (as the sub) know that you can absolutely trust this person to take you to terrifying and exciting places and not break you into pieces. I love humiliation—it makes me so wet—and for a long time I was ashamed of that fetish. I was also scared, because while I wanted someone to go there with me, I didn't want them to actually think of me as nothing or treat me like dirt every day. I wanted love and trust, and a safe space to go there and come back to love and trust again. And one of the humiliating things that made me the most wet? Being cheated on. Knowing that the man I loved was off enjoying himself with some sexy young thing while I was sitting home alone, or tied up in the next room ... or sitting at the end of the bed watching and unable to do anything.

Don't get me wrong, I'm scared of being abandoned. The idea of actually being dumped for the hot young thing makes me want to curl up in terror ... but I've discovered something very special about myself and my sexuality. I'm a very sexual person, but my sexuality is kind of diffuse ... instead of being all about fucking and sucking (although I'll never turn that down) it can find itself attaching to all kinds of things. I've learned that if I attach it to something that frightens me, the sexual thrill can pull me close enough to explore it, and over time I'm not afraid of it any more. And that makes me feel so powerful! I know, what business does a slave have feeling powerful? Well, my master says that it's a great power, a power that I use for good, to face my fears and heal myself of my wounds.

In practice, this means that I encourage my husband to find other people to have sex with. He is bisexual, so he has both male and female lovers. He has a male slave who is not live-in (Ross comes over about two days a week and stays over maybe once a week) and two long-distance slaves, one female and one male ... and a whole lot of casual sex. I am almost never allowed to have sex with other people, unless he orders it. (Lest you think that I am being abused, please understand that the difference in privilege turns me on and reinforces my position. I love it, even when I hate it. I know that is contradictory, and I will explain later. But I'm here of my own free will. I even suggested it.)

I worried for a long time before writing this essay and sending it in, because I'm afraid that everyone who reads it is just going to think that I'm crazy or self-destructive or doing bad poly or should just get over it. I'm afraid that poly people are going to say that this practice has no place in real polyamory. But I was assured by the editor that this book is as much about power exchange and kink as it is about nonmonogamy, so I'm being brave and writing about this tiny percentage of the poly/power exchange bunch, those of us whose kink it is, and who find so much power in it—on both sides.

My master and I talked about this for a long time before we went forward with it. We'd been discussing polyamory, and I was having a lot of qualms about it. I was terrified that he'd find someone better and leave me, and that as his slave I wouldn't be able to do anything about it until I was dumped on the street. My brain ran through all kinds of terrible scenarios—and we hadn't even started looking yet! But my wicked cunt eventually sabotaged all this obsessing, because I noticed—to my horror—that those painful scenarios were turning me on. Actually, the more humiliating they got, the more of a turn-on they were. One day, while he was looking at a BDSM dating site—not seriously, just daydreaming—I imagined him finding someone else on the site and wanting her (or him) more than me. I felt like I'd been kicked in the stomach. I wanted to lay down on the floor and cry. At the same time, I realized that I was incredibly wet and wanted to masturbate right there. That's right, lay on the floor and cry and beat off.

It was confusing as hell ... but I knew I couldn't keep this reaction from my master. If anyone would accept it, it would be him. He has taken me to amazing places in humiliation play and never once made me feel afterwards like I was any less of a person to him. He gets it. He doesn't make me feel ashamed for wanting that. He accepts every part of me, even my twisted sexual desires. I've never come up with anything that disgusted him. I've been covered in garbage, licked the mud off his feet, been used as a human toilet, been ordered to screw other people, and that's not all. But that was all part of playing. This was a real, painful taboo, a limit in myself that I wanted to cross.

Bringing another person into your emotional edgeplay is dangerous business. You don't know what their triggers are and what might make them uncomfortable. Also, the master needs to be really careful not to break their slave. These things take a delicate hand and a lot of talking. Before my master would play with this, we did a lot of deep discussion—and a little bit of sexy storytelling in my ear about such a scenario while using a vibrator on me. When we were ready to act on my new fetish, he decided on a technique he called calibration—he would flirt with a woman with me watching, and then we would talk about it later, and I would report my reaction. If the pain was greater than the arousal, he'd stop. If it went well, he'd try kissing someone, then having a nonsexual scene with them, and finally scaling up to screwing them, but with me at home. Obviously—I'm now a dedicated cuckquean slave—it worked out. The first time I sat home while he was in a motel room with a female acquaintance, I couldn't concentrate on anything. I wanted to cry, and I wanted to masturbate. I had been forbidden to do the latter, so I did a lot of the former. By the time he got home I was desperate to be fucked. He told me he didn't have any fucking left in his cock, he'd used it all up on her. He made me smell him all over, to sniff the scent of her. He made me sniff his cock, which had been in her and which he hadn't washed, just so he could bring it home to me. Then he threw me a dildo and told me to choose—I could sleep on the floor and get off as many times as I liked, or I could sleep in bed with him, with my head buried in his crotch so that I would smell her all night, and not be allowed to touch myself.

I threw myself at his feet and kissed them. I had never felt so submissive before, so humiliated … and so grateful. He was cruel and that was exactly what I needed. After a minute of kissing his feet, I asked for permission to sleep in bed with him.

There's almost nothing written about women who enjoy being cuckqueans. I know that we are statistically rare. There's a little bit about submissive men who enjoy cuckolding—most of it erotic fiction and not stuff by actual people doing it—but it even has a dot com. When I read the words of female submissives who are looking at polyamory with their masters, it seems like three-quarters of them are angry or terrified or demanding that it not happen or being miserable—and not in a good way—because it already is. The other quarter are happy being poly and don't seem to be all that worried. I don't feel like I fit in anywhere. As we've done this more and more, has my actual comfort with his extramarital activities grown? Yes and no. Certainly my faith in our marriage is much, much higher. I have no rational fear whatsoever that he will actually leave me.

Irrational fears? Lots of them. They will probably never go away, so I make them work for their tears—entertaining my cunt, and my master. I also feel much more like a real slave.

Eventually we went from casual sex in cheap motels to bringing the girls home. At this point, we had to have a big talk about ethics. He hadn't been telling the half-dozen women he'd had casual motel sex with about his marriage—and to be fair, they didn't seem to want to know more about him than his ability to keep it up half the night. But if they were going to be meeting me, things had to be different. First, we made an agreement to restrict our cuck-fucks (that's what he calls them) to kinky polyamorous people. No dishonesty, no helping someone else cheat. I know that a lot of cuckold/cuckquean couples indulge in all sorts of dishonesty to get their needs met, because they figure that most people just aren't going to believe it—"What do you mean, it turns your wife/husband on!"—or if they do believe it, they will be disgusted and not want to get involved. But we made a commitment to honesty, which makes it harder to find partners, but we can feel better about ourselves.

We've found that it's more effective if he explains it first, and then I talk to them over the phone and explain it again. They need to hear it from me so they won't think he's just lying to get into their pants. Of course, admitting my humiliating need to strangers is even more deliciously humiliating. Then there are the ones who are fine with fucking a married man—even if he was cheating—but they are weird about having the wife watch. Some of them are mean girls, which I don't mind because I know they are just one-time deals, and we've talked about how maybe they would be more comfortable having me there if my master emphasized how much power they had over me—let them insult me and verbally humiliate me. But we'd both really rather have people who understood and were fine with everything. Which is rare.

Sometimes I will just watch, kneeling at the side of the bed while my cunt burns like a fire. I torture myself with thoughts about how much prettier and better she is than me, how much I want him to notice me and touch me (but I am not allowed to make a sound or touch myself), how much lower I am than this new interest. How much of a slave I am for being there, getting off on his "infidelity". I seethe and I burn. Sometimes, if the woman is OK with it, he will say things to me about her body and how much he wants her. Sometimes she will say things like that back to him. Watching him come inside another woman makes me want to scream and come at the same time.

Then I will be sent to get them towels and clean them up. I fantasize about being forced to lick his cum out of their cunts, but we have safe sex and it isn't an option yet. (Maybe if we find another slave girl someday!) I fix them drinks and call her a cab, then I crawl into bed and smell her on him. It's all I can do to keep my hands off my cunt until I can fall asleep. The next day I replay the whole thing in my head, complete with all the emotions, and that night we have explosive sex. I know that some cuckqueans don't get hardly any sex, but I'm lucky that I get a lot of it. My master is a horny guy and he doesn't want this fetish to rule who he wants and doesn't want to fuck at any time, including me.

Once, we brought home a woman from a fetish club and had our usual cucking night. Afterwards, she asked me some questions, and I realized that she didn't understand as well as I thought. She got that I was turned on by watching, and she was cool with that. But when I explained that I found it painful and scary and humiliating, but that I liked that part too, she got really uncomfortable. She wanted me to have only positive feelings about the poly sex. I know that it's hard for people to understand—but when it comes to cuckqueaning, just because you might be terrified and sick to your stomach before every event, just because it's painful to watch, doesn't mean that it's not a success. It's a kind of emotional masochism. Without the emotions, it's just kind of pale and boring. While I know that the worst-case scenario isn't going to happen, I can't keep my mind off that scenario, and I even get off on the vague feeling of betrayal. More even than humiliation, this is about eroticizing fear. It's safe jealousy. It's a thrill of risk, the adrenalin of risking the relationship that your whole life is based on. The fact that I can risk it, feel that fear, and have it all be all right afterwards (not to mention the bang-up orgasms I get the first time

I'm allowed to have sex after) really does give me power over that fear. It's like the high of playing dice in Vegas, only I actually do win every time.

When my master goes hunting for boys, it's easier for him, but harder for me. Gay men are cooler about casual sex, and most of them don't care if his girl is sitting there watching, so long as they are not expected to do it with me. A few of them are grossed out enough by anything female that they don't even want me in the room, but my master screens them out before bringing them home. In those cases, he does motel sex, calling me before and after to describe it. Sex with men is more difficult in a lot of ways than sex with pretty women, even. I know for sure they have something I don't. They have cock. They are less needy and clingy, or seem that way to me. They have a tighter-knit leather community that I can't ever get into. They have the Old Guard. They can take a heavier beating than me, and if my master wants something really extreme, they have probably already done it with five other guys. And did I mention cock? I know that not all leathermen are like that, but it's what I tell myself while my master is doing it with them. It's the most humiliating thing of all—for that hour, I am a female nothing in a male world, good for nothing but bringing them drinks afterwards. (I should say again that while this is extra painful, it is also extra hot, and makes me feel extra submissive. And some part of me really is happy that my master is getting needs met that I can't fill.)

Occasionally we will find a F/m couple who is into cuckolding, and with a woman that my master is attracted to. (Or, more rarely, a non-dominant girl whose boyfriend or husband has cuckold "fantasies" and my master is the "stud", which is what they call the cuckolding male.) Then the two of them will have sex together while the two of us kneel on opposite sides of the bed, or take pictures, or help clean up. I remember watching the look on the sub-boy's face the first time we did that—I kept wondering, do I look like that? Suffering, but absolutely alert, attentive, never taking his eyes off them? His breath coming hard, in a way that is more than just pain? He would have been hard if he hadn't been locked in a chastity harness. I kept sneaking looks at him until his mistress noticed that I wasn't paying enough attention and said something degrading that brought me right back to the action. After they were done, we each got to clean the cum off the other person—it was the first time he had ever dealt with cock, licking his wife's juices off my master's condomed cock.

Later I talked to him—and other men like him. We understood each other. Only twice have I connected with other cuckqueans, though. We're just too rare, and when we speak up on Internet forums for submissive women, we horrify the other slave girls and they shout us down for being sick, or doormats.

Cuckold erotica puts a lot of emphasis on the man not being able to satisfy his wife. She degrades him for being a lousy lover or having a tiny cock. That's something that my master has never done with me. He never puts any emphasis on my not being a good enough lover for him, because he says that it would be too obviously a lie for me to convince myself otherwise, and anyway he doesn't want me thinking that. He wants me to believe that he loves me as a lover, but just chooses to be with other people because the one thing I can't give him is variety. That's good, because I can get off on being lower on the totem pole, or being a disgusting slut, or even being nothing, but I can't get off on being completely unattractive or a bad lover. I know that some of the cuckold men I've talked to can get off on that. The human mind is an amazing thing and I'm always blown away by what people can find arousing. Maybe if I tried, I could go there, but I haven't felt the need.

There's also a whole secret vocabulary about the cuckold lifestyle... "hotwife" who wants a monogamous relationship with her "bull" and gives the husband no sex, "slutwife" who has many lovers called "studs", and so forth. Some people into this lifestyle aren't so much into the power dynamic, it's just a kind of threesome foreplay. Some go all the way to entirely celibate husband/slaves with dominatrixes. Somewhere in the middle are submissive women who have masters and whose sub husbands are sub to them, bottom of the totem pole and liking it. All the cuckqueans I've met had male masters and were slaves. Maybe no woman who wasn't submissive would ever do this, I don't know. I've never met gay male cucking couples, even with all of Master's gay exploits, but maybe that's because jealousy and monogamy don't have the same charge for them? I did meet one lesbian cucking couple online, though. But we don't have secret vocabularies yet. I think we're still too ashamed to talk about it, even in fetish circles.

But what about "real" poly in all this, or rather what about more permanent relationships? Well, that happened eventually as well. My master picked up Ross at a gay leather event and brought him home. He had several nights with him, at our place and at his, and then one night we sat down together and he asked he what I thought of Ross. I told him that I liked Ross a lot as a person—he was cute, he was a good slave in that very formal leatherman way, he was always polite to me, and he made my master happy. In fact, he was such a good guy (and I was getting to know him so well) that it was hard for me to feel enough pain about his presence to be turned on. I told my master that. I knew what was coming. He wanted to keep Ross, to collar him. When he told me that, all those feelings came rushing in like crazy. He just looked at my face for a minute, and then he threw me down on the bed and screwed me. He told me later that while he figured it might be more exquisitely tormenting to leave me to my suffering, I was so sexy in that moment of fear, humiliation, and arousal that he had to fuck me right there.

Later that month he collared Ross, and later that night he fucked him in front of me. It was the first time that he had ever fucked anyone but me without a rubber. We'd all exchanged tests and waited the requisite time with no other partners, and the three of us were now fluid bonded. After it was over, he made me clean his limp cock and Ross's ass, which included eating Master's cum. Ross isn't into women, which made it even more humiliating—I was just a maid to do the cleanup. I brought them towels and slept on the floor that night. The next night, Master brought me into bed to talk to me and hold me while Ross slept in the next room. I was torn between wanting to repeat the last night and needing to be in his presence. He somehow knew that my "cunt was getting a little ahead of my heart", as he said, and made me cuddle him and sleep with him. There would be more cuckquean nights, he told me. Right now I needed love. And he was right.

After Ross had been coming over for a while, his presence in my master's bed didn't do it for me anymore. I knew that my master wasn't going to leave me for Ross, and I knew that Ross liked and respected me. Most of me was really happy that I had a slave brother who liked me and was good to me. The parts of me that want to have good poly were happy. But there was that little part of me that wanted the pain, and the sexual high that came with it. I confessed this eventually to Ross, being quick to emphasize again and again that the internal majority vote was absolutely that being secure around him was great. I liked him too much to want him back in that category of random stranger.

I think that if he'd been a woman, he wouldn't have understood me. But gay men are a lot more open to strange fetishes, so he just looked at me quizzically and nodded. Later that week Ross was kneeling on the floor in the bedroom, waiting for our master to come in and use him. Master was in the shower, and I was walking by, and Ross called me in and whispered for me to get down next to him. I did, and he said conspiratorially in my ear, "You know he likes my cocksucking better. You know I give better blowjobs than you. I'll bet that every time you suck his cock, he was wishing it was me." He was grinning at me as he said it, and I knew he didn't mean it … but it made me really hot. Suddenly I was back to feeling like that with him, but it didn't affect the affection we had for each other. It was like we could turn it on and off as needed. Over the next few weeks, he periodically tormented me verbally with images of how much better he was as a slave than me, and even came up with some pretty creative misogynist insults. He's not a misogynist, and he admitted that it took him a while to think them up. We told our master about it, and he laughed for ten minutes, then said that Ross could torment me verbally all he wanted.

So now I know that I can handle "real" poly without a hitch— and it's not like my master isn't going to keep bringing over more strangers to fuck in front of me. He's teased me with the idea of making Ross the alpha slave just to further my cuckquean fantasies, but in the next breath he says that he never will because I'm the live-in married partner who actually runs the house and Ross likes living in his own place. I've toyed with the idea—it's sexy—but I also kind of think that would be going too far for my own comfort. Or maybe not! I am completely sure of my place in my master's heart and life, and who knows how far I can go with eroticizing this lifestyle? Maybe someday he'll have a whole houseful of slaves, and I'll be the bottom of the bottom, only allowed to have sex with him every other Thursday, and forced to watch him get it on with all the rest. You know, I think I could live with that ... and even in that situation I know that if I needed him for some emotional reason, he would be right there for me. He's that kind of wonderful and trustworthy man. How many men could do this and still make me feel loved and worthy at the end of each day? That's why I can trust him to hold this part of me in his hands, and I know he'll never drop me.

PART IV
FAMILIES SPEAK

I'm Poly And You Are Too ... But Only When I Say So

John Riedell and Jennifer

Polyamory is, simply put, a lifestyle choice where each person in a relationship has additional relationships with other people. In the vanilla lifestyle, poly tends to be fairly egalitarian—that is, within a set of agreed-upon guidelines with their primary relationship, each person has the ability to pursue additional relationships as they would like. But what happens if one person in the primary relationship is Master over the other(s)?

Polyamory in a Master/slave relationship is a different animal from polyamory in a vanilla relationship. In a vanilla relationship, partners tend to be equals, while in an M/s relationship, the Master often has unlimited control over their slave(s). Likewise, in vanilla polyamory, both partners will often agree to the same set of guidelines as they enter into additional relationships. In an M/s relationship, these guidelines are more often directives given from the Master to the slave. As our relationship evolved into a stronger M/s dynamic, our views of polyamory, as well as the rules we followed, had to change.

Our History

For some background: When we met, John had three other relationships; two submissives and a mostly vanilla girlfriend. For the most part, he had regular weekly dates with one submissive, meeting the others on a more secondary basis while he lived on his own. On the other hand, jennifer was in a vanilla marriage, with no other serious partners aside from her husband. Jennifer was looking for a Dominant, as it was a role her husband was not comfortable with, and she had agreed with her husband to a once-weekly relationship with John. For various reasons, John's relationship with his primary submissive ended, and jennifer became his primary submissive. At this point, jennifer's marriage was also coming to an end, a process that had begun well before she and her husband became polyamorous.

As jennifer negotiated more time with John, they recognized that their relationship had evolved into more of a Master/slave dynamic. In our dynamic, John prefers to define jennifer as a "daughter-slave". By this, John recognizes the deep emotional bond they share, and also defines his role as a mentor and protector. In contrast, you could picture an "object-slave", or, one who is merely a piece of property to be used as the Master sees fit. While not a perfect picture of our relationship, you could look at "The Nine Levels of Submission" by Diane Vera, as published in *The Lesbian S/M Safety Manual*. Jennifer started off near a level one (Kinky Sensualist), but is now closer to a level eight (Full-Time Live-In Consensual Slave).

She was collared, and by the next year we moved in together to live as a 24/7 Master/slave couple. Shortly after moving in, John presented jennifer with her slave contract. This contract dealt partially with her duties as a slave, but was mostly crafted to define how the relationship would function with the change to an M/s relationship. As jennifer strives to get to a point of giving up all her decisions to John, some basic understandings had to be put down on paper. Part of this was to make John's rights and responsibilities clear as her Master, but it was also to remind jennifer what she had agreed to as John's slave. As we had both started out in polyamorous relationships, the transition from a more vanilla style of polyamory to an M/s polyamory was reflected as well. The contract was written by John, with some input from jennifer, so all first person statements are from John.

The Contract

I own you. I will protect you.

This first statement sets the stage. Primarily, it defines jennifer's relationship to John as his property. It also offers the reassurance that, no matter what, as his property, she is valuable to him. Just as one would not crash their own car for fun, John will look to jennifer's care and use the power she has surrendered to him to take care of her. As this applies to our polyamorous lifestyle, these words also mean that John will protect her from STDs by practicing safer sex, as well as protect her mentally and emotionally by not associating with persons who are not trustworthy. Lastly, this also reflects John's role as a father figure in their relationship.

> **Relationships:** I am free to pursue other relationships totally at my own discretion. You are limited to pursuing additional subs/slaves for my household (may be female, male or transgendered) and relationships with single females or where your only sexual contact would be with the female of a male/female couple.

The first section of jennifer's contract deals directly with polyamory. Both of us agree that as Master, John is allowed the freedom to pursue whatever relationships he would like to. As slave, jennifer's interactions are much more limited. This is parallel to the idea that just as a daughter wouldn't tell her father what to do or whom to date, jennifer wouldn't tell John these things either. But, as her authority figure, John has the right to approve of the women she is dating. Likewise, he also has the jurisdiction to tailor her interactions to suit his tastes and desires. Jennifer had a very limited sexual history, and has become more interested in exploring her interest in other women. As John would like to add another female slave to the household in the future, jennifer is encouraged in her explorations.

> I will give careful consideration to the compatibility of who I allow into my household, and both of us will work mindfully towards harmonious integration.

This clause serves two purposes. First, it is a reassurance for jennifer that John's primary interest in adding slaves or submissives into the house is to add to the pleasure of the environment. John is not interested in polyamory as a contest, or in having slaves for the sake of having slaves. Also, as jennifer joined the house as a daughter-slave, John would like to find an addition to serve as a similar daughter- and sister-slave. Both John and jennifer have made a commitment to each other as primary partners, so any additions to the house should match well with both partners.

Second, jennifer requested the addition of "both of us will work mindfully towards harmonious integration" to serve as a reminder for her. While not having a final say in any decision, jennifer serves an additional role of trusted advisor, and she knows that her opinions and thoughts are considered when John is making any decision. She is often stubborn, and one of her personal goals is to practice patience and be able to take a step back in the heat of the moment and look at the whole situation.

> ***Sex:*** *You will have sex when and with whom you are directed to. Proper protection will always be used with any individual with whom we are not fluid-bonded.*

Again, this clause serves two purposes. First, it reminds jennifer that John is the Master in this relationship, and his word is law. If he decides that someone should be considered as a potential member of his household, it is jennifer's job to make sure that this person feels welcome. As is also stated in her contract, jennifer is expected to be completely obedient in her tasks, so she will make certain that she also performs this duty with genuine enthusiasm. For John, this also reaffirms that he has pledged to protect jennifer, so that if he is not completely satisfied that a potential partner is trustworthy and disease-free, he will insist on proper protection to maintain safer sex practices.

For jennifer, this clause also serves as a reminder for her. In this case, jennifer knows that she is sometimes quick to rush to judgment, or to dismiss someone because they are not her ideal. As part of her growth as a person, jennifer is committed to learning that real life is not a fairy tale. As part of this learning experience, she also needs to learn to let John control all aspects of any new relationship. By having more than one set of eyes look at a potential addition to the household, you can more easily get a complete picture of what this potential addition actually is.

> ***Orgasms:*** *You will not purposefully cause yourself to orgasm or allow yourself to orgasm unless you have permission.*

With so much of this contract, this clause serves to once again establish John as the primary authority figure in the relationship. No matter what the sexual situation, whether it is just John and jennifer, jennifer and another partner, or John/jennifer/another slave, jennifer must always remember to ask for permission before she allows herself to orgasm. This kind of control has been a challenge for jennifer to learn, but it has also made her incredibly mindful of what she is doing, and how those actions might lead to an orgasm. With this kind of mindfulness, she is indirectly always thinking of John. As other slaves are considered to join the house, this contract is shared with them. By doing so, not only will they understand the nature of John and jennifer's relationship, but they will also know what kind of controls they will be expected to follow as well. This is a clause that John will expect of all his slaves.

> ***Initiative:*** *Obedience to all expected standards is admirable. You are also commanded to use your creativity to envision better ways of serving me.*

While this clause comes further down the contract, it also has found its importance in polyamory. For example, John is currently considering another slave, whom jennifer is dating as well. Of course, she is showing obedience in primarily acting as a good example to the potential slave, as well as paying careful attention to her own sexual duties to John. But in addition to serving her own duties as John's slave, she has independently taken on an informal role as mentor to the new slave. Not only is jennifer sharing John's preferences in things such as how the house is kept clean, but she is also sharing what kinds of stimulation she has learned that John particularly enjoys. One might think jennifer would want to keep these "trade secrets" to herself, so she could better keep herself as John's primary slave. But in sharing these tricks, she is better serving John, as she is making sure that he would always be cared for as he likes.

> *This contract may be amended as new situations arise.*

Just as John and jennifer's relationship has progressed quite a long way in the past two years, it is unrealistic to assume that the way things are now is the way things will always be. When another slave is added to the household, jennifer's role may also include official duties to mentor her sister-slave. If John chooses instead to add a Domme to the household, there will have to be changes made in the other direction, providing definition and guidance to jennifer in relation to her new Mistress. Both John and jennifer are fans of flexibility; John doesn't want to play the endless game of "What if..." and jennifer doesn't *always* want to be tied up, as it were.

Our Advice to You

Do we claim to be unquestionable experts in M/s Polyamory? Absolutely not. But there are some things we have learned on our journey that are worth taking into consideration as you embark on your own path. First, for both Master and slave, you should have a good idea of what you want, and whether it is realistic. As a Master, do you want a household where you are the Matriarch/Patriarch, or just the less formal person in charge? What kind of relationships or interaction do you desire between your slaves? Two individuals could be very pleasing slaves by themselves, but they may not fit well in a household together. As you build your household, be sure to communicate to prospective slaves what you envision for your household.

Likewise, as a slave, you should know what role you find most rewarding. Do you need to be valued as a precious jewel, or are you happier being used as an object? Would you feel more secure as a primary slave, or a secondary slave? How much of a say would you like to have in who joins your Master's household? If you are looking for a household to join, knowing your preferences and limits are useful for starting a discussion with a Dominant/Master, and will also help you to find a place where you feel most comfortable. As a wise man once said, it is impossible to explain to another what you want if you don't know yourself.

Above all, practice patience. There are probably quite a few people out there who are a great fit for what you are looking for. The problem, of course, is finding them. For those of you in a primary relationship, we're sure that you had to kiss quite a few frogs before finding that prince/ss. With each experience you have that doesn't quite work out, there is a lesson to be learned. By practicing patience, you can help to keep yourself from getting discouraged in your journey.

If you are already in an M/s relationship, and would like to open yourselves up to polyamory, remember that any good M/s relationship is built on trust. A slave must be able to trust their Master/Mistress completely in order to give up control to them. Once that trust is damaged, as in a scene gone horribly wrong or a sudden addition of another player, it can be very difficult to build back up. From the beginning of our relationship, we have always agreed to full honesty and complete disclosure. With this solid foundation, we have faced many different situations, from breakups to new beginnings, and knowing that we can always trust each other has made it easier to face any new situation that may arise.

Polyamory, M/s and Parenting

Kyra of Mists

One topic that people often ask about is living poly and/or M/s while also living with kids. We are a poly M/s family. The three of us live together and we have four children that range in age from 11-17. We have lived together since December of 2007 and have been in a relationship since April of 2005 when the kids ages were between 6-12. The youngest two children cannot vividly remember a time that I was not in their life.

His parents know about us, Alandra's mom knows, and my parents have a really good idea but they have no desire to know the details. For all of them, what is important is that we are happy and the kids are happy. As a family friend who is a Catholic priest describes our relationship, we are a "marriage of three". That is how we live our life.

We do not hide that the three of us are in a relationship inside our home; outside our home we are more discreet depending on where we are. We do not hide that he is the boss in our relationship. The kids are fully aware that Daddy is the ultimate decision-maker in the family. They are also aware that Alandra and I need his permission to do certain things.

As an example, she and I are not allowed to have junk food without his permission. When the oldest makes cookies she will ask me if I want her to save me cookie dough so I can "ask Dad for some". She will also hear me ask permission for it; once she didn't hear me ask permission for a second spoonful and when I went to get it she said, "Hey, you only asked permission for one spoonful!" I just looked at her with a little grin and stuck the spoon in my mouth. Her comment then was "Oh, I guess you asked for a second one." They all know that he is the boss and that their mom and I would not disobey him.

They know that our relationship is different and that others will not have a relationship like ours. They see Alandra and I tie his shoes, put his jacket on, lay out his clothes and we also refer to him as "my Lord" in front of them. They also know that we all sleep in the same bed and they see physical affection that is appropriate between the three of us. We hug, kiss, hold hands, cuddle and to them it is normal behavior for their family. They also know that I am fiercely protective of their mom and will not let them get away with being disrespectful to her. They know that their mom and I let their dad fight his own battles. They know that when their mom and I speak that it is as good as their dad telling them to do it. He is the ultimate decision-maker and we are his senior officers carrying out his orders.

We have all three gone to parent-teacher conferences for the kids. We went for the oldest last year in the 11th grade and her teacher's comments were "Wow, it is great to see so many people caring about her education." The teacher didn't ask any questions about who I was or what I was doing there; she just thought it wonderful that our daughter had three adults caring about her education.

The kids refer to me as "Mom's friend" at school and they understand that some things are private and for family only. The youngest has had a friend over many times and his comment is "It is so cool that you have two moms." His parents are split up and he has a single mom; he thought it was awesome that his friend had two moms. At various times all the kids have referred to me as Mom, then they kind of laugh or shake their head at themselves and say "I mean Kyra."

The kids are also aware that in having three adults in the house that they get privileges that they otherwise would not be able to enjoy. Having three incomes in the house greatly increases our ability to do entertaining things like spend two weeks at Disney World, send the oldest two girls to New York on a school trip, and put all three girls in dance lessons. We also have several gaming systems, computers, large house, multiple pets, multiple cars ... all things that are not necessities that having three incomes makes possible.

Also, all three of us are on the title of the house and vehicles. We all share bank accounts, though there are several so that certain funds come out of one and not the other. Our life is extremely integrated together, and the kids know this and there is no negative impact on their life. They have sleepover parties, hot tub parties, birthday parties, friends over, boyfriends over and any of the other normal kid stuff. At one point a boyfriend was over and our daughter was supposed to be doing dishes, but she had her boyfriend doing them. She was standing in the doorway of the kitchen making sure he did it right. As she was standing there, she realized that her shoe was untied and very casually said, "Oh look, my shoe is untied." Her boyfriend stopped washing her dishes, walked over, knelt down and tied her shoes. When he was done, she thanked him and he went back to washing her dishes. So even though she sees her female parental figure submitting, she knows she can make her own choice for her relationships regardless of gender.

The bonus for the kids is that they have three adults to turn to when they need or want us. Just recently, our oldest came to us wanting birth control pills. She had a boyfriend and she wanted to have the option open to have sex with him. Alandra and I spent a lot of time talking with her about the pros and cons of having sex, and her comfort level was strong enough that she even talked to her dad about it. We didn't freak out over her request, but we did make her do research. She was telling a friend about what she asked us and her friend's comment was "You did what? You told your parents!" Then our daughter said, "Yeah, I have to do research about it." The friend laughed and said "Another research project from your parents!" Apparently we have her research a lot of things from her friend's perspective. (This is the same friend that came and sat with Alandra and myself during our daughter's last birthday party. All the kids were downstairs and her friend would come upstairs to sit and hang out with us. She doesn't have as comfortable of a relationship with her mom and envies our daughter's relationship with us.) In the end, our daughter broke up with her boyfriend without having sex. It was a rather painful breakup because he lied to her about prior sexual information and she felt betrayed. We were there for her then too; we supported her in her decisions and in grieving over the loss of the relationship.

Honestly, I could go on and on about all these little examples that show how well the three of us fit together and how happy the kids are in an open poly M/s relationship. Alandra and I use hand signals to ask permission to speak with him. They work so well that a few of the kids have picked up the habit as well. They will try to get their dad's attention verbally and if that doesn't work, they will use a hand signal and it works really well. They haven't been told to do this; they just see what works for us and they are learning the most effective way to communicate with their dad as a result.

This is just a small taste of what we as a family are like. The M/s activities and poly life for us is not hidden or feared in this house. It is a life that we embrace and acknowledge with the children as being different and unique from the norm of society. Of course, what is the norm? We are living our way of life in a manner that is enhancing and growing for all members of our family even though it's not the way of most.

Interview With A Polyamorous Power Exchange Household

This interview was conducted by Raven Kaldera with a polyamorous household in western Massachusetts, whose members practiced a variety of interesting power exchanges involved. I interviewed them about how they manage their household and interesting combination of relationships. They were wonderfully open and honest with me about their continually evolving and intricate balance of love and power, and there's much wisdom to be found in their musings about power exchange, polyamory, legalities, spirituality, and practical relationships.

The Household

Micah: *38 years old, the "top/dominant/daddy/master/guy in charge/whatever's working that day" of Aimee, although he points out that they don't use titles much.*

Aimee: *29 years old, bottom/submissive of Micah, and legally married wife of Michelle.*

Michelle: *30 years old, legally married wife of Aimee for 10 years (poly for 4 years). Involved with Ian, and his submissive, but somewhat dominant (to an extent) over the others. She says, "Aimee and I both identify as switches. She's a much more submissive-leaning switch, which is what led us to open up our relationship. I'm a more dominant-leaning switch, but that fluctuates with the day."*

Ian: *39 years old, "for the most part a dominant," and involved with Michelle, who also says, "Ian and I have been involved for about three years. We had a dominant-submissive contract for a year— with me being on the submissive end—but now we're trying to figure out where to go next."*

The Interview:

RK: So how do your individual power dynamics work? What are the rules?

Micah: Aimee and I have a contract. We first started with a year and a day contract, to mesh with our Pagan philosophies and faith. That expired in June. We then signed a seven-year contract, so now she's really stuck with me! Our contract very much reflects who we are as people, because part of our dynamic and part of our personalities is that both of us are "littles". So if you read our contract, that would shine through loud and clear. The title of the contract is "Da Rulz" and it says things like, "The dominant, he can haz the power." And it just gets sillier from there. So it very much reflects who we are.

Aimee: There's some serious stuff in there, mixed in with the silly, but I think we kept most of it very light-hearted, even where there are very D/s things. Like I'm supposed to ask him before I eat, that kind of very structured thing. But we're very playful about most of our relationship.

Micah: For example, she's not allowed to smoke cigarettes—because it's no fun to kiss ashtrays—and that's actually in the contract, along with a whole host of other things like that.

Aimee: But the actual written contract ... came after a year or more's worth of talking about it. The circumstances in our lives had to change before we could actually do it.

Micah: When we first met, I was living with someone else. That relationship ended 2 years ago this December ... It put a serious limit on what we could do and how we could express our dynamic. She knew about it, but she kind of wished that she didn't. The dynamic that she and I had was switching daily. Even days was one, odd days was the other, and that worked for a while. But I don't think that she was ever comfortable with me having another partner that was mostly submissive all the time, because it felt like a threat to her. It also didn't help that my previous partner was slightly older than me, and Aimee is ten years younger. So there was also the threat of "the beautiful younger woman who is a lawyer, she's better than me and has more education" and all that stuff. For a lot of reasons, that relationship collapsed, and when it did, we almost immediately started taking the theoretical conversations we'd been having and turning it serious.

Aimee: But it still took us a good six months before we actually wrote it all down. We started implementing some rules and some protocol, but it was about six months before we were ready to sign something.

Micah: We signed it on my birthday the following June after I moved in. You were the best birthday gift ever.

Aimee: When we sit down to talk about something, we talk about it as equals.

Micah: Yeah, we step out of our roles. Technically we're 24/7, but it's not like I'm always In-Charge-Grrr-Domly-Dom! That's not how we operate. It's not like Aimee is always simpering and following around behind me, trying to anticipate my every move. That's just not the way our relationship works.

Aimee: I wouldn't be able to do that. Not with my job. I need to have my days mostly free of restrictions on what I'm doing, otherwise I wouldn't be able to get anything done.

Micah: And that 24/7 thing wouldn't work for us anyway, because if she's always in submissive headspace ... well, how does that work with her wife? How does that work with Ian? Because we all live together, and that type of thinking and acting, all day, every day, just wouldn't work. There is still an undercurrent of "you're the one in charge, and that's good," though.

Aimee: There are rules that I always follow; I can ask for a break from them if I'm going out on a date with Michelle, so that I can have that time off. Like, I want these three hours to not have to check in with you about food.

RK: What can you say no to, and how do you go about that?

Aimee: One of the biggest rules for us is about food. I'm supposed to ask him before I eat something. That's because I have health problems, and he's keeping an eye on me, making sure I'm not doing too many things that are bad for me. But I get one meal off a week so that I can eat what I want, when I want. I usually use that for going out to dinner with Michelle and her family, or going on a date with Michelle, or I have to go to some lawyer-schmoozey thing and I don't want to have to text him to say, "Can I have a cocktail?" It would be awkward. We've also recently come to an arrangement where between the hours of 9 and 5 on a typical workday, if he asks me to do something, I have the option of saying, "I really can't right now, I'm too busy with work."

Micah: Because this way, her work time is her time, and the rest of the time is mine if I want it. Of course, in the real world, we're really busy people, so entire weeks will go by where we don't really have the opportunity to do anything except what we're obligated to do. But it's now written in so that if it's ten o'clock at night and I tell her to do something, she's expected to do it, and if she doesn't there's consequences. We do use a punishment dynamic, although we don't do that very often, not because she's a perfect sub, but I think of it the same way you would discipline a child. The threat of the rod is often worse than the rod itself. So if she does something so bad that I have to take Lord Voldemort to her ... er, I'm sorry, we have a leather blackjack that we jokingly referred to as the Dark Lord and it stuck, and being littles, he's now Lord Voldemort. So if I have to take Lord Voldemort out, it was really bad. I try not to do that too often. It's written into the contract that I can if I want to, but it's at my discretion. Everything's at my discretion. If I wanted to, I could beat her every day ... but what's the point in that? It starts to lose its effectiveness if you're doing it every day.

A punishment scene is never fun. One of the things that we do most often for fun is spanking scenes. Aimee got her start in kink as a spanko, so we do a lot of OTK, we do a lot of caning. But when we do a punishment scene, all of the things that we do that she likes for fun, none of it happens. There's no warmup. She prefers to be spanked with my hand; that doesn't happen. She's not over my lap. Everything about it is as impersonal as possible, so it emphasizes This Is Not Fun. Which is why I don't like to do it very much, and thankfully I don't have to.

RK: And Michelle and Ian?

Ian: I was married to another person when I moved into this house, and I'm currently going through a divorce. That process has put a lot of pressure on us. First, it's shifted all the dynamics in the house. Everything came into question and we had to reset it. Michelle and I are working through what the new dynamic is. Similarly, we went through a long process as equals to form a contract...

Michelle: ... and very specifically set it for a year and a day, and set it as a speculative period of exploration. During that time, we moved in together.

Ian: And then a wide variety of life started happening. We all moved in together, and that was very stressful. I ended up getting laid off.

Michelle: Aimee was laid off. Then Micah was laid off. And I went from being in academia and working on my PhD to holding a 9 to 5 job., so I completely changed my life as they were completely changing their lives.

Ian: And then I started going through this divorce. So through that process, the contract did not get the attention that it needed. Life had come down as a ton of bricks, and while I was able to start my own practice and be an independent contractor, it's still very volatile and difficult to predict one week from another. So in the midst of all this chaos, Michelle and I are continuing to question and explore how the roles are going to fall out.

Michelle: We began with Aimee and I living together, separately from Micah and his ex-partner, and Ian was living with his wife at the time over an hour away. We met online for the purpose of meeting once a month to play. It evolved very quickly into a relationship. Part of the reason that Aimee and I initially opened up our relationship is that we had gotten into the BDSM world.

Aimee: We'd been exploring between the two of us, trying to play with power exchange, but because we are both switches, one or the other wasn't being fulfilled at any given time. I'm a very submissive-leaning switch; I top only when it's fun. Michelle found it very difficult to always have to be the one in control, so our opening up was to allow us to explore in that way.

Michelle: Because while you have fun topping, you have no interest in dominating.

Ian: Yeah, oftentimes when you top, there's another one of us in the scene instructing you one what to do!

Micah: But that works. There are fewer things in life more sadistic than a 6-year-old child.

Aimee: And when I'm in that role, I can be a very mean little 6-year-old!

Michelle: So anyway, when Ian and I met, the intention was once a month, nothing deep; but that quickly changed when we found out that we had a lot in common. We had a lot of the same goals and vision, and I got along really well with his wife. We became friends, and then all of us became friends! But the more I got involved in the BDSM scene, and the closer Micah and Aimee got, the more I had a craving to explore what it would be like to have a formal arrangement with somebody, in terms of being a submissive. So eventually that's the route that we took. Our contract at the time was much more serious and formal-protocol based than Aimee and Micah.

Ian: We were also chasing a lot of traditional models at the time that turned out to not necessarily be us. We are exploring a lot about service and tradition and protocol, much more than just kink. Service is important to both of us.

Michelle: We've gone from trying to fulfill a dominant-submissive model that we had seen in other people's relationships in the public scene, and things that we had read, to something that works more for the dynamic we actually have, which is much more of a "head of household/mistress of household" way of doing things. One of the models he talks about is the "southern gentleman"; he's very into service himself, but as a way of...

Ian: ...Of being a good host, being gracious, providing for my guests, but still with a level of control.

Michelle: Part of why that works is that I end up fulfilling a majordomo role. I'm taking care of the finances, the correspondence, the daily running of the household, the calendaring. That's a service to the whole house, and to the quad. Although I don't see Micah or Aimee as my dominants, the ideal of our household is something that I'm serving.

Aimee: I'm also in service to the household in my own way. I like to cook, to make sure that everyone has a nice meal, that the house is clean. I spent most of Wednesday mopping the floors and scrubbing out the fireplace. I like that kind of service to the household. I'm definitely the bottom of the totem pole when it comes to our family.

Ian: I heard you once talk about the "rock star dominant"—Michelle does a lot of service for the household, but she also does that kind of service for me. I travel a lot, and she helps me with finding out about the new location, who I should set up appointments with and see, how I get from one place to another. Which I appreciate to no end! It's a very different dynamic than Aimee and Micah have. But there's also a dynamic between the four of us in the house. Michelle alluded to that. There's an element of a parental role between Michelle and myself towards the other two.

Micah. Absolutely. We're the "littles". You're the "bigs". Sometimes I'm Aimee's "big", but usually when you two aren't around.

Michelle: My submission is discretely bound in time and place. While I prefer to be in a dominant role, I enjoy being able to be "little" once in a while and enjoy macaroni and cheese and coloring in a coloring book, in order to release some of that. I'll have Juice Box Night, where I get to be little and I don't have to worry about the finances or my adult responsibilities. But that's very much an occasional fun role and not a natural part of my life. It's a balancing mechanism. Whereas for them, it's much more natural.

Micah: Aimee and I drift in and out of "little-space" constantly, and even from the very beginning we were very adept at reading each other's cues, and picking it up and running with it when the other would signal a change. We just seemed to instinctively "get it". It was kind of frightening, actually.

Aimee: But at the same time, having adults around when you're being children is a very important thing.

Michelle: Because we can regulate you when you're getting a little exuberant.

Micah: Of the four of us, Ian is always the "big", the house Daddy. But he enjoys being a "big" to "littles". That's a part of ageplay that people don't know much about. They hear "ageplay" and they think "diapers", adult babies, all that sort of thing. They don't stop and think about all the other ways you can play with age.

Michelle: But I'm a very serious person. I take myself and my life very seriously all the time, and I need the influence of people who can embrace the levity.

RK: What labels do you use for yourselves? What fits?

Michelle: Well, we all embrace polyamorous.

Micah: To use the lingo of an LJ community I'm on—Bi Poly Pagan Geek Gamer Kinkster—I'm a 5 out of 6. I'm only situationally bisexual, which means I'm open to the idea, but they'd better be licking my boots. Which is why I think that the one experience I had in that area didn't work—we came to it as equals, and it had no interest for me whatsoever. But ... having a little boy to play with ... that's different. I don't call myself queer usually, but that depends on the day. I'm definitely a dominant. I tried the switching thing and it just did not work for me. And now I've got this fun little subbie-girl here who enjoys service, so when I tell her to do some activity normally associated with the bottoming side to me, I can tell her what to do and she'll do it. So it's domming from the bottom.

Aimee: I usually call myself queer. I'll call myself pansexual if I think that the other person will understand that term, but usually I'll go with queer or bisexual because it's more easily understood. I identify as submissive with occasional topping tendencies, but not dominant. Of the four of us, I am the odd man out—I am not a geek. I am a geek-lover.

Michelle: I also have the issue of using pansexual when I think the audience will understand. I used to teach gender studies at the university, and it was really great to screw with the kids' heads and get them to think about what that meant. But mostly I end up identifying as bisexual and as a switch. I'm all over the D/s spectrum; it depends on the day. I top Aimee, I have other friends in the public scene that I top. Publicly, lately, I tend to top rather than bottom or submit.

Ian: I don't identify as queer, although Michelle calls me a lesbian.

Michelle. Yeah, I call him my big fuzzy dyke, because he is more of a lesbian than my wife has ever been.

Ian: I'm not religious on the labels. I do use polyamorous, I do use kinky and dominant, but none of those are rigid terms.

RK: When you guys decide things as a household, is it all egalitarian?

Aimee: It depends on what kind of household decision we're making. In general, Ian and Michelle handle the operational things like getting the bills paid. But if we have to make a really fundamental decision we sit down as equals.

Ian: The majority of the decisions are made as equals. But there are times when Michelle and I, in this pseudo-parental role, will also make decisions for them, or definitely have a path already proposed, with an explanation. "We need to do this" versus

"What shall we do?" But that's also because we have insight into the operational facets.

Michelle: I think that we end up taking charge of the operational day-to-day because we have a sense of the overlying philosophy that we all share. So because we have a sense of our values as a quad, we can then make some of those day-to-day decisions without their direct input. It's also the way that we use our individual strengths. I'm a very organized, concrete, sequential sort of person. And Aimee's ... not.

Ian: I tend to be much more a "path" or "vision" person. This is one reason why Michelle and I work really well together. We have insights, and then figure out how we get that done, and what are the details, and do we have to change the vision or the operation?

RK: Can you be voted down? Does your authority stick?

Ian: We rarely do the "This is the way it's going to be," against the wishes of the rest of the group. That doesn't tend to work well here. Even Aimee, at the bottom of the totem pole, has the right to block a decision if she thinks it's wrong. Whenever anyone tries to make a unilateral call, it has an impact across the quad.

Michelle: Every decision impacts everyone else. Every dynamic affects everyone else. When they put together their contract, all four of us talked about it, and provisions were put in for other partners.

Aimee: We wrote in how Michelle got worked into the dynamic. And when they wrote their contract, it was the same idea. There was a provision for Ian's wife, and for me.

Michelle: It was important to me that there was a way to step outside of the roles. Our contracts have ways to step out of role built in, as protocol. There had to be a way for me to request that.

It's a very rare and serious thing, to get a safe space to step out of our roles and communicate as equals. Especially when it came to communication with his wife! I did not want to feel like I had to be submissive to her.

Ian: Furthermore, we are active in the community, and we've taken leadership roles, and I did not want her to be in a leadership and a submissive position at the same time. I wanted her to go out there and be herself and teach.

Michelle: As an example, I was on the board of a BDSM organization, and while we were at that particular club with me as his submissive, I wasn't allowed to use the furniture. However, when I became a board member, we discussed that rule and decided that when I am there in my capacity as a board member I have permission to use furniture as I see fit. It's what's appropriate for the circumstance.

Ian: Our contract was about growth, and part of that growth was working in our community, so she had to go there and be authoritative and take that position. It was very important for me, in service to that contract, that she be the best person she could.

Michelle: And while the whole point of my not being able to use furniture was to remind me of the role that I was taking, being able to then sit on the furniture reminded me of the role I was taking as a leader in my community. It was all very conscious.

RK: How much clout do you have with each other's dynamics?

Aimee: Micah and I don't let it change things too much. But we also have an understanding that if, say, Michelle and I want to go away for the weekend, then that weekend is off the rules because I'm not going to be around him, I'm going to be around Michelle the whole time. But we needed to come to that agreement before

I went away. Some rules still apply—I would never dream of having a cigarette just because I'm out with Michelle.

Ian: But it's all a matter of negotiation. I enjoy pipes and cigars. One of the things that we've talked about but haven't executed is that Aimee has a curiosity about cigar service. We've already started the discussions about her lighting them in service, though not smoking them.

Michelle: There's definitely a respect for their rules, and the things that they've decided. That's because they don't have any major rules that are arbitrary. They're based on health and betterment. There's nothing that is limiting to how we can interact.

Micah: It also helps that Michelle knows that I am not a dick. The rule around here is "Don't Be A Dick." I don't pull any of that bullshit power-play crap with the other members of the quad. When Aimee and Michelle went away together last spring, that meant that Michelle was in charge of her and managed things, and everything was fine. So because I show that I'm flexible, Michelle is also willing to work within the system that we've worked out.

Michelle: And when Ian and I have had a more formal system, Aimee and Micah were definitely a part of helping us. Even though I tend to be a more dominant personality than Micah and Aimee, and I tend to take a dominant role in terms of our everyday life, when it came to an agreement I had made to a certain submission, and they wanted to take an active role in enforcing that submission to Ian, that worked for me. Because I respect them as people. A lot of our dominance and submission was based in us working towards becoming better, stronger, more capable people. When I was working on my dissertation and I had orders to be studying eight hours a day, they were willing to help me focus on that, and I was willing to let them help me even if I might not listen if it was them randomly telling me to do something. That worked because we have a close dynamic between the four of us.

Ian: Mixing the poly with the power exchange ... we do sit down and talk. We talk a lot, and we respect each other.

Micah: It's not just respect, it's love. And trust. Ian and I are not romantically or sexually involved, but we do love each other very much. Our family unit is pretty solid.

Ian: Even with all the crazy dynamics ... Aimee and I have had several conversations of "Aimee, can I pour you another cup of coffee?" And when I do that, I'm also asking her, "Am I crossing a boundary?" Just because it's only Aimee and I here on a given day, I'm not going to take dominant advantage of her without asking, "Does this violate a rule you have with Micah?"

Aimee: And sometimes it is OK, and sometimes it's not.

Ian: And that's perfectly acceptable. So we're back to "Don't Be A Dick."

RK: Besides "Don't Be A Dick", if you could give people advice on how to do this, what would you tell them?

Micah: The second thing is to never stop talking. Communicate, communicate, communicate. Because if you don't, you're going to fail.

Aimee: And also, talk as equals, at least in the beginning. When you're actually trying to arrange a poly dynamic and make all the pieces fit, everyone has to have some control over how it's going to be. Yeah, I'm Micah's submissive, but when we're sitting down as the four of us, we're equals, and that helps. At the very least, equal in that my input is taken seriously, and that Micah can't tell me what my opinion is on a particular subject that affects the four of us.

Ian: We all come from a wide variety of experiences, and we respect that in each other. If Aimee mentions something about a legal precedent, nobody's going to stomp on her. That's part of her expertise.

Michelle: We do meet as equals. Not everyone is involved in everyone else's power dynamic. When we lived with Ian's wife who wasn't into BDSM, the five of us made decisions as a group of equals, and it was very important that the power dynamics were off the table then. I think it might be very different in a situation where the power dynamics were observed between everyone, so that somebody was the submissive of the house, or the submissive of the whole group.

Aimee: Where the difference here is that, for example, the two of you might be resentful if you thought that my voice was being tempered by what Micah was telling me to do.

Micah: I think that the biggest mistake that people make when they try to do this is that they fall for the fantasy of it. They think that 24/7 means that the master is always going to be sitting in his Barcalounger, waiting for his martini every night, and the submissive is always going to be naked, or dressed provocatively, always attentive and ready to serve—the eternal scene! And that's just not possible! Maybe for a weekend, but even that's hard to maintain! Just a few hours is hard at the end of a long week. And then when reality doesn't match the fantasy, they quickly become disillusioned.

Ian: I think there are some balances that have to be made between life and these roles. Putting a BDSM relationship together with a poly relationship is not easy. It's about being willing to work. It's not always going to be what you expect, but don't give up! Don't abandon what you have in front of you. It's not just going to take sweat, it's going to take blood—but it comes back tenfold. For those who are willing to go through the hard work, it's worth it.

Michelle: I think that one of the biggest things that I've learned is that open communication is absolutely critical with partners who are not involved with the D/s aspect. I would not get involved in another situation where someone was not comfortable with the power dynamic.

RK: How do you include partners who are not involved with that? I notice that two of you have broken up with partners you weren't in power dynamics with.

Aimee: It was difficult when Ian's wife lived in the household and she did not approve of the power dynamics, partially on feminist grounds. She didn't like the way that Micah talked to me, and it didn't matter that I said, "No, I really enjoy this, I like getting him his dinner." It bothered her when she would be in the room and Micah would tell me to fix him a plate. That would be fairly innocuous for some people, but because she knew we had that dynamic, for her it had a lot of baggage—she read a lot into the way that we related to each other even though I didn't feel that we were being particularly D/s at that moment. It's just that the way that he talks to me always has that taste, I guess.

Micah: Any request I made of Aimee, because I was the dominant, meant to her that we were "scening" in front of her, playing in front of her, and not respecting her boundaries, when it was just part of how we do things.

Aimee: Micah and I tried hard not to be obvious about our D/s in front of her, but she was hyperaware of it.

Michelle: She had another boyfriend and was also poly, so it wasn't a poly issue. It wasn't a kink issue either, because she and her boyfriend were kinky, but in a bedroom way, not a D/s way. The D/s component made her very uncomfortable. She and Ian had been together for 20 years, but when she was around, I wasn't comfortable having any kind of a power dynamic, because I did not want to be submissive around her. So it affected our dominance and submission as well.

Micah: So the point is that if you involve someone who isn't part of any D/s dynamic, they have to at least be tolerant of it. They can't be hostile, because that just doesn't work.

Ian: I think it has to go further than that. they have to have some appreciation for it, because they need to be able to go to their partner and say, "I recognize that you have this need."

RK: So how do you deal with the practicalities of having a four-person relationship?

Michelle: Aimee and I are legally married in the state of Massachusetts. We have a civil union in Connecticut, which will soon be a marriage there as well. So we have a legal tie. Micah is legally divorced from his former wife. Ian is in the process of legally divorcing his wife. So we're all in different legal states.

Aimee: We have a plan; we just haven't implemented it yet. We're waiting for the final divorce to go through. I'm an attorney, and I like working with alternative families and doing estate planning for non-hetero-normative families. So my plan for us is to take advantage of small business law and create an LLC (Limited Liability Corporation) where we would all be members of the LLC, and the LLC would own our property. It would be a way of protecting us from liability and giving us legal ties to each other. And since we own a company together, we can have life insurance policies on each other, that kind of thing. One of the things I really want to do is to make sure that I have a durable health care proxy and power of attorneys reciprocally for all of us, because right now if Michelle was to be in an accident, I'm the only one who would be legally allowed into the hospital. Ian would have no rights.

Micah: If both of them were involved in an accident, Ian and I would not be able to do anything. We'd be at the mercy of their families. You never know what's going to happen, and you might not be able to defend yourself. You just don't know.

Aimee: You never know what grief is going to do to someone. So you need those legal provisions. Further, the four of us are talking about having children—biological children—and thinking about the legal complications of that, and what influence all the different dynamics will have.

Micah: Well, to cover all the bases what we'll have to do is to have Ian and I marry! *(Laughter.)* Yeah, we've all joked about it, but in all seriousness it might be a good way to protect us.

Ian: We've gone through several silly scenarios, like where Micah and Aimee would have a child and Michelle and I would adopt it, and vice versa. And there is a legitimate argument for Micah and I getting married.

Micah: It would work like this: Massachusetts has a presumption of paternity in a marriage. So if Aimee and I make a baby, then it is presumed legally that Michelle is one of the parents. So if I marry Ian, he's also presumed to be a parent.

Aimee: This is all very theoretical, of course. I don't how it would work in practice. I think that it would be worth the argument in court; I don't know how well it would fly. It's all untried legally, it's shaky ground.

Micah: Completely untried territory. But I bet we could make it stick. It would be worth the argument, and then you could write a law review article about it.

Michelle: Especially since in and of itself, Aimee and I are a same-sex couple. Which is new ground already. What does presumption of paternity mean in a situation where we could never have a biological child together?

Ian: So we are charging into the gray area of the law. But I think that there's also a conscious decision to challenge these things. We've been involved in leather leadership, we've been involved in poly leadership, and Pagan leadership too—we definitely have an activist streak. Hey, what are we going to do today? Go out and get arrested? We're up to the challenge!

About the Author

Raven Kaldera is a Northern Tradition Neo-Pagan shaman, homesteader, astrologer, herbalist, vampire, and intersexual transgendered FTM activist. He is the King of a very small Pagan kingdom, and one of the founders of its current incarnation, the First Kingdom Church of Asphodel. He is the author of far too many books to list here, but any web search will tell you far more than you want to know. 'Tis an ill wind that blows no minds.

www.ingramcontent.com/pod-product-compliance
Lightning Source LLC
Chambersburg PA
CBHW020606270326
41927CB00005B/199